Walkable Cities

Walkable Cities

Revitalization, Vibrancy, and Sustainable Consumption

Carlos J. L. Balsas

Published by State University of New York Press, Albany

For information, contact State University of New York Press, Albany, NY
www.sunypress.edu

Library of Congress Cataloging-in-Publication Data

Names: Balsas, Carlos J. L., 1971– author.
Title: Walkable cities : revitalization, vibrancy and sustainable consumption across the Atlantic ocean / Carlos J. L. Balsas.
Description: Albany : State University of New York Press, [2019] | Includes bibliographical references and index.
Identifiers: LCCN 2018052657 | ISBN 9781438476278 (hardcover : alk. paper) | ISBN 9781438476285 (pbk. : alk. paper) | ISBN 9781438476292 (ebook)
Subjects: LCSH: Urban renewal—United States. | Urban renewal—Europe. | Sustainable urban development—United States. | Sustainable urban development—Europe. | Walking—United States. | Walking—Europe.
Classification: LCC HT175 .B356 2019 | DDC 307.3/4160973—dc23
LC record available at https://lccn.loc.gov/2018052657

10 9 8 7 6 5 4 3 2 1

Contents

Figures

Tables

Abbreviations

3Rs	reduction, recycling, and reuse
BID	business improvement district
CCA	*centro comercial abierto*
CNG	compressed natural gas
CU	commercial urbanism
DCP	Department of city planning
EEC	European Economic Community
ENDS	National sustainable development strategy
EU	European Union
GTL	Technical advisory committee
HORECA	hotel, restaurant, and cafeteria sector
IDB	Inter-American Development Bank
LULU	local unwanted land use
MSC	medium- and small-size Iberian cities
NIMBY	not in my back yard
NYCDOT	New York City Department of Transportation
PAYT	pay as you throw
PERSU	Strategic plan for urban waste

PNPOT   National Program of Territorial Management Policy

SRU   urban rehabilitation societies

TCM   town center management schemes

UAC   *unidade de acompanhamento e coordenação*

UK   United Kingdom

US   United States

WB   World Bank

Acknowledgments

Multiple chapters of this book were presented in various forms at scholarly and professional conferences. Specifically, parts of Chapter 1 were presented as a keynote speech entitled "Urbanismo comercial: Mitos e boas práticas na revitalização de centros urbanos" at the International Conference of the Research Center on the Technology of Architecture and Urbanism—NUTAU'02 at the University of São Paulo, Brazil. A revised article based on the proceedings paper was subsequently published in *Sociedade e Território: Revista de Estudos Urbanos e Regionais* in 2003.

An earlier version of Chapter 2 was presented as "Commercial Urbanism in Iberian City Centers: A Study of Pedestrian Precincts in Portuguese and Spanish Cities" at the 13th NECTAR International Conference in Ann Arbor, Michigan in 2015. A different version of Chapter 3 was presented as "Walking and Urban Vibrancy: An International Review of Commercial Pedestrian Precincts" to the IIIrd *Seminário Internacional Cidade, Comércio Urbano e Consumo* in São Paulo, Brazil, in 2012 and published in a subsequent issue of the journal *Cidades*.

Chapter 4 was presented at the 2007 International Conference Eradication of Poverty and Exclusion, Strategies for the 21st Century, in Lisbon. Chapter 5 was presented at the 2008 Conference *Comércio e Cidade: Uma Relação de Origem* (CinCci) in the Faculty of Architecture and Urbanism (FAUP) at the University of São Paulo (USP) and appeared in Portuguese in *urbe: Revista Brasileira de Gestão Urbana* in 2017. The chapter benefited from additional field work research in Phoenix at the end of 2015. I would like to thank *urbe*'s editors for suggesting the publication of this research in English.

An earlier version of Chapter 6 was presented and published in the proceedings of the IIIrd Place Management and Branding Conference in

Poznan, Poland, in 2015 and was subsequently presented at the 2016 APA NY Upstate Chapter Conference in Buffalo, New York. An earlier version of Chapter 7 was presented at the 2002 International Conference Partnerships for Economic Development in Small Port Cities: The Case of Figueira da Foz. Chapter 8 was presented as "*Urbanismo Comercial, Consumo e Resíduos*" to the sixth International Seminar City, Retail and Consumption at the University of Lisbon in 2017. Finally, some of the recommendations presented in the conclusion were initially distilled in the author's dissertation at the University of Massachusetts, Amherst.

I would like to thank the *Universidade de São Paulo, Editora Afrontamento, Universidade Estadual Paulista "Júlio de Mesquita Filho," Pontifícia Universidade Católica do Paraná*, Manchester Metropolitan University, Poznań University of Economics, and the *Gabinete de Estudos e Prospectiva Económica do Ministério da Economia (GEPE)* for publishing some of the aforementioned original materials and partially updated in this book. Unless otherwise noted, illustrations are my own.

I would also like to thank the following colleagues, friends, and family for their conference invitations, readings of earlier versions of these chapters, sponsoring some of the research and travel, and providing logistical and emotional support: Heliana Comin Vargas, Lineu Castello, Teresa Barata Salgueiro, Herculano Cachinho, João Freitas, Maria Marques, Magarida Pereira, José Teixeira, José Fernandes, Silvana Pintaudi, Sidney Vieira, José Gasca, Duarte Silva, John Mullin, Zenia Kotval, Meir Gross, Piper Gaubatz, José Lúcio, Sherry Ahrentzen, Katherine Crewe, Hemalata Dandekar, John Meunier, Tom Angotti, Nan Ellin, Paulo Pinho, José Gavinha, Richard Smardon, Carlos Rodrigues, Artur da Rosa Pires, Miriam Fujita, Constantino Rodrigues, Maria da Luz, and José Carlos. I would also like to thank the participants at the various conferences where this research was presented, the two anonymous manuscript reviewers, and the acquisitions editor, Michael Rinella, for their thoughtful and encouraging comments.

Introduction

Retail is one of the most dynamic economic sectors in cities with important impacts on the habitability of urban areas. Traditionally, city centers have occupied a privileged position in the urban hierarchy of city functions. However, with the suburbanization of housing and jobs, soon, thereafter, retailing also relocated to the suburbs from the downtown's CBDs. Although this phenomenon has been occurring in the United States practically since the end of World War II, this trend was only experienced in Southern European countries much more recently. Furthermore, the scale of an agglomeration tends to dictate the number of subcenters and their relationships, usually via higher-density developments near expressway interchanges and railroad/subway stations.

This book is concerned with the revitalization of city centers in cities of various sizes across the Atlantic Ocean. The main research assumption is that the automobile has been greatly responsible for enabling the relocation of households and families to the suburbs. The building of highways and expressways facilitated regular movement between suburbs and central areas and among peripheral neighborhoods, in certain cases even without the need to drive through the center of town. An automobile-centric lifestyle has had devastating consequences for city centers. Directly and indirectly, city centers had to create space for the increasing number of vehicles passing through and, in most cases, demanding parking at relatively low costs. With the building of suburban shopping malls and commercial plazas, incrementally, city centers began losing their centrality as marketplaces. This cycle of decline has been discussed extensively in the literature.

This book explains how cities of various sizes mostly in the Iberian Peninsula (i.e., Braga, Guimarães, and Porto in Portugal; Burgos, Valladolid, and Barcelona in Spain), Latin America (i.e., São Paulo in Brazil and Mexico City in Mexico), and relatively low and dense North American cities (i.e., Phoenix, Arizona, and New York City, respectively) have been conducting urban revitalization processes where walkability improvements contributed to strengthening downtown and midtown centralities and various other urban functions, including vibrancy, livability, partial eradication of homelessness, pedestrian and bicyclist safety, tourism, and sustainable consumption, among others.

This book is organized in three parts. Part 1 is about small, medium, and very large cities in the Ibero-America world. Part 2 is about two polar opposites: Phoenix in Arizona and Manhattan in New York. Finally, Part 3 is about one particular variant of commercial urbanism: tourism planning in the context of urban revitalization and consumption in Figueira da Foz, and how the implementation of commercial urbanism projects throughout Portugal in the 2000s has impacted consumption and solid waste generation.

The presentation of the case studies in the book follows a regional and scale-oriented criterion, from relatively small and medium-size towns and cities to the largest mega-cities in South and North America, all to a certain extent centered on privileged historic and cultural relationships across the Atlantic Ocean. The main case studies range from a little less than 100 thousand for the medium-size cities to about 10 million for the large American ones. Also, the case studies were selected based on my direct contact through either extended periods of residence or multiple study visits to the various cities during the last two decades.

Following this introduction, the book includes eight chapters and a conclusion. After reviewing some of the myths and best practice theoretical principles on the revitalization of urban centers in chapter 1, chapter 2 analyzes pedestrian precincts in four medium-size Iberian cities: Braga, Guimarães, Burgos, and Valladolid. This chapter also examines the impact of commercial urbanism improvements on the overall livability of the four city centers. The research was based on mostly qualitative methods that included multiple site visits to the four case studies at different times during the late 2000s and again in early 2014, extensive literature synthesis, and twelve approximately one-hour-long semi-structured interviews with employees and business owners in various economic sectors, residents, and administrators.

Chapter 2 identifies five major findings. First, major changes in the digital economy may have impacted walking levels for customary services in city centers. Second, the improvement of city centers has contributed to an increase in the leisure and night-time economy. Third, neighborhood specialization might have detrimental impacts to the overall city center livability. Fourth, local governments are relying on their expertise, creative funding strategies, and established collaborations to maintain existing programs and eventually start new ones. Fifth, cities' scales, proactive collaboration climate, and political leadership are found to influence the dynamics, complexities, and opportunities for the continued success of commercial urbanism projects in medium-size cities.

One of the chapter's takeaways is that to be fully effective, walkability improvements to public spaces in downtown areas need to be coordinated with other appropriate legislative and management programs. Furthermore, city scale (structure) and political leadership ability (agency) influence the dynamics, complexities, and opportunities for the continued success of the initial commercial urbanism improvements.

Chapter 3 analyzes four walk-only commercial precincts in the Ibero-American world. The research assumption is that the downtowns of global cities in Latin America have undergone transformative experiences relatively similar to those of the global north, with a slight time lag and with a higher presence of the informal sector. This chapter's argument is that the study of governance practices within contexts of urban revitalization is important to understand whether similar phenomena in distinct contexts have been dealt with differently and have produced relatively unique outcomes in terms of improved public spaces, a reinvigorated built environment, and more robust governance networks, especially at the neighborhood and city levels.

The pedestrianization of main streets seems to offer an important opportunity for this type of analysis. The key findings of chapter 3 include the realization that the promotion of a culture of walking is critical to the survival of livable cities and that walk-only commercial precincts play an important role in ensuring urban vibrancy. Public intervention is not only needed to create quality urban spaces but also to maintain adequate levels of urban vitality, free of crime and without the monopoly of strong interests that often tend to privatize and exclude citizens from the public realm.

City centers go through cycles of growth, decline, and revitalization, but not everybody benefits equally. Using Phoenix as a case study, Chapter 4 utilizes an eclectic array of data sources from personal interviews, focus groups, media sources, public reports, and technical studies to identify how institutional and civic leaders and citizens have traditionally responded to the presence of homeless individuals in the city prior to the 2008–2009 global financial crisis. The argument is that ending homelessness ought to be an integral part of the process of revitalizing urban areas. The chapter advances seven recommendations for addressing homelessness in contexts of downtown revitalization.

Chapter 5 recognizes that commerce has always influenced the development and growth of cities. The relationship between urban development and trade has given rise to the emergence of different types of spontaneous and planned commercial formats, depending on people's needs, technologies of production and distribution, sale and storage techniques, and the technical innovation of firms. The Phoenix metropolitan area in Arizona is an interesting case study due to its multitude of recent commercial developments with a mix of modern and postmodern formats and the transformations and adaptations that resulted from the global financial crisis.

Therefore, Chapter 5 analyzes the innovative characteristics of four commercial formats in the Phoenix metropolitan area (i.e., the Phoenix public market, a "lifestyle center" in northern Phoenix on the border with Scottsdale, the Tempe Marketplace in Tempe, and the shopping area in terminal four of Phoenix's Sky Harbor International Airport). Finally, it also discusses a set of implications for the future of commercial developments in the Western world: local-global, material-sensorial, essential-dispensable, and authentic-illusory.

Chapter 6 examines the motivations, designs, and expectations behind the recent walkability improvements to New York City's Times Square district. This chapter emerged from the research assumption that the existence of safe, attractive, and comfortable walking environments is critical to the vibrancy of downtowns in global cities. Such a policy goal is a significant departure from the traditional transportation planning approach that has catered mostly to the needs of drivers.

The argument of Chapter 6 is that the creation of an almost exhilarating "theme park" setting in the core of Manhattan is as much an example of American neoliberalism as it is a demonstration of liberty, and a human desire made so by marketing campaigns, which increasingly broadcast Times Square and American-inspired globalization to the rest of the world. The impacts of the redesign works from both management's and users' perspectives are identified and discussed, including: first, a world-class status; second, localized street improvements as part of a comprehensive public spaces redesign; third, real vibrancy gains for the district; and fourth, demonstrative potential for the creation of walkable areas elsewhere.

Tourism, like other economic sectors, is also subjected to major market fluctuations. Established tourism destinations are impacted by internal socioeconomic changes and leadership options as well as by exogenous forces and tendencies, events, and sectoral innovations. Chapter 7 answers the research question of whether cities can augment their endogenous tourism potential while reducing their volatility to outside forces by devising and implementing a tourism planning strategy as part of their community economic development programs. The chapter analyzes the case of a traditional "sun and sea" tourism city in central Portugal: Figueira da Foz. It is argued that over the last fifty years Figueira da Foz has had to reinvent its tourism branding and positioning multiple times through a myriad of city marketing and infrastructure development strategies to circumvent territorial and societal hurdles. The key finding is that tourism reinvention beyond consumption-oriented planning is necessary to withstand major socioeconomic and territorial transformations.

Chapter 8 analyzes the relationships among physical improvements to public spaces, increased levels of consumption, generation of solid waste, and associated environmental climate change pressures in the context of the Portuguese commercial urbanism projects of the 2000s decade. It ought to be clear by now that revitalizing city centers to become mostly privileged arenas of consumption has negative consequences from a triple–bottom line sustainability perspective. Commerce involves high levels of exchanges and consumption. Although commercial urbanism in contexts of urban revitalization has been used by decision-makers to improve the urban livability of cities, these revitalization interventions have increased the pressures on other more peripheral and fragile, but equally important, urban areas.

Therefore, Chapter 8 also discusses the relationship between merchants' participation rates in Portuguese commercial urbanism projects and waste generation in four regional jurisdictions (i.e., *distritos*) of the north-central coastal region of Portugal. The chapter closes with a set of four implications for future policy actions. The first implication is the need for reduction, recycling, and reuse. The second, more emphasis on sustainable consumption. The third, the promotion of a circular economy. And the fourth, the implementation of a zero-waste city strategy.

Finally, the conclusion discusses the need to base urban revitalization interventions on more sustainable consumption practices that do not necessarily entail higher growth levels but instead aim at improving quality of life in cities.

1

Commercial Urbanism

Introduction

Retailing is one of the most dynamic economic sectors in cities with major impacts on the habitability of urban areas. New commercial formats and transactions have evolved over time and are in constant development. Examples range from shopping centers, franchise stores, retail parks, factory outlets, and leisure complexes to catalog sales, television, and the internet. For example, in many cities in the United States of America, many shops in the city center were forced to close not only due to the opening of shopping centers in more peripheral locations with more convenient vehicular accessibility and ample parking options, but also due to a lack of entrepreneurship of the economic actors located in central areas. At the present moment, the closure of stores in many first- and second-generation shopping centers is easily observed due to an increasing saturation of the marketplace.

Although the effects of these transformations have been known in the US for quite some time,[1] in Europe and in some Latin American countries it is only recently that city and state administrations have become aware of the profound impacts associated with these changes.[2] However, it is often found that local authorities are not technically prepared to manage these economic impacts sustainably. The objective of this chapter is to present a set of myths and principles of best practices on the revitalization of urban centers. These myths and best practices are structured in response to six main questions:

---

1. Jackson (2001).

2. DoE (1997), Balsas (2000), and Vargas (2000).

What? Where? Who? Why? How? When? And they cover areas ranging from competitiveness, multifunctionality, urban actors, accessibility, public space improvements, urban management, and public-private partnerships.

The argument is that it is important not only to understand the myths that are used to justify certain revitalization options instead of others, but that it is also important to know best practices of urban revitalization in order to maintain and increase quality of life in cities. These myths and best practices are the result of research conducted over the last two decades, mostly in the United States, Southern Europe, Latin America, the Pearl River Delta, and Japan, which comprised many interviews with city planners, architects, place managers, retailers, business owners, politicians, and shoppers; extensive bibliographical reviews; and intense debates at many conferences and congresses.

This chapter is structured in five sections. The first section analyzes the city-commerce relationship and how profound changes in this sector have contributed to the decline of the city centers in the US. The second section presents several strategies used in the revitalization of urban centers, namely, the Main Street program and business improvement districts (BID) in the US, city center management schemes (also known as town center management schemes or TCM) in the United Kingdom, and commercial urbanism (CU) projects in Portugal. The third and fourth sections present a set of myths and best practices used in the commercial revitalization of urban centers, respectively. The last section offers some concluding remarks.

Urban Centers and Commerce

Urban centers are privileged places for commercial activity. Their organic mix of functions and uses means that many people travel daily to urban areas in order to carry out a great diversity of activities. It is well known that city centers are fragile and constantly changing places, mainly due to alterations in their economic and commercial structure. Commercial activity in Western cities has undergone tremendous changes in recent decades. The appearance of new commercial formats on the periphery of cities and the lack of entrepreneurship of traditional retailers has partly influenced the decline of urban centers. There is perhaps no country more suited to illustrate these changes than the United States of America.[3] Before World

---

3. Burayidi (2001).

War II, the centers of many North American cities were the privileged place of their respective communities. The city center was not only the economic and business center, but it was also an important part of social dynamics; people strolled the streets on the weekend to meet friends, window shop, or to watch some cultural performance.[4]

In the post–World War II period, the construction of the highway system, subsidized housing loans, and the extraordinary growth in vehicle fleets led to unidirectional developments toward the suburbs. This large and multifaceted suburbanization process, which practically involved all sectors ranging from housing, commerce, industry, services, and leisure, contributed greatly to the hollowing out of urban centers. Commercial developments in peripheral locations and in close connection with the abandonment of traditional buildings and establishments in city centers have led to serious economic and social problems and to the degradation of the urban environment in central areas. Declining sales in city centers has caused shops to close their doors and to relocate, often to new shopping centers in newly constructed suburbs.[5]

This resulted in a reduction of economic activity and less appealing urban centers, with mostly underutilized infrastructure. The fact that many of the buildings were abandoned, their windows and doors boarded up, and garbage accumulated on the streets gradually reinforced the public perception that these areas were in decline and not worth caring about. This whole situation results in what has been dubbed a "spiral of decline," with buildings slowly deteriorating due to a lack of rehabilitation, which had tremendous negative consequences for urban livability, resulting in problems of vitality and viability of the affected areas.[6] This situation repeated itself in city after city throughout the country.

If in the 1960s the prevailing attitude toward this exodus was to deny that the suburbs would occupy a prominent place in urban development, in the 1970s the attitude changed to a growing concern about the negative impact of this spatial imbalance. Thus, rather than revitalizing city centers, retailers and those responsible for downtown areas began to imitate the suburbs and to replicate many of their characteristics in the central areas of cities. National urban renewal policies contributed greatly to the demolition

---

4. Mullin (2001).

5. Jackson (2001) and Burayidi (2001).

6. Ravenscroft (2000).

of large urban areas and the irreparable loss of many historic buildings in urban centers. Cleared urban blocks left vacant became surface parking lots. Traditional retail establishments have tried to imitate their new counterparts in the suburbs by closing entire streets to traffic and creating pedestrian areas, modernizing the facades of historic buildings with inexpensive materials reminiscent of those used in shopping centers. In addition, stakeholders installed gigantic advertising signs, thinking the size of advertisements was proportional to their power to attract consumers. Soon it was discovered that these ineffective methods did not change the declining situation because they did not correctly identify the main problem, which was not only the decrease in attractiveness but also the loss of economic competitiveness of the center to the suburbs.[7]

Thus, neither the denial of the problem, nor the imitation of the suburbs, nor the existence of large public investments served to alter substantially this course of events. In the late 1970s, there was a need to find innovative solutions to problems that had already existed for several decades. These solutions were radically different from those tested in the past and had three main characteristics: they were local, small scale, and were shared by public and private entities.[8] During the 1980s, the first urban revitalization programs delivered some initial successes. These solutions were not based on large projects; instead, they were centered on various partnerships and small revitalization operations, such as the modernization of establishments with substantial historical and architectural value, the rehabilitation of the original facades, various promotional campaigns and street fairs, festivals and other popular events, and the centralized, commercial management of downtown retail. The victories of a few bold leaders rapidly gave visible results, which in turn led others to join subsequent revitalization initiatives.[9]

The suburbanization phenomenon and the visibly felt decline of city centers reached European cities after the reconstruction operations of World War II.[10] Large European shopping centers and hypermarkets were built mainly in the 1980s and early 1990s. This shopping revolution only reached Southern European countries, and Portugal in particular, during the 1990s. But its consequences have been seriously felt by the older retail establish-

---

7. Balsas (1999).

8. Gratz and Mintz (1998), Winterberg and Bender (2002).

9. Jackson (2001).

10. Fernandes (1995).

ments in downtown areas. Also, in Latin America, these suburbanization trends have been observed over the past three decades. However, the impact of retail activities in the urban environment of São Paulo was a relatively recent phenomenon too.[11] These trends demonstrate well the universality of peripheral commercial developments and the need to find timely responses to minimize their impacts in the decline of urban centers.

Return to the Center and Urban Revitalization

In the cities of Western Europe and North America, the decades of the 1990s and the 2000s were visibly impacted by city center revitalization interventions.[12] After earlier decades being mostly characterized by the growth of suburban peripheries and centrifugal movements to the cities' edges, the last 10 to 15 years were impacted by a general interest of the population, economic agents, and public authorities in reactivating city centers as places to live, work, shop, and recreate.[13] This growing interest in the city center has resulted from a growing awareness of the crucial role that centers hold as privileged places in the economic, social, cultural, historical, political, and territorial organization of urban areas. In this sense, urban revitalization comprises the improvement of the physical, socioeconomic, cultural, historical, and political dimensions of cities. Often the main objective of urban revitalization operations has been to increase or improve the livability and sustainability of the local community by attracting and increasing employment, residential, recreation, and leisure opportunities and by ensuring more and better support services for the various socioeconomic groups.

In the United States and Canada, after several decades of suburbanization, more attention has been paid to the investment of funds and other resources in an attempt to make the future of these areas more viable in the long term.[14] Key intervention strategies have included the creation of BIDs and the implementation of the Main Street program.[15] While BIDs aim to provide a mechanism through which property owners can contrib-

---

11. Vargas (2000).

12. Gratz and Mintz (1998), Ravenscroft (2000), and Wachs (2013).

13. Gotham (2001) and Ehrenhalt (2012).

14. Porter (1995, 1997).

15. Seidman (2004).

ute financially to the provision of additional services in the public spaces surrounding their buildings,[16] the Main Street program aims to help local communities develop a strategy of integrated commercial revitalization that stimulates economic development in a context of historical preservation. This program adapts to the needs and opportunities of local communities in four important areas: economic restructuring, organization, promotion, and design. The ultimate goal of the Main Street program is to create a pleasant and attractive space that encourages visitors to return to the center more often. These two mechanisms of commercial and urban revitalization of city centers are being widely implemented in many North American cities.[17]

Across the Atlantic, the European experience shows great diversity in terms of the nature, timing, processes, scales, and types of revitalization interventions.[18] While many of the interventions can be considered international in character, it is quite clear that historical, geographical, cultural, and economic conditions in the different European countries have greatly conditioned the various planning processes. However, it can also be said that commercial revitalization of city centers in Europe is usually associated with urban regeneration programs, which include not only the commercial area but also areas such as transport, public spaces, safety, the urban environment, and more recently the establishment of partnerships for the revitalization and management of central areas.

Also in Europe, the revitalization of city centers has been increasing in importance since the early 1990s, mainly because of the possibilities that commercial planning and city center management provide for the creation and maintenance of pleasant and livable cities.[19] In the UK, town center management schemes such as the "4 As" approach—accessibility, attraction, amenities, and action—is being used to identify the problems and potential interventions in city centers and to propose management tools for these areas.[20] However, the fact that these programs are based on voluntary partnerships between public and private entities has led to the need to identify sustainable financing modes to assure their future existence and further development. Thus, most interventions at the international level have been concerned not

---

16. Mitchell (2001).

17. Robertson (1997) and Winterberg and Bender (2002).

18. DoE (1997).

19. Page and Hardyman (1996).

20. DoE (1997) and Brown (2001)

only with keeping commercial areas and public spaces attractive and pleasant (i.e., physical space approach) but also with developing well-managed, funded, and promoted strategies (i.e., organizational approach).

In Portugal, commercial urban development projects, subsidized through the PROCOM program, were timely strategies in attempting to stop (or at least remedy) possible spirals of commercial decline in the centers of Portuguese cities.[21] Although the overall scope of these projects has been quite broad in their revitalization proposals, low levels of adherence on the part of local merchants and the difficulties in coordinating their implementation have led to the conclusion that there is still a need to find innovative mechanisms to promote commercial activity and at the same time increase the effectiveness of collaborations and partnerships between economic agents and local authorities.[22] The main difference between the international developments and the Portuguese reality is that abroad there has been a greater concern with the involvement and participation of property owners and retailers in the financing and raising of funds to carry out the revitalization actions, which are likely to lead to mutual benefits. In Portugal, a certain dependence on public subsidies has resulted in often passive attitudes and a lack of collaboration that have limited the investment opportunities of many economic agents and local authorities.[23]

It is therefore one of this chapter's assumptions that, although each city is unique and needs to develop its own strategy of commercial and urban revitalization, there is a vast amount of knowledge that must be procured in order to enhance the solutions that cities can implement. It is also believed that the analysis of international practices of commercial revitalization can contribute to draw very positive lessons to other geographical contexts. The next section is a discussion of a set of six myths and six best practices that may be useful for the development of commercial urbanism programs and the revitalization of urban centers.

Myths of Commercial Revitalization

The myths of commercial revitalization are generally preconceived ideas, based on a superficial, often unfounded, and short-term analysis that leads

---

21. Fernandes (1995).

22. Teixeira and Pereira (1999) and Marques (1999).

23. Fernandes, Cachinho, and Ribeiro (2000).

to certain ideas becoming accepted as true by a specific group of individuals. Often, these myths are conjectured by urban actors who may feel penalized by public or private actions. Their origin is relatively well circumscribed but they spread rapidly to wider geographical areas. The diffusion of myths about commercial revitalization takes place not only through informal conversations between urban actors but also through the media, sometimes more interested in maintaining the status quo than in contributing to an in-depth analysis of those problems. Usually myths are generated and scattered because certain individuals or groups are interested in benefiting from a specific set of circumstances.

With the identification of these myths, it is hoped that the various urban actors with responsibilities or interests in city centers think differently about their realities. These myths are structured in response to six main questions: What do we face? Where does the problem lie? Who is responsible? Why did the problem arise? How can it be resolved? And when should we act?

What?—The Problem Is an Increase in Competition

Reality check: It is also the lack of entrepreneurship and not only the increased competition

Often the decline of a city center is mostly attributed to increased competition. This idea is known in professional circles as "putting one's head in the sand," because the main problem is not identified in its entirety.[24] There is no doubt that increased competition leads to a decrease in market share if the number of customers does not increase. The loss of market share is due not only to the added competition created by new commercial areas but also to the loss of entrepreneurship of older retailers operating in the city center. In this context, competition is seen as disruptive to businesses.

But it is also very often the case that traditional retailing cannot meet the needs of its customers in terms of diversity of products, services, and prices. Their products are out of fashion, prices are sometimes high, their establishments are not attractive, and their service is not courteous. Against this background, customers prefer to patronize new buildings with a wide

---

24. Palma (2000).

variety of shops and often a greater assortment of products and after-sale services.

Often, merchant groups and their representative associations conduct promotional campaigns to influence customers into shopping locally. However, in today's global economy and with increasing levels of mobility, customers are able to cover a wide geographical area. Therefore, it is important to do a good market analysis before proceeding with promotions of this type, and to know exactly who a business owner wants to attract to the establishment, and only then craft marketing strategies.[25]

Where?—The New Developments in the Outskirts of Cities Are the Problem

Reality check: It is also the decline of the center and not only the attractiveness of the periphery

The decline of the city center is often associated with the opening of other commercial ventures on the peripheries. In this context, the periphery is seen as a more suitable area and with a set of attractions that is not easily located in the center of the city. For example, the size of the properties is generally greater, the locations near major road intersections are more convenient, the possibility of securing a large number of car parks is higher, and the proximity to suburban consumers is also much greater.

But the truth is that it is not only these factors that must be considered. Retail trade is dependent on the global environment of the urban area. Thus, variables such as security, cleanliness, mobility, and commercial composition have a substantial impact on the quality of the act of purchasing and the number of people who decide to move to a certain place. For example, it is well known that in a privately owned shopping mall the retail mix of the stores is done with great care because a poorly located store can lead to the bankruptcy of five adjacent stores,[26] but in the center of the city this concern is practically nonexistent. Another aspect to consider is how outdated municipal regulations condition private investment in city centers and indirectly contribute to the center's decline.[27]

---

25. Stitt (1996).

26. Stitt (1996).

27. Winterberg and Bender (2002).

Who?—The Others Are Responsible for the Problem

Reality check: Others include also the independent retailers and not only the lobby of the big investors and elected officials

In the opinion of many urban actors, those responsible for the decline of city centers are always the others. Often there are high expectations that others will do something. The others in this case are not only the big investors, developers, and owners of shopping centers or hypermarkets but also the local, regional, and national government workers and elected officials who allowed the opening of these new spaces.

Before accusing the other urban actors, it is necessary to raise a set of questions in order to have a clearer idea of the responsibilities for the decline and revitalization: What can I do to improve the situation in the city center? When was the last time that I attended a public meeting? Am I willing to invest time and money in order to improve my establishment? Am I willing to adjust the opening hours of my establishment to better serve my clients? All too often, the same attitudes toward these issues do not bode well to higher levels of cooperation.[28]

It is therefore important that retailers not only maintain attractive establishments but also actively collaborate in the revitalization efforts of the center as a whole. It is important that community leaders develop relationships of trust with the various urban partners involved in urban revitalization and contribute to finding endogenous resources and learning to be self-sustaining. Multiple participation strategies, such as the organization of events, the coordination of promotions, festivals, and the production of advertising materials are effective ways to mobilize merchants to the revitalization of the center.

Why?—The Problem Stems from the Lack of Public Intervention

Reality check: It is also the inactivity of some merchants and their associative structures at local and national levels and not only the inability of the public authorities

The explanation for the problem always seems to pertain to insufficient public intervention in the center. Frequently, municipalities and national gov-

---

28. Stitt (1996).

ernments are indicated as those who must propose revitalization solutions. However, it is often the small retailers and their associative structures at the local and national levels that do not have coherent and effective promotional strategies. Since these organizations' main goals entail the advancement of their members' overall interests, chambers of commerce can play a critical role in articulating and resolving some of their members' complex problems, therefore helping to resolve the problems that have partially caused the city center's decline.

The fact that chambers of commerce usually have a wider territorial scope than the downtown area may create some inertia in defending retailers' interests, which, in the long run, can become the source of institutional conflicts. However, since in many cities the stores located in the core constitute the main commercial area of a city, it is relatively consensual to justify the renewed interest in the city center and its institutional collaborative involvement in the central area to the association's members.[29]

In certain communities, the commercial association is the first institution to host a city center management unit, allowing a downtown manager to share resources (e.g., facilities, equipment, administrative support, etc.) of this newly created entity.[30] The chamber of commerce may also promote good business management practices to its members, as well as organize or coordinate professional training activities aimed at increasing the competitiveness of economic activities.[31] In addition to this, and in cooperation with the city center management unit and the municipality, the chamber of commerce can develop and promote alternative business models. For example, it can identify traditional products and goods in the region, as well as mobilize and provide computerized means for the creation of virtual stores on the internet.[32]

The existence of national associations dedicated to the management of urban centers is also important for the definition and implementation of commercial revitalization agendas in urban centers. Similarly, other supra-municipal level associations (e.g., the International Downtown Association [IDA] and the Association of Town Center Management [ATCM]) have these core goals: the representation of multiple publics in matters

---

29. Balsas (1999).

30. DoE (1997).

31. Waits and Henton (2001).

32. Balsas (2000).

pertaining to commercial planning policies; the promotion of open communication and the holding of multidisciplinary meetings on issues affecting the core areas; the provision of technical and advisory support; the delivery of vocational training; the implementation of research programs conducive to the satisfaction of specific research on the main needs of urban centers, including good management and economic development practices; the establishment and maintenance of management units, partnerships, and funding.[33]

How?—The Problem Is Solved through the Treatment of Public Spaces

Reality check: The organizational and management approaches are as important as the public space approach

The way to solve the decline problem is perhaps where most myths are found. Among them there are four preconceived ideas that are more often mentioned: (1) the arrangement of public spaces, (2) the completion of a major project, (3) more parking, and (4) the failure to consider the organizational approach to revitalization. Many revitalization strategies favor the arrangement of public spaces through the installation of new pavements on the sidewalks, the landscaping and installation of trees and urban furniture (i.e., benches, rubbish bins, information kiosks, etc.), and the improvement of *façades* in commercial areas. What the best practices show is that this approach alone does not work if these arrangements are not integrated into a more global revitalization strategy. In most cases the commercial vitality needed to attract investments and consumers back to the center is in serious danger of failing.

It has been pointed out that many of these initiatives have contributed to creating more equal and homogeneous cities,[34] since similar urban furniture is sold to different local authorities by the same companies. Many urban actors have mistakenly believed that the economic growth of these establishments is directly proportional to the local authority's investment in upgrading the public space of the downtown area. In addition, oftentimes large sums of money are spent on physical improvements, which soon thereafter become ruined once again, and subsequently no other funds are available for either maintenance or other future management initiatives.[35]

---

33. DoE (1997), ATCM (1998), Brown (2001).

34. Teixeira and Pereira (1999).

35. Balsas (2000).

Certain authors argue that the implementation of a project of considerable size is enough to revitalize urban centers. Among the most common projects we find convention centers, parking garages, and pedestrian streets. Also, the implementation of these projects in isolation does not produce sufficiently long-lasting results to help revitalize urban centers. Best practices show that multifaceted projects that consider the needs of the various city users bring more benefits to the community than this type of intervention. Therefore, the emphasis should be on the revitalization process and not just on the project itself.[36]

Another paradoxical example of this tendency to privilege physical arrangements is the lack of car parking spaces, or the perception of a parking problem, in the city center. This is perhaps the most often invoked reason utilized to justify the need to intervene in the center. It can be argued that certain urban actors, usually merchants, are even irrational about car parking spaces, which never seem to exist in sufficient numbers, nor are those spaces located in the most suitable places—ironically just in front of their shops.[37] However, once again the best practices show that the problem is not so much the lack of parking spaces but their poor management. Often, customers find it difficult to find parking spaces in a particular location because many of them are occupied daily by the business owners' cars, the cars of their employees, or are not properly signposted. Thus, in these cases the problem is a better management of the existing places and not the creation of more parking. Parking is a necessity, but it is not the only factor influencing commercial success.[38]

Finally, another myth in the area of revitalization solutions is inconsideration of the need to modernize or restructure the organizations responsible for maintaining and improving the urban center.[39] If existing organizations are not doing their part or delivering minimally visible results, then it is a sign that their roles and competencies must be rethought, the people who lead those organizations replaced, their staff and budgets adjusted. These organizations include not only trade associations but also the various municipal departments with responsibilities over the urban centers. In addition to organizational restructuring, it is also important to think about professional place management activities in urban centers through the establishment of a

---

36. Palma (2000).

37. Mullin (2001).

38. Palma (2000).

39. Stitt (1996).

management unit based on public-private partnerships and the appointment of professional managers.[40]

When?—The Problem Is Solved by a Short-Term Intervention

Reality check: The intervention must be prolonged in time

In most cases the problem arises almost always associated to the opening of a certain commercial enterprise or set of ventures. Thus, the most frequently mentioned solution is the establishment of a moratorium prohibiting the opening of other commercial formats of significant size in the area. Usually, short-term urban development projects and arrangements are then implemented to mitigate the first signs of urban decline. In most cases, this solution known as "silver bullet" does not give significant results. This is because just as the problems of the city center are structural in nature and result from an accumulation of prolonged inaction or neglect by multiple urban actors, the solutions to resolve those problems need to be developed and implemented in a phased approach. And certain revitalization actions need to be implemented in the short term (six months to a year) while others ought to be implemented in the long term (three to five years).

Best Practices in the Revitalization of Urban Centers

Best practices in the context of urban revitalization comprise actions and capabilities to achieve a city center that is livable, capable of generating wealth, and capable of attracting investment in a self-sustaining way.[41] Important aspects that characterize best practices include: being effective, having achieved testable and measurable results, and being replicable. Best practices are influenced by legal, social, economic, and cultural contexts and may vary from country to country. Best practices should not be synonymous with "magic formulas" that cure all evils of urban decline. To a certain extent, the aim is to help the stakeholders involved in the revitalization activities make informed decisions based on policies, measures, and projects that guarantee the ultimate goal of maintaining or increasing the livability

---

40. DoE (1997), Marques (1999), and Brown (2001).
41. Ravenscroft (2000).

of a given urban center. While circumstances may vary from country to country, this does not prevent urban actors from sharing information on the procedures and experiences that have given positive (or negative) results in other similar situations, thus helping to avoid steps in the learning process.

The fact that the decline of city centers in the United States and Western Europe has been known for some time has allowed organizations and professionals in these countries to synthesize more best practices and principles of intervention than those that can be explained in this chapter.[42] For example, the good practice guide produced by ATCM includes various areas ranging from cleaning and maintenance (street cleaning and walking, graffiti and abusive advertising removal, recycling, and waste management), marketing and promotions (public relations, media, festivals and events, entertainment, and local guides), safety and security (initiatives to reduce crime, homelessness and vagrancy, alcohol and drugs), urban planning (design guides, lighting, paving, public art, trees and gardens, public bathrooms), property (markets, rentals, signs, use of vacant properties), transport and access (car parking, park and ride, pedestrianization, traffic-calming, mobility for the disabled, cycling), night economy (cafes, residential uses, attractions and tourism); participation (customer service, visitor management, young people in the city center) to city center management (strategic vision, public participation, SWOT analysis, action plans, and funding).[43]

In order to be consistent with the previously identified myths, the best practices outlined in this section attempt to answer six main questions: What?—a culture of entrepreneurship; Where?—a central and multifunctional location; Who?—those most interested in having an updated knowledge of the market; Why?—individualism does not generate synergies; How?—a physical and organizational approach; When?—an ongoing and regularly monitored intervention.

A Culture of Entrepreneurship

The most entrepreneurial individuals and organizations are those that find their own niche market and conduct their business in a different, authentic, and genuine way.[44] It is quite clear that it is not possible to compete in all

---

42. Cabrita (1991), Waits and Henton (2001), Roberts and Sykes (2000), and Brown (2001).

43. ATCM (1998).

44. Waits and Henton (2001).

branches of activity with hypermarkets or shopping centers in the suburbs, but retail located in the city center may have a comparative advantage over these same commercial formats if it exploits a niche market instead, sells products and provides services that are not available anywhere else, and above all provides a unique experience compatible with its urban location. Thus, differentiation should not necessarily be on the basis of cheaper prices but rather on the selection and quality of specific products and services.[45] Besides differentiation, the organization and concentration of establishments by theme in a given geographic area also has advantages in terms of expected turnover. Different shops of the same commercial branch located in a certain well-perceived area increase the number of choices and attract a greater number of customers.[46]

A Central and Multifunctional Location

The central location and the organic mix of functions in the city center is an important advantage. Often the city center is the main commercial area in a city and includes both planned and unplanned commercial formats. The main characteristic of central areas is that they provide a wide range of services; allow diverse needs to be satisfied in one single trip; serve various business, cultural, or leisure objectives for the community; and finally constitute a convergence center for public transport. The continuation of its vitality depends largely on its ability to attract people who spend time and money downtown. One important aspect of a downtown's multifunctionality is that commercial activities occupy the vast majority of ground floor spaces. A city center is more than a shopping center. However, if it loses its attractiveness as a trading hub, it can hardly survive as a center. Commercial activity is definitely one of the essential components of city center living.[47]

Urban revitalization projects should capitalize not only on the particularities of a site, its unique character, architecture, diversity of uses, and proximity to transport interfaces but also in terms of their contribution toward the qualification of commercial activity. Above all, it is necessary to value the preexisting urban settings.[48] All cities are different and require

45. Mullin (2001).

46. Palma (2000).

47. Salgueiro (1999).

48. Loukaitou-Sideris and Banerjee (1998).

revitalization strategies that are adaptable to their idiosyncratic characteristics. Successful plans are those that capitalize on endogenous elements and historical preservation to create new opportunities or to capture investment and generate wealth.[49] It is extremely important that every possible effort is made to rehabilitate the historical heritage in the city center. On the other hand, high densities must be maintained in order to prevent suburbanization.[50]

The revitalization of its urban center should be a public policy priority for each city. It is the responsibility of a municipality to promote the identity and diversity of its urban centers through active leadership and broad-based public-private partnerships. In order for economic activities in urban centers to be competitive, municipalities need to review licensing processes to facilitate investments in central areas. Thus, intervention processes in urban centers ought not only to be expeditious but also to assure that they are implemented with high standards of quality.[51]

An Updated Knowledge of the Market

The economic actors located in the urban center ought to have the highest interest in possessing an updated knowledge of the market. Only this up-to-date knowledge allows marketers to meet the needs of their customers. Retailers ought to ask themselves the following questions: What is the area of influence of the center? Who are our current customers? Who do we want to attract in the future? What goods and services do current customers prefer? What are their future preferences? How can these products and services be secured in the future so as to retain customers? These questions can be answered with diagnostic studies and market analysis. These studies and analyses should be more than simple questionnaires; in order to understand exactly what consumers' tastes and preferences are, these studies should be administered not only to customers of the establishments located in the center of the city but also to customers in shopping centers. It is important to keep in mind that customers have a wide array of options and that competitive prices, quality products, variety and selection, personalized treatments, and after-sale services contribute decisively to maintaining customers' loyalty.

---

49. Gratz and Mintz (1998) and Winterberg and Bender (2002).

50. Robertson (1999).

51. Balsas (2000).

Collaborations and Partnerships

Most retailers are by nature very individualistic, secluded and self-centered, and many of them are in business not because they are entrepreneurs but because they want to be their own bosses.[52] However, best practices show that the creation of public-private partnerships is a key element in the successful revitalization of city centers.[53] The main characteristics of these partnerships include joint decision-making and the sharing of responsibilities between the various actors in order to benefit the community as a whole. Although a partnership may be initially led by the public sector, best practices show that collaborative partnerships are often much more effective. Furthermore, there is also evidence that partnerships initiated and led by the private sector tend to be a lot more effective as well. Also, in addition to public and private partners, many partnerships also include the participation of civic, voluntary, and resident associations.[54]

More than discussion arenas, partnerships should be used to locate all potential partners with interests in the city center and to invite them to contribute to the success of the revitalization. Community leaders should also be encouraged to participate in solving their own problems, and to encourage the self-sustainability of the initiatives. Above all, the municipality and public authorities should be seen as partners and not as, which happens frequently, the main funders, conceivers, and implementers of the revitalization efforts.[55]

In order to achieve successful partnerships, it is necessary to promote local leadership. There is no one better informed about a particular urban area than the people who live or work there. Thus, adequate public participation should be possible before, during, and after the formulation of revitalization plans and programs. Very often, urban revitalization processes need to establish a new relationship with existing levels of power. In particular, urban actors who have more power must learn to share it, and those who seem to lack power must learn to acquire it. Revitalization efforts must still be based on mutually supportive self-help, that is, community leaders

---

52. Stitt (1996).

53. McQuiad (1999).

54. Brown (2001).

55. Carley et al. (2000).

must learn to promote economic development, preserve historic areas of cities, and keep the results of revitalization through time.

A Physical and Organizational Approach

Urban revitalization should include both physical and organizational approaches. The physical approach should translate into ensuring solutions that increase accessibility to and mobility in the center for all users. Elements and actions that increase the attractiveness of the center should also be privileged. For its part, the organizational approach implies the professional management of the urban center. But these two approaches to revitalization should be integrated into an inclusive strategic planning process and the implementation of an action plan.[56]

First of all, it is necessary to realize that timely political and technical leadership is critical to the success of the revitalization, and that the revitalization of urban centers requires professional assistance.[57] The planning process should begin with the formulation of a strategic, consensual, and shared vision for the entire urban center and its translation into an action plan that defines priorities, identifies responsibilities, and describes the phasing of the revitalization activities. The main question underlying the strategic vision can be stated as follows: What do we want our center to be like five to ten years from now? The action plan should delimit the center, make an inventory of existing uses, and be based on a full diagnosis of the strengths and weaknesses of the intervention area.

The action plan should also translate the strategic vision into achievable short-, medium-, and long-term objectives; identify specific actions and their temporal implementation; define and direct human and financial resources; identify potential sources of funding; and describe methods for assessing and monitoring the implementation of the plan. Two extremely important aspects of the action plan include setting priorities and defining incremental and phased implementation.

Priority setting is necessary because resources (e.g., technical, human, time, energy, financial, and volunteer resources) are always limited and urban centers are vast, with multiple problems needing attention. More than trying

---

56. Balsas (1999) and Palma (2000).

57. Mullin (2001).

to change existing conditions through the immediate resolution of complex problems, the most important action is to divide them into subproblems and to try to solve them individually. The adequacy of these resources to time-bound and geographically well-defined priorities makes it possible to reach visible and demonstrable results more easily. But this does not mean that the intervention is not comprehensive and does not include a critical mass of establishments, since an investor's ability to make a profit on a real estate project depends on the value of the properties adjacent to it.[58] Prioritized and phased interventions also allow for the possibility to learn from the mistakes made in the first phase and to prevent similar situations from occurring in the future.

Regarding physical approaches, accessibility always appears as critical to the success of the revitalization.[59] While city centers should always focus on pedestrians, this does not mean they are not accessible and ensure adequate levels of mobility for all modes, such as public transport, cars, bicyclists, pedestrians, and mobility impaired individuals. The management of car parking places and the supply of commercial establishments via logistical platforms are extremely important. The attractiveness of the center is guaranteed by the maintenance and reinforcement of its multifunctionality. As stated earlier, retailing (through its promotion of ground-level activity) should be an integral part of urban revitalization schemes. However, this does not mean that housing rehabilitation programs (through the reuse of upper floors) and cultural facilities such as libraries, theaters, museums, and so on, are not to be given priority.[60] Synergies with leisure and entertainment activities, such as restaurants, cafés, and cinemas, prevent the desertification of the centers and promote the continued use of these areas, especially in the late afternoon, at night, and on weekends, when the majority of businesses and other administrative activities are already closed.

Daily public services with high levels of patronage, such as city halls, post offices, and decentralized public departments, should be centrally located.[61] The pleasantness of a center is reflected in its high levels of cleanliness and safety and in a positive image that reinforces its character and identity as

---

58. Winterberg and Bender (2002).

59. Newman and Kenworthy (1999).

60. Evans (2001).

61. Mullin (2001).

a civic and collective venue for multiple urban actors. Festivals and other public uses that ensure enjoyable collective experiences are key to attracting people back to the center.

The professional and self-sustaining management of the city center should be the main component of the organizational approach. The main idea to bear in mind is that the city center should be regarded as a large open-air shopping center that needs good management in order to function efficiently. Just as a private shopping center cannot function without a management structure, neither can city centers neglect this critical aspect of urban revitalization. The management of urban centers begins with the formation of a public-private partnership and with the appointment of an urban manager to coordinate the making and implementation of the action plan developed and approved by all partners. The urban manager must be able to generate consensus, coordinate the work of volunteers, and keep the channels of collaboration between the different actors open and receptive. Furthermore, funding sources and work toward the technical, human, and financial self-sustainability of the revitalization initiative ought to also be identified.[62] Finally, the existence of the partnership does not mean that the different urban actors (municipality, retail association, economic activities, and other public agencies) involved in the revitalization no longer perform their respective functions in an active and committed way in order to create and maintain increasingly prosperous urban centers.

A Continued and Regularly Monitored Intervention

The formulation of an urban revitalization strategy, the creation of partnerships, the achievement of consensus, and the development of professional management take years to produce results. Their regular evaluation and monitorization can be accomplished through the use of performance indicators and benchmarks. Regular monitoring of progress is important for two main reasons. First, to inform the current (but also potential) sponsors of the success of the activities and, second, to enable the partnership to gain insight into the impacts of its strategies. Number of vacant properties, footfall, crime rates, street cleaning, and the number of jobs created are some indicators often used in monitoring activities.[63]

---

62. Marques (1999).

63. Brown (2001).

Conclusion

It is now widely accepted that cities are privileged centers of economic, social, and cultural activity in each country. Cities are also constantly changing, reflecting the culture, experiences, and priorities of their residents, workers, and visitors. However, what is happening nowadays is that these changes are increasingly very rapid and intense, mainly due to the internationalization of capital, new consumption habits, and altered travel and leisure patterns. Thus, and especially in the context of an increasingly open and competitive global economy, it is important to create wealth-generating cores, not only for the survival of cities but also for the prosperity of those who live, work, and entertain there.

This task is too important to be achieved only by the governmental intervention of local authorities. It has become increasingly urgent that local communities, private investors, nongovernmental organizations, and citizens organize and collaborate in revitalization actions that promote the interests of cities as a whole. What the international experience shows is that successful urban revitalization cases have largely resulted from creative partnerships between the public and private sectors.[64]

Revitalizing urban centers is a difficult, complex, and long-term task. The key finding of this chapter is that the problems of urban centers in Western cities have been created by relatively similar phenomena and that their revitalization can be better achieved if preconceived ideas and best practice principles are shared and implemented by all actors in the urban revitalization effort.[65] The list of myths and best practices is necessarily incomplete and is not intended to exhaust or be fully accepted by all involved one way or another with urban centers. This chapter aimed to synthesize a set of aspects that have appeared repeatedly in my professional and academic work in different countries. Above all, it is hoped that these best practices can be understood as suggestions for the creation and promotion of cities that are increasingly more sustainable and offer a higher quality of life for everyone.

---

64. McQuiad (1999), Robertson (1999), Waits and Henton (2001).

65. Jackson (2001).

PART I

IBERO-AMERICA

2

Placemaking

Introduction

Iberian city centers are old and have remarkable histories easily observed in their patrimonial heritage and vibrant socioeconomic nature. Different layers of urbanity and architectural influences can be found in most cities. Common to most Portuguese and Spanish cities are their narrow streets, punctuated by plazas and courtyards, and in other cases also riverfront locations. Spanish cities have their unique main squares in most cases due to redeveloped built environments.

Most of their city centers hold key social, economic, administrative, and cultural activities, despite recent suburbanization trends. Their historic centers have been the location of important activities (i.e., seats of government, churches and cathedrals, courts, public markets, and retail shops). Contrary to cities in Northern Europe, their Iberian counterparts allow and regularly promote year-round open-air activities, which contribute to high levels of sociability and vibrancy.[1]

Extensive suburbanization from the 1970s onward, anchored by new peripheral shopping malls and satellite residential subdivisions, have led to the weakening of many city centers, despite their size and location in the urban system.[2] In order to reverse the decline of those centers, many jurisdictions have implemented commercial urbanism (CU) regulations and various urban design projects in the last 15 to 20 years. These projects

---

1. Hass-Klau (2015).

2. Castillo-Manzano and Lopez-Valpuesta (2009).

25

aimed to modernize small, mainly independent, and mostly family-owned retail establishments in central locations and to revitalize city center shopping districts. Among commonly utilized strategies, one finds public space improvements, pedestrian precincts, and city center management strategies with public-private partnerships.

The urban design improvement of central areas—where retail has a relatively high concentration of establishments—has been a widespread strategy with very visible impacts in the appeal and attractiveness of historic centers of large cities.[3] Although published literature on city center livability, retail modernization, and placemaking is increasing, it focuses mostly on individualized and disconnected programs or projects of historic preservation, urban design improvements, retail modernization, transportation, and delivery logistics, mostly in large cities. Research on medium-size city center revitalization and integrated placemaking in Southern Europe is still quite meager and urgently needed to understand how peripheral regions are coping with the pressures of globalizing neoliberal tendencies, while preserving their cultural heritage, traditional lifestyles, and genuine authenticity.

This chapter analyzes pedestrian precincts in four medium-size Iberian cities: Braga, Guimarães, Burgos, and Valladolid, and it attempts to examine the impact of these pedestrian precincts on the overall placemaking livability of their city centers (see Figure 2.1). It also attempts to understand the extent of their benefits for different city users (i.e., residents, merchants, workers, and visitors). It confines itself to the following three research questions: Are the initial perceived advantages maintained after their continued implementation? Besides the obvious increases in comfort and safety for pedestrians, what are the impacts on retailing? How do institutional interests organize themselves to promote, maintain, or oppose the implementation, continuation, or reduction of these pedestrian schemes?

The argument is that to be fully effective those public space interventions need to be coordinated with appropriate legislative and institutional programs in order to generate partnerships with multiple civic and business agents for the continued management and improvement of those areas. At least 20 years of CU interventions have led mostly to the improvement of physical spaces in inner-city areas. However, the root cause of the problem—the continued upgrade and management of those same areas—requires better coordination and dedicated funding streams from public and private sources, and that can only happen with comprehensive and

3. RUDI and Academy of Urbanism (2009) and New Solutions Group (2013).

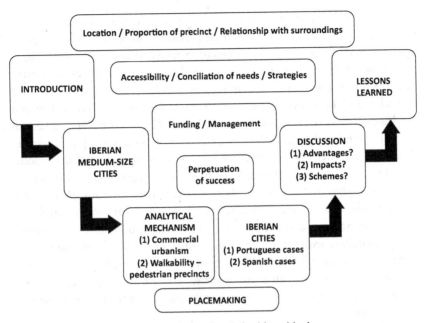

Figure 2.1. Placemaking's building blocks.

collaborative institutional arrangements. Therefore, it is hypothesized that city scale (structure) and political leadership ability (agency) influence the dynamics, complexities, and opportunities for the continued success of the initial CU projects.[4]

This chapter is based on four case studies and mostly qualitative research. The four cities were chosen because they exemplify recent urban dynamics and similar city interventions in various other medium-size cities throughout the northern part of the Iberian Peninsula, including Viseu, Vila Real, and Guarda in Portugal and Salamanca, Léon, and Bilbao in Spain.

The research techniques comprised multiple site visits to the case studies at different times during the late 2000s and again in early 2014, extensive literature synthesis, and 12 approximately one-hour-long semi-structured interviews with employees and business owners in various economic sectors, residents, and administrators.

The interview selection process utilized a snowball sampling method based on ethnographic and evaluative *derives*—that is, the canvassing of case studies on foot without a rigid predefined path but aimed at discovering the

---

4. Building on the work of Prytherch (2007) and Barber (2013).

initial character and urbanity of the cities' historic districts[5] and to assess the veracity of data and information found previously in local plans, programs, and studies examined during the literature review phase of the research.

One of the initial tasks was to conduct an inventory of pedestrian spaces in the selected cities. The other was to zero-in on specific streets and to understand how those particular streets and squares functioned within the historic centers. This was followed by an identification and review of the roles performed by the different entities responsible for capital improvements and their regular maintenance and an extensive review of their recent programs and activities. Although the findings are significant mostly to the four case studies and are not without limitations when considered as the partial results of an evaluative study, the longitudinal information, multidisciplinary assessment, and the precision of the descriptions will surely enable other researchers working on the same topics to utilize results confidently in their own research.[6] Arguably one of the major findings is that local governments are relying on their expertise, creative funding strategies, and established collaborations to maintain existing programs and eventually to start new ones.

Iberian Medium-Size Cities

Iberian cities are part of a large family of Southern European cities; as such, they share common development traits.[7] Iberian countries have been suffering both from macrocephaly and from high concentrations of urban development on the Atlantic and Mediterranean coasts. In Portugal, this is the littoral area from approximately Viana do Castelo to Setúbal and the southern Algarve region. In Spain it comprises the Mediterranean coast from the northern Costa Brava to Costa del Sol on the southern tip of the peninsula. Even though they share common traits, they constitute two distinct urban systems influenced by two different sovereign arrangements that shared a common border for many centuries.

These cities vary in terms of attractiveness, functionality, dynamics, and hierarchical networks. They compete with each other in many areas and they attempt to collaborate in others. Economic and infrastructure development exemplifies the former and attempts at reducing desertification and

5. Shortell (2016).

6. Kennedy (1979).

7. Salvati (2014).

depopulation in the border region is an example of the latter.[8] To refer to Iberian cities as a research subject is a superlative,[9] perhaps even a pretentious, gesture done only to capture an imagined place with a centuries-old common ancestry, barely present in today's urbanscape.

From a macro-geospatial perspective, one could identify seven large urban areas; three metropolises are internationally renowned (i.e., Madrid, Barcelona, and Lisbon), and four are relatively smaller regional metropolises (i.e., Valencia, Seville, Bilbao, and Porto). Besides these large areas, there are networks of medium-size cities in each country, which in general correspond to the capitals of the autonomous regions in Spain and to the district capitals in Portugal. Although the three megalopolises concentrate most of the commanding economic activity in the peninsula, the medium-size cities are organized according to geographical concentrations of development and, often, engage in regional planning activities, usually under European Union coordination programs and initiatives. The Atlantic Arc Commission comprising approximately 60 million people in Portugal, Spain, France, the United Kingdom, and Ireland is a good example of one of those supranational cooperation efforts.

Within each country, the largest cities are concentrated along the coast and development has occurred more vigorously during the last 50 years.[10] In Portugal, coastal development along highway A1 and the Northern railroad represents about 28 percent of the country, with a population of about 60 percent. The rest of the population lives mainly in medium-size cities throughout the country. The two metropolitan areas suffered a late suburbanization progress, which occurred mostly after the political revolution of 1974.

Portugal and Spain joined the European Union (then the European Economic Community [EEC]) in 1986, which led to high economic growth rates and large investment programs in transport infrastructure, health, higher education, and research and development during the 1990s.[11] Portuguese medium-size cities received increased attention in the mid-1990s. The Program for the Consolidation of the National Urban System and Support for the Execution of Municipal Master Plans (PROSIURB) aimed at strengthening these cities' roles in the structuring of the national territory in strategic planning terms. Medium-size cities were eligible to receive

---

8. Fernandez (2007).

9. Beauregard (2003a).

10. Pérez (2007).

11. Farrell (2005).

public development funds pending the making and adoption of master and strategic plans.[12] These attempts at influencing territorial development priorities with central administration programs was continued in the 2000s with the enactment of the National Program of Territorial Management Policy (PNPOT) and the National Sustainable Development Strategy (ENDS).[13]

Spain's capital, Madrid, located in the center of the Iberia Peninsula, dominates the Spanish geospatial urban system. The seventeen autonomous regions—each with its capital city and a system of provinces with hierarchically smaller cities, towns, and villages—are in different stages of development with a major distinction between the Mediterranean metropolises and the relatively depopulated interior part of the country.[14] The openness of the economy, influenced by neoliberal tendencies, has instigated regional political movements in several of these autonomous regions, namely, Catalonia and the Basque country. These attempts at seceding from Spain are not new. However, the impact of the global financial crisis and the real difficulties in controlling public spending might have renewed them due to the implementation of austerity measures.[15]

This chapter analyzes urban revitalization dynamics in small and medium-size Iberian cities, mostly because said cities have been understudied in comparison to the peninsula's large cities and metropolitan areas (i.e., peninsular macrocephaly). Therefore, attention is dedicated to urban development cycles and debates on current and future uses of historic districts and their public spaces, especially their pedestrianized precincts. In the case of historic districts, it took public authorities almost two decades to realize that careless suburbanization developments, subdivision, and planned-unit developments along major arterial roads in exurban areas of medium-size cities would contribute to the decay of more central districts.[16] By the same token, continued investments in historic districts have led to increases in property values and to revitalized spaces. The trend toward renovating public spaces in urban areas seems positive, and to a large extent it has been welcomed by those who are benefiting from those improvements the most. However, those interventions seem to be limited in their capacity to generate tangible economic improvements and long-lasting positive impacts in the built environment.

---

12. Ferrão, Henriques and Neves (1994).

13. Balsas (2012).

14. Lima and Cardenete (2008).

15. Harvey (2010).

16. Balsas (2000).

Analytical Mechanism

Commercial Urbanism

In Iberia, commercial urbanism projects and several mega events have helped to improve city center shopping districts.[17] Although improved public spaces are easily observable because of their physical designs, new pavements and street furniture, public art, trees, and other landscaping improvements, their indirect effects on the adjacent economic activities and building stocks are usually difficult to quantify and assess. One of the main premises of this chapter is that a review of the contributions of these improvements is critical to demonstrate their added value and to strengthen public policies not only aimed at improving central areas but also extending results and similar practices to other neighborhoods.[18] Retail development has evolved from small traditional retail establishments to shopping malls, outlets, discount stores, and internet shopping.[19] The primacy of retailing along the high street and in public markets was widespread until quite recently. Changes in the retail sector reached Southern Europe, mainly in the 1970s and 1980s.[20] Cities in metropolitan areas were the first to receive retail innovations. After a certain saturation of these areas, and usually as part of diversification strategies, shopping mall developers began targeting medium-size cities in the countryside.

The responses to these changes have been well tested and refined in countries like the United States, the United Kingdom, and the Central and Nordic European countries.[21] Centralized retail management, business improvement districts (BID), and town center management schemes (TCM) have been widely implemented.[22]

Southern European countries have privileged the utilization of CU interventions during the late 1990s and early 2000s. "Open-air shopping centers" were conceptualized in both Portugal and Spain to improve the livability of those shopping districts by attracting and retaining shoppers and by competitively marketing the central areas regionally and

---

17. Sanz (2007).

18. Gospodini (2004) and Filion et al. (2004).

19. Guy (2007).

20. Salgueiro (1996).

21. Karrholm (2008) and Frechoso-Remiro and Villarejo-Galende (2011).

22. Coca-Stefaniak et al. (2009).

internationally.[23] Portuguese CU projects were better institutionalized than the more ad hoc Spanish interventions, mainly led by autonomous regions, provinces, and individual cities. In fact, 35 percent of 23,000 potentially eligible retail establishments in Portugal received funding to modernize their stores under the EU's PROCOM program (1997–2007).[24]

Broader retail planning also comprised other regulatory measures, such as quotas for the opening of new shopping centers over a certain floor area and the regulation of retail trade schedules of hypermarkets and large shopping malls.[25] From relatively simple interventions in the public space, CU projects have evolved to attempts at maintaining and even bolstering positive impacts through the creation of public-private partnerships, regularly held events, and attempts at reducing the "free ride" effect—impacts caused by those who benefit from collective improvements without contributing their own fair share in anticipation of risk reduction and of future rewards. European Union funds were critical to the success of the first and second generations of CU projects, both in Portugal and Spain.[26]

Also, in Portugal, the management of open-air shopping areas, following their subsequent physical improvements, was ill conceived and produced very limited results. In many cases, city center managers lacked the political clout and the funding allocations needed to implement continued management, animation, and promotional actions. In Spain, the philosophy of the *centro comercial abierto* (CCA) has been implemented with different degrees of success. The combination of CU projects with urban-regeneration initiatives was relatively successful. In fact, Spain has strived to be part of European efforts and professional networks since the initial CU projects were featured at the first city center management congress in Malaga in 1998.[27]

Internationally, the continuation of major structural societal changes has contributed to the further decline of the high street and to the decline of many market towns in the UK, France, and in many other countries.[28] The UK has implemented legislative measures prompted by the Portas report to improve the conditions of town centers. One such initiative was the

---

23. Hall (1997) and Fernandes and Chamusca (2014).

24. Cavaco (2010).

25. Guy (2007).

26. Barreta (2012) and Fernandes and Chamusca (2014).

27. Frechoso-Remiro and Villarejo-Galende (2011).

28. Parker et al. (2014).

adoption of business improvement districts quite similar to the US and Canadian approaches. Unfortunately, Iberian cities have not adopted highly effective strategies both to halt the decline of city centers and to assure the long-term rewards of the mainly public-sector-driven modernization efforts conducted in the 2000s. These regeneration models are relatively time and space specific; nonetheless, it is argued that in democratic contexts where the imposition of economic development clawbacks is relatively difficult to implement, the most adequate strategy may be to assess progress at specific moments and to enact innovative public policies tailored to nascent issues as they arise.[29]

For instance, the 2008–2009 global financial crisis and the attainment of EU Objective 1 status by certain Iberian regions has meant that less funding is available to dedicate to the implementation of revitalization and management strategies, with considerable constraints on consumption levels and the possible closing down of small, family-owned, and independent retail establishments.[30] Resilience strategies going beyond the modernization of retail stores and into practical training of business owners and employees, in order to endow them with the skills and capabilities needed to face increased competition in a more globalized world, are strategies commonly implemented by local and regional chambers of commerce. Furthermore, initiatives such as the *Portuguese Fazer Acontecer Regeneração Urbana* under the aegis of the EU COMPETE program (2010–2014) and the URBANA initiative in Spain (2008–2013) have attempted to foster integrated urban (re)development and social cohesion interventions.[31]

Slow City and Sustainability

In certain European regions there is a growing emphasis on becoming ever more sustainable through the creation of urban sustainability programs aimed at preserving endogenous local cultures, traditional production methods, and at utilizing community development as a response to globalization trends.[32] Many of these almost spontaneous movements to preserve traditional environments and lifestyles have been supported by governmental

---

29. Tallon (2013).

30. Barreta (2012).

31. Garcia, Rodríguez, and Moreno (2015).

32. Beatley (2000) and Mayer and Knox (2006).

programs aimed at creating pedestrian precincts; redeveloping brownfield sites, waterfront areas, parks, and historic neighborhoods; as well as improving accessibility and environmental and social conditions.

Many communities throughout the Iberian Peninsula have benefited from developing Local Agenda 21 (LA21) strategies to identify, prioritize, and fund their sustainability actions at the local level.[33] In certain cases, these responses have attempted to reverse shrinking tendencies in urban areas through intermunicipal collaboration arrangements. The shrinking cities phenomenon is characterized by major demographic and spatial changes in European countries. As population ages, fertility rates decrease and families get smaller, their lifestyle needs and habitation arrangements change, and there are important implications for how cities function and develop over time. Directly related to this trend, and to a certain extent influenced by the sustainable development visions of society, the slow cities movement has emerged as a way to embrace, celebrate, and preserve unique practices, histories, know-how, and attempts at resisting exogenous trends imposed by globalization tendencies.[34]

Sustainability has been relatively more associated with environmental aspects. However, the social components of sustainability can be discussed in terms of attempts at preserving local economies by modernizing independent retail shops, while maintaining traditional urban lifestyles (living above the store and being able to walk safely and comfortably everywhere), and serving the needs of local populations in small and medium-size cities.[35] It is well accepted that changes in retail structure and the closing of decades-old grocery stores have contributed to the decline of livability conditions in city centers, despite their size and urban morphology.[36] Furthermore, the most recent global financial crisis has led many Spanish cities to also utilize alternative development tools. These have ranged from agro-ecological production to cooperatives, time-based currency, bioconstruction, and solidarity economy networks.[37]

The slow city or CITTA Slow movement and philosophy reflect an attempt at valuing what is local in terms of lifestyles, production modes, and products with certificate of local origin. Membership in this interna-

---

33. Fidélis and Pires (2009).

34. Inskeep (1988) and Servon and Pink (2015).

35. Capel (2009), Bell and Jayne (2009), and Mehta (2013).

36. Ruth and Franklin (2014).

37. Castells et al. (2012).

tional association is only for cities and towns below a certain threshold (50,000 inhabitants). Its fundamental approach to maintaining local idiosyncrasies could be extrapolated, and attempts at implementing relatively similar strategies have been accomplished in many Iberian cities, even prior to the emergence of this particular associative movement. The Basque city of Bilbao has accomplishment major strides by combining a strategy of local entrepreneurship that boosted the utilization of local raw materials and ancient technologies and partnerships with a strong cultural visibility due to the construction of the Guggenheim Museum—a paradigmatic example of a "glocal" action.

Another example in Iberian cities is the movement toward the preservation and rehabilitation of public markets in core city and neighborhood areas. Depending on the city, a public market was usually built to remove trading activities from streets and squares, where markets would occur either daily or on a regular basis, to a permanent building with higher cleanliness standards. The rise in supermarkets and hypermarkets with fresh produce has contributed to the decline of public markets. Although public markets in many Iberian cities have been renovated and are still important social and community places, like the ones in Barcelona, Lisbon, and Porto, there is still much work to be done in the case of small and medium-size cities. The work to date on the evolution of Portuguese public markets within a 2030 horizon has been relatively successful in the cities of Coimbra, Viseu, and Figueira da Foz.[38] These cities have modernized their public markets during the early 2000s and managed to keep them as strong magnets of community livability.

Another type of strategy worth mentioning is the "transition towns" initiative that basically allows cities and towns to adapt their local economies, built environments, and democratic governance practices to a post-carbon-intensive scenario. Energy conservation campaigns, reductions in greenhouse gas emissions, and fostering community resilience, while strengthening local employment creation and maintenance are some of the initiatives' main goals currently under way. Within this framework, relatively spontaneous social networks have been formed to implement alternative production and consumption models and practices, which also appear to have the potential to create renewed roles for retail establishments, public spaces, and their strategic management in historic districts.[39]

---

38. Barreta (2011).

39. Matos (2012) and Coca-Stefaniak and Bagaeen (2013).

Walkability—Pedestrian Precincts

The urban morphology of most Iberian city centers has enabled the creation of pedestrian precincts in many historic districts.[40] In fact, Southern European cities and towns have seen an increase in the number of pedestrian precincts in the last decade and a half.[41] This emphasis on creating city center pedestrian areas has resulted mainly from the need to preserve and conserve public spaces and their adjacent urban fabrics in historic neighborhoods.[42]

Varied EU multisectoral regeneration initiatives and programs (e.g., European Regional Development Fund [ERDF] and the Joint European Support for Sustainable Investment in City Areas [JESSICA]) have been implemented by many Iberian jurisdictions to revert blight and decay in both central and peripheral suburban areas. RECRIA, PROCOM, and POLIS are just a few examples of these initiatives implemented in Portugal under different political frameworks and governments,[43] and URBAN I and URBAN II are examples of urban regeneration programs in Spain.[44]

For instance, the POLIS program (2000–2006) in Portugal aimed to improve the urbanity of dilapidated areas by implementing joint urban and environmental regeneration strategies. The POLIS XXI program implemented after 2007 widened the scope of the prior POLIS program by emphasizing the economic dimensions of the regeneration in terms of talent and creative capacity.[45] The urban pilot program entitled Building León: A Development Proposal for the Old City 1995–1999 is an example of an innovative city center regeneration program in Spain.[46]

The decline of the city center has had structural reasons, and the responses, despite in most cases being holistic and comprehensive in nature, take time to change decades of neglect and inattention.[47] The appeal of suburban shopping areas, the ease of parking, the cleanliness and the combination of retail with office and leisure activities has had distinct impacts

---

40. Castillo-Manzano, Lopez-Valpuesta, and Asencio-Flores (2014) and Arranz-López et al. (2017).

41. Tejedor, Jerez, and Sánchez (2009).

42. Banerjee (2001) and Hass-Klau (2015).

43. Portas, Domingues, and Cabral (2002).

44. Fernandez (2007) and Garcia, Rodríguez and Moreno (2015).

45. Fadigas (2015).

46. Fernández (2007).

47. Pèrez-Eguiluz (2014).

depending on the relative hierarchy of the cities, their regional competition and governance practices, and the leadership efforts of their elected officials.

New technologies (i.e., internet, smart phones, GPS, etc.) seem to have belittled time and almost erased space to a trivial instance. Coupled with the immense power of multinational firms, which tend to exploit logistics systems to carry the largest amount of goods to the highest number of people at the lowest prices, the urban landscapes of many cities and towns have lost their historical heritage and, in certain cases, became clones of each other.[48] As temporal stages of development became noticeable and information availability about products and prices increased with the possibility of comparison shopping, attention shifted to placemaking strategies capable of bolstering the unique characteristics of localities.[49]

Many cities simply widened sidewalks to create more comfortable areas; others, partially or fully, closed one or several streets in their cores not only to accommodate shoppers but also to enable greater utilization of their newly created public spaces; yet others introduced limited vehicular speeds to 12.4 miles per hour, revamped public transit with CNG or minibuses, and constructed traffic-calming schemes aimed at controlling car traffic volumes and at preserving neighborhood characteristics.[50]

The automobile technology has allowed major revolutions in cities. Travel distances have been shortened as a consequence of more direct and faster routes and highways. However, the day remains only 24 hours long and good, attractive cities can still be distinguished from disinteresting ones.[51] Many of the cities built in the last half century are perceived as examples of wasteland, social isolation, automobile dependence, and partial culprits of greenhouse gas emissions. On the other hand, certain authors have argued that older cities are congested, their built environments are inappropriate by today's standards of living and expected comfort levels, and that newer neighborhoods have been properly planned to facilitate consumption, withstand change, and to adapt to the needs of future residents.[52] Despite these positions, walkability has remained a very important and desirable characteristic in both old and new cities.[53] In Portugal,

---

48. Castello (2010).

49. Sepe (2013).

50. Whitehead, Simmonds, and Preston (2006).

51. Hall (2014).

52. Jayne (2006).

53. Speck (2012) and Forsyth (2015).

universal design has been more than an election campaign tagline. Multiple associations have created plans, programs, and campaigns to reduce mobility barriers, mainly for special populations. The Ministry of the Environment has helped to prepare plans for 40 small and medium-size cities in the late 2007. Nonprofit organizations have created programs and networks to incentivize municipalities to retrofit their public spaces to universal mobility standards.[54]

Spain has also been incentivizing the creation of better walking conditions in cities for many years. Barcelona's *ramblas* and the city centers of many historic cities were pedestrianized many decades ago.[55] *Plazas Mayors* in most Spanish cities hold important identity, character, and meaning not only in the built environment and Iberian culture but also in the hearts and minds of most Spaniards.[56] Although this almost spontaneous cultural trait is difficult to find with its animation intensity, splendor, and joie de vivre in other places outside of the Iberian Peninsula, it is important to keep in mind that pedestrian-friendly areas are characterized by connectivity, legibility, comfort, pleasantness, traffic and urban safety, universality, and accessibility.[57]

Many of these characteristics are easily encountered in the pedestrian precincts of most small and medium-size cities.[58] In addition, the most vivid and easily observable functional change besides pedestrian precincts has been accomplished with the installation of traffic bollards to prevent automobiles from parking illegally on the sidewalk, obstructing pedestrians' right to walk safely and comfortably on the sidewalk.[59]

Iberian Cities

The cases for this chapter were preselected based on a combined record of best practices in CU projects and patrimonial heritage (see Figure 2.2). They contrast with other Iberian cities in the sense that they were among

---

54. Teles (2014).

55. Sepe (2013) and Castillo-Manzano, Lopez-Valpuesta, and Asencio-Flores (2014).

56. Luna-Garcia (2003).

57. Hass-Klau (2015).

58. Balsas (2014).

59. Loukaitou-Sideris and Ehrenfeucht (2009).

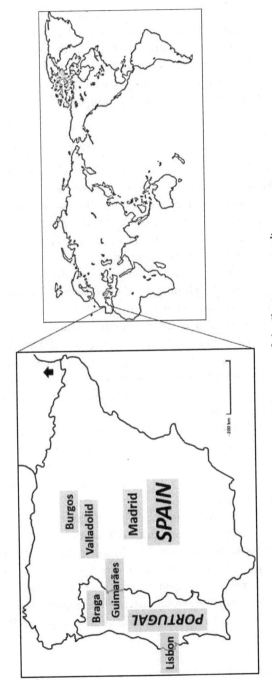

Figure 2.2. Location of the Iberian case studies.

the first to implement CU improvements. The preservation of their historic districts was also a major goal in regional and revitalization plans. Braga and Guimarães are located in the District of Braga in the Ave Valley. The two Spanish cities are located in the autonomous region of Castilla y León—the largest autonomous region in the country, covering an area of 36,380 square miles, and the third largest region in the European Union.

Portuguese Cases

The city of Braga is known as a center of culture, religiosity, and industrial activity.[60] Its historical roots go back to the time of the Roman Empire in the farthest, most western part of Iberia. The passage of time saw the construction of protective walls, which remained through the medieval era. Due to multiple vicissitudes, the city experienced major changes in subsequent centuries, which led to the demolition of the wall, the opening up of squares and small parks, and later on to large urban blocks.

The city possesses a high number of churches and convents, including the city's cathedral and two major sanctuaries. Being the capital district, it has a relatively high number of deconcentrated regional services. The city's chamber of commerce and its business elite (agency) have had a strong dynamism. The city center has a strong inner-city retail sector presence. The Rua do Souto is perhaps the most important pedestrian street in the city, which with approximately 143,518.8 square yards is one of the largest pedestrian precincts in the whole country (see Figure 2.3).

Together with the two very famous religious sanctuaries (i.e., Bom Jesus and Sameiro), this pedestrianized precinct is the most touristic and visited area in the city. The University of Minho in Braga has been responsible for the successful R&D transfers to the bustling entrepreneurial activities throughout the northeast.

Guimarães has an important place in the history of the country. The city center has very exiguous streets and a rich architectural patrimony going back to the 10th century. The Praça do Toural is the main square outside of the formal city wall. The Largo da Oliveira and the Praça de São Tiago are located right in the historic center, and the Domus Municipalis was the place where the city councilors would meet before important decisions about the future of the city had to be made (Figure 2.4 on page 42).

---

60. Bandeira and Vilaça (2013).

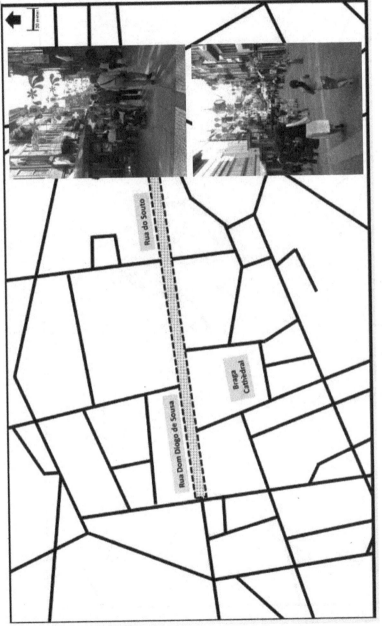

Figure 2.3. Historic center of Braga.
(Images of Rua do Souto)

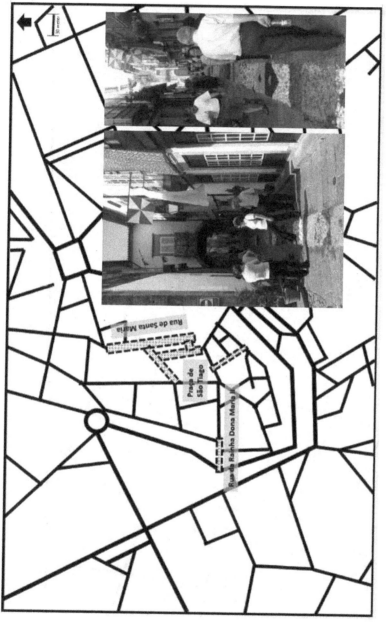

Figure 2.4. Historic center of Guimarães.
(Images of Rua de Santa Maria)

The city had leather tanneries for at least 400 years. In recent decades the city benefited from the opening of a campus of the University of Minho. The city's patrimonial heritage was recognized as a world heritage city of the UNESCO in 2001. In addition to the historic district, the city also has new expansion areas. These areas are more attuned to the needs of modern consumers. The many banks and other retail establishments are located along modern wide avenues within a few short blocks of the historic center.[61]

Guimarães had its football stadium renovated for the 2004 European Championship, which according to an interviewee augmented the tourism potential of the historic center. In addition, it contributed to the city also hosting the 2012 European Capital of Culture event—an opportunity to celebrate culture, upgrade several cultural facilities such as the leather tanneries, and to implement a major promotional campaign. Still in cultural terms but with an annual frequency only, some of the narrow streets of the historic district are decorated with carpets of flowers to host religious parades during the summer city festivities (i.e., Festas da Cidade).

Spanish Cases

Burgos is an important regional city in northern Spain. It is well known for its gothic cathedral that was classified as world heritage site of UNESCO in 1984. The Arlanzón River separates the historic center from the newer neighborhoods and it helps to structure the urban form of the city in an elongated linear arrangement, almost reminiscent of Arturo Soria's linear city.[62] The *Plaza Mayor* is bordered by the city hall located in the historic center. The municipal theater is emblematically located across the river from the city's convention center.

The streets in the historic center have retail establishments on the ground floor and residences and offices in the floors above (see Figure 2.5 on page 44). The transportation hubs are on opposite sides of the city, the regional bus station is across the river from the cathedral square and the new and very modern train station is literally outside of the city, in an expansion area near the Burgos University Hospital.

Residents and visitors happily patronize the stores in the city center's pedestrian precinct in the vicinity of the city's cathedral, mainly in the

---

61. Rahaman, Lourenço, and Viegas (2012).

62. Neuman and Gavinha (2005).

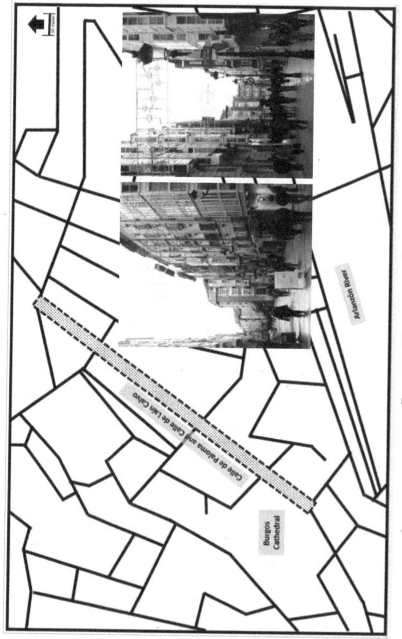

Figure 2.5. Historic center of Burgos.
(Images of Calle de Laín Calvo)

evening and on weekends and holidays, as was observed by and related to the author during various interviews with Burgos's business owners, residents, and workers. There is also one underground parking garage in the historic center with capacity for about 500 cars. During the field visit, very few vacant or for sale/lease buildings were found in winter 2013–2014. The ecclesiastical monasteries and religious schools are relatively recondite from the city center.

Valladolid is the capital of the autonomous region of Castilla y León.[63] The city is bordered by the Pisuerga River, which until recently constrained most of the city to the eastern bank. The city hall is located on the *Plaza Mayor*, where in addition to this turn-of-the-19th-century building there are many other colonnaded structures, typical of Spanish architecture of the last century. The *Plaza Mayor* is pedestrianized with vehicular circulation surrounding the central area. The pedestrian street network is comprehensive with streets leading to and from the *Plaza Mayor* to other surrounding public spaces in the city center (see Figure 2.6 on page 46), such as the Plaza de España and Campo Grande park.

The city's most important employment sectors are services and industry with about three-fourths and one-tenth of total employment, respectively. Retail in the city center consists mostly of traditional stores, with the exception of an *El Corte Inglês* department store located a short distance from the *Plaza Mayor*. Various interviewees in Valladolid confided that the city has a relatively small and mostly regional tourism market, although the extensive pedestrian street network and the high concentration of various important public and private services and public parks in the city center enable everyone to reach a high number of destinations in safe and comfortable conditions simply by walking. Furthermore, the city's new bike share scheme also makes daily life without a car a viable option for residents and tourists alike.

Discussion

Tables 2.1 and 2.2 summarize the selected pedestrian precincts. The tables compare the case studies in terms of nine main characteristics deemed

---

63. Sanz (2007).

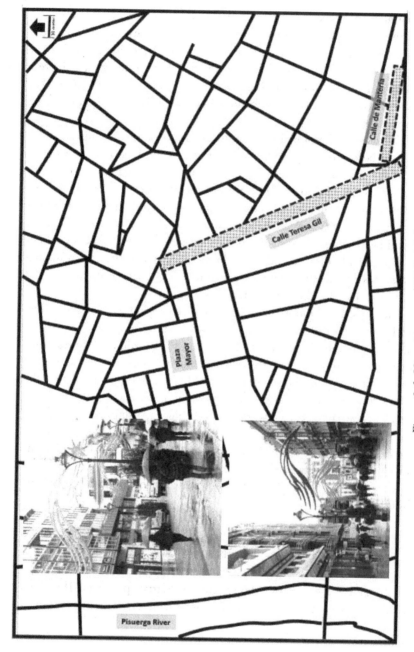

Figure 2.6. Historic center of Valladolid.
(Images of Calle Santiago)

important when analyzing pedestrian precincts. This chapter has formulated these three questions: Are the initial perceived advantages maintained after their continued implementation? Besides the obvious increases in comfort and safety for pedestrians, what are the impacts on retailing? How do institutional interests organize themselves to promote, maintain, or oppose the implementation, continuation, or reduction of these pedestrian schemes? This section attempts to answer these questions. The first question is answered by reflecting on the first six rows of tables 2.1 and 2.2. The second question is answered mainly by row seven; and finally, the third question is answered by rows eight and nine. Evidence is also provided on how benefits for different city users materialized before and after the placemaking interventions.[64]

Maintenance of Perceived Advantages?

Before answering this question, it is important to review the cities' most pertinent characteristics, similarities, and differences. These pedestrian precincts are located in historic centers. They constitute a combination of interconnected streets, squares, and alleyways. The old pedestrian streets in Portuguese cities are much narrower than the Spanish ones, an estimated average of 5.4–7.6 versus 8.7–10.9 yards. This is partly explained by the era when those centers were built, by each city's urban morphology, and also by the degree of urban redevelopment or renovation experienced over the years.

A comparative analysis of the demographics in the case studies shows that only one of the four municipalities had fewer than 100 thousand inhabitants in 2011: Guimarães. Portuguese cities have the highest urban densities. City centers have experienced different demographic trends as a direct result of residential, commercial, and service dynamics and preservation policies. Valladolid's population has decreased slightly in 2001–2011.

The urban form of each city explains, at least partially, its fundamental socioeconomic trends. Although neighborhood blocks in the Spanish cities are relatively regular, allowing for modern living conditions, such is not the case in the historic districts of Braga and Guimarães, where certain residences in Braga are dilapidated—as it was revealed by an interviewee—and in the latter, it is virtually impossible, for instance, to park a car in certain streets of the historic center.

---

64. Balsas (2004b).

Table 2.1. Synthesis of pedestrian areas in the Portuguese medium-size cities[65]

	Braga	Guimarães
Location of the main streets / squares	Historic center, Rua do Souto, reduction in stores 53 to 46 1995–2008, Rua Dom Diogo de Sousa in the alignment (old Cardo Maximus) to the Arco da Porta Nova.	Historic center, Praça de São Tiago, Largo da Oliveira, Rua da Rainha Dona Maria II, Rua Egas Moniz, Rua de Santa Maria.
Population (2001; 2011) and area	110,000; 136,885 inhabitants; 12.3 square miles.	50,000; 47,588 inhabitants; 8.8 square miles.
Proportion of the pedestrian precinct	Eleven pedestrianized streets and squares (0.046 square miles), largest pedestrian area in Portugal.	Streets inside the medieval walls restricted to residents, regulated (un)loading.
Relationship between the streets and the surrounding areas / activities	The main shopping area in the city, stores/offices increased 2% 1995–2008 to a total of 788 establishments.	Historic district serves mainly residential and commercial functions.
Accessibility to the pedestrian precincts and movement in the street	Underground garages 2,500 spaces (Av. Central, Arcada, Av. Da Liberdade, Praça da Galiza, Campo da Vinha), restricted access 8:00–11:00 p.m.	Regulation restricts mobility and accessibility to residents.
Conciliation between the needs of different street users	Some vandalism of street furniture, aesthetically inconvenient use of pillars to stop abusive car parking.	Physical measures (retractable and fixed bollards) to control access to the historic center, license plate readers.

65. www.ine.pt, Domingues (2006), Guimarães (2009), Bandeira and Vilaça (2013).

	Braga	Guimarães
Strategies to respond to competition from new and emerging centers	PROCOM (1995–2000): renovation of 22 streets and the modernization of 171 establishments (47% participation rate), eight streets were pedestrianized, partnerships, animation programs.	Skill-building programs, cultural and tourism-oriented activities in the historic center.
Funding of improvements and continued management and promotional activities	First, commercial urbanism PROCOM; second, commercial urbanism URBCOM, 7 million Euros invested 1985–2010.	PROCOM (12 million Euros of potential investment); URBCOM (1 million Euros of potential investment).
Perpetuate success and avoidance of decline	Multisectorial interventions (housing, retail, public space, parking, promotion, etc.), conservation plan.	Technical advisory committee (GTL) 1985.

Table 2.2. Synthesis of pedestrian areas in the Spanish medium-size cities[66]

	Burgos	Valladolid
Location of the main streets / squares	Historic center, area surrounding the cathedral, the *Plaza Mayor*, Calles Paloma, and Laín Calvo.	Historic center, Calles de Manteria and Teresa Gil between the *Plaza Mayor* and Plaza de España.
Population and area	167,962;178,574 inhabitants; 41.3 square miles.	318,293;311,501 inhabitants; 76 square miles.
Proportion of the pedestrian precinct	1.5 square miles of car-free pedestrian streets.	Ample plazas and streets.

continued on next page

66. www.estadistica.jcyl.es/, Asociación Vallisoletana de Comercio (2011).

Table 2.2. Continued.

	Burgos	Valladolid
Relationship between the streets and the surrounding areas / activities	The *Plaza Mayor* has services and retail functions, the pedestrian streets are bordered by retail on the ground floor with housing and services above.	Commercial with services and residential uses in upper floors, increase of 102 stores (2009–2011) total 2,811, and 30% higher vacancy rate (457 spaces).
Accessibility to the pedestrian precincts and movement in the street	Sixteen access points, shared bicycle (Burgos BICI).	Vertical signage adverting of nature of the streets, shared bicycle scheme (Valla BICI).
Conciliation between the needs of different street users	Restricted mobility with retractable bollards, ceramic tiles, and concrete and stone curbs.	Mixed tiles, different materials used to design sidewalks, and travel lanes.
Strategies to respond to competition from new and emerging centers	Logistics system with electric distribution vehicles in the pedestrian precinct.	Master plan recommendations to encourage city center retail activity, street furniture, fountains.
Funding of improvements and continued management and promotional activities	Investment of 30 million Euros.	Inventory of commercial establishments Valladolid.
Perpetuate success and avoidance of decline	Phased implementation (2003–2006), public celebration upon launching each phase, traffic control center, CIVITAS sustainability network, commercial promotions.	Commercial urbanism regulations.

The length of the pedestrianized streets also varies from short streets and courtyards to the relatively long high streets. In the cities of Braga and Burgos, the main commercial streets comprise a continuous and straight alignment of the following streets, Ruas do Souto and Dom Diogo de Sousa in Braga and Calles de Paloma and de Laín Calvo in Burgos.

The relationship between the streets and the surrounding areas both enhances and conditions the land uses in the adjacent urban fabric. Streets were pedestrianized to create better walking conditions for everyone. The criteria included a combination of commercial or civic uses on the ground floors and the elimination of traffic safety concerns. Accessibility to the pedestrian precincts varies from unrestricted in Braga and Valladolid to restricted in certain streets in Guimarães and Burgos.

The most common feature used to control access to the pedestrian precinct is a bollard system activated by a user's card, which grants vehicular access to the area. Interview testimonies confirmed the author's observation of the value of traffic-calming improvements on several streets surrounding the historic centers, with narrower travel lanes protected by short metal bollards to prevent the abusive invasion of sidewalk space by automobiles.

Another common measure in these pedestrian precincts is the existence of (surface and underground) parking garages or on-street parking in the immediacies of the precincts. Also, there are public transportation stops and mass transit stations in very close proximity to the precincts. These two transportation features are essential to their proper functioning. Finally, the four cities also regulate the delivery of goods to the retail establishments located along the pedestrian streets to no later than 11 a.m. on weekdays and Saturdays.

The conciliation of the needs of different street users in most cities has been accomplished through the use of different pavement materials and design features to create distinct, at level, paths for different users. This central travel lane is sided by areas dedicated to pedestrians, despite pedestrians being allowed to use the full width of the street. This allows universal design principles to be implemented almost everywhere and to still create in the minds of users the alertness needed for the eventual presence of vehicular traffic, such as emergency vehicles.[67]

In the US, many pedestrian precincts were demolished in the 1980s and early 1990s and streets reopened to vehicular traffic.[68] Such a phenom-

---

67. Southworth (2005).

68. Hass-Klau (2015).

enon has not happened in any of the Iberian cities reviewed in this chapter. Although, there have been critical observations of the extensiveness of the pedestrianized areas. The common criticism that the improvements have influenced automobile-dependent shoppers to go elsewhere often results from a combination of more diversified and appealing retail offers in other locations, usually also at more affordable prices.

It is known that retail stores located in city centers still have to compete with stores located in peripheral shopping centers. Those commercial spaces are fully designed real estate investments, mostly created to lure shoppers away from other existing trade areas. Retail in city centers benefits from the uniqueness that cannot be recreated in shopping malls. Their niche markets are different and instead of mainly replicating peripheral shopping malls, their advantage might be in differentiating themselves from other shopping areas, which might have contributed to the 2 percent increase in stores/offices in Braga's main shopping area to a total of 788 establishments during 1995–2008.[69] Variations in sales might not be directly attributed to the pedestrianized streets but to a combination of internal and external factors, such as quality and variety of goods, prices, retail schedules, capacity to haul away, lifestyle changes, disposable income, accessibility, parking, and other area amenities.

Impacts on Retailing?

The impacts on retailing can be assessed through a combination of sales volumes, store turnover, retail rents, and duration of commercial activity. The pedestrianized spaces can either supplement or constrain certain activities in the adjacent built environment. Each effect varies for different types of commercial activities, and even for the same type of activity, it depends on where in the street such activity is located and on the density and characteristics of the surrounding activities. The improvement of streets and squares is the visible part of the revitalization. However, most of these improvements involved the replacement of old underground infrastructure, such as water mains, sewage pipes, and electric and fiber optic cables. The pavement installed in many of these pedestrianized precincts ranged from ceramic tiles, such as the ones in most of the streets in the Spanish cities, to granite slabs and cobblestones in the Portuguese cities.

---

69. Guimarães (2009).

A measure of vibrancy of pedestrian areas is footfall, which certain cities care to monitor over time. In many Iberian cities, official walking figures at the municipal level show that walking mode share has been decreasing over time, perhaps due to growing automobile ownership and usage. Ferreira (2010) has also conducted ethnographic research on how other activities besides the ones located in Rua Direita have helped to create footfall. It is accepted that simply replacing the pavement is no guarantee that additional people will flock to the pedestrian precincts. The activities in the built environment and the mix of multiple sectors of activity are what attracts people to city centers.

The CU projects in Portugal included an animation component that ranged from fashion shows, holiday season fairs, street performances, and many other regularly held festivals and cultural events. Also, in Guimarães, the night-time economy (i.e., bars and pubs) in the city center has experienced a revival in recent years.

The Spanish *la movida* characterized by a gregarious tendency to go out at night, party, drink, and recreate until quite late at night is well known in the big cities of Madrid, Barcelona, and Seville. Smaller cities might not generate the same crowds, but they also have a considerable entertainment component, especially in cities with colleges and universities, such as Braga, Guimarães, and Valladolid. In Valladolid, it is believed that night-time economic activities have had a detrimental impact on some of the city's retail activities, as expressed by an interviewee and documented by the Asociación Vallisoletana de Comercio with the increase of 102 stores (2009–2011) to a total of 2,811, but with a 30 percent higher vacancy rate (457 spaces).[70] In addition to examining the direct and indirect impacts on retailing, one can also examine what other activities are being implemented to respond to added competition from new and emerging centers. Public art, street furniture, maintenance of important public and nonprofit institutions in city center locations, residential renovations, modernization of retail establishments, installation of cultural facilities such as museums and municipal art galleries, in addition to training and business acumen workshops and capacity-building for retailers, have been devised and implemented recently to different extents in the four cities.[71]

---

70. Asociación Vallisoletana de Comercio (2011).

71. Barreta (2012) and Frechoso-Remiro and Villarejo-Galende (2011).

Institutional Interests?

Pedestrian streets are regulated by municipalities. These jurisdictions are responsible for their construction, maintenance, circulation patterns, and overall utilization by multiple publics. Streets have been closed to traffic, fully or only partially, as a result of public decisions recommended by technical advisors and approved by elected officials. Residents, and especially merchants and trade association leaders, have lobbied municipalities to have certain streets pedestrianized. In addition to their business activities, many merchants are members of political parties or have organized themselves independently to make their concerns and ideas heard by elected officials. Acts of leadership by elected officials and by civic volunteers are critical to the success of city center revitalization efforts.

On the other hand, certain municipalities, such as Braga, Guimarães, and Burgos, have created technical advisory committees (GTL) and municipal corporations, or they became part of new organizations (e.g., urban rehabilitation societies—SRU in Portugal), in order to implement revitalization strategies. Funding for many of these activities usually has multiple sources ranging from the European Union and national and local governments to the private sector. Certain funding arrangements pay only for capital improvements, while others pay for management, animation, and promotional activities.

In the case of Portuguese cities, the role of institutionalized partnerships involving central and local governments and the merchants and their representative associations was very important to the implementation and continued success of commercial revitalization. The Portuguese *Unidades de Acompanhamento e Coordenação* (UAC) and the Spanish *Centros Comerciales Abiertos* (CCA) are relatively similar to many of their counterparts in Europe and North America, and as such they also suffer from similar problems, mainly the need to find creative ways to sustain and enhance the revitalization outcomes achieved in previous years.[72]

Obtaining funding for new projects has been a major barrier to their continued existence. Since many of the CU projects were sponsored with EU funds and many of them were not formally institutionalized at the local level, the leaders of those organizations have had difficulty continuing their work. The lack of required contributions to pay for some of the improve-

---

72. Coca-Stefaniak et al. (2009).

ments, animation, and promotional activities has drastically curtailed their effectiveness.

Once the material improvements have been made to a city center, it is also understood that there is a change from mostly capital improvements to maintenance and promotional activities, which are relatively less costly than the former. The perpetuation of success and the avoidance of decline is likely to be accomplished with regulatory actions, such as those in Valladolid that favor central locations and prevent the sprawling of suburban areas. Commercial partnerships between merchants and their trade associations are regularly utilized for animation and promotional campaigns, while elected officials at multiple levels are responsible for regulating new commercial developments in and outside of city centers.

Lessons Learned

The type and characteristics of an urban environment impact the quality of life of those who inhabit it.[73] Cities have been around for millennia and planners, of different guises, have been attempting to build better cities for a long time. As new technologies appeared and urbanization became an instrument of wealth maximization, almost completely detached from social networks—and no longer an opportunity to create ever more livable and vibrant humane places[74]—it seems that individuals were sidetracked and deluded into believing that ancient city-building and societal rules and principles were no longer valid.[75] While cities have the capacity to regenerate themselves, certain characteristics, apparently fundamental to the maintenance of specific cultural traits and values, are put at the mercy of capitalistic logics, perhaps beyond the control of those responsible for the destinies and livelihoods of local communities.[76]

Retailing has occurred in central locations for many generations. Most cities reviewed in this chapter were created more than 2,000 years ago.[77] Their creation resulted from civic, trade, and defense purposes. They have

---

73. Fernandes and Martins (1988).

74. Ravenscroft (2000) and Arefi (2014).

75. Hall (2014) and Balsas (2017).

76. Harvey (2010).

withstood the test of time. Some of their heritage has been preserved, while many of their functions are still in existence today. These four cities have attempted to create better public spaces in hopes that exogenous urban development models, propagated by global forces, do not destroy local cultural heritage and legacies nor contribute to the further homogenization of cityscapes.[78]

This chapter has characterized pedestrian precincts in four medium-size cities. An attempt was made to examine the impact of these pedestrianized precincts on the overall livability of their city centers. The three fundamental research questions were answered and it was argued that to be fully effective those public space interventions need to be coordinated with appropriate regulatory and institutional programs like the ones identified in the analytical mechanism and that are capable of generating partnerships with multiple civic and business agents.[79] This chapter is limited by its scope, since it reviews urban policies enacted after 1995, and by the ethnographic methods derived mostly from the design disciplines, which confine the scientificity of its results.

This chapter has identified six lessons learned with relevant implications for similar realities. First, traditionally, transportation hubs, major employers, supermarkets, banks, and publicly run services such as post offices, *Lojas do Cidadão*, and schools tend to generate high pedestrian activity. With major changes in the economy, many services are now conducted remotely with visible reductions in walking for customary services. Second, the improvement of city centers has contributed to an increase in the leisure and night-time economy. Third, neighborhood specialization might have detrimental impacts to the overall city center livability. Such areas require planning interventions to minimize land use conflicts and abrupt changes in property values.

Fourth, big Iberian cities, such as Lisbon and Barcelona, had the means to conduct retail censuses of their cores and to even create citywide commercial atlases (i.e., *Cartas Estratégicas do Comércio*) with the intent of providing information to customers and decision-makers.[80] Medium-size

---

77. Bandeira and Vilaça (2013).

78. Hall (2009).

79. Guy (2007).

80. Carreras (2003) and Barreta (2012).

cities like the ones studied in this chapter might not even need such a planning instrument. However, they will require a proactive planning attitude to prevent positive results from getting lost (overall livability improvements), mainly due to contradictory future actions (inadequate prioritization of sectoral programs instead of structural quality of life goals). Fifth, local governments are relying on their expertise, creative funding strategies, and established collaborations to maintain existing programs and eventually to start new ones. Sixth, city scale, proactive collaboration, and political leadership are found to influence the dynamics, complexities, and opportunities for the continued success of CU projects in medium-size cities.

3

Walkability and Downtown Vibrancy

Introduction

Vibrant urban places are those that enable people to perform many and diverse activities. Successful city centers are nurtured to allow people to recreate and experience a myriad of behaviors.[1] Such an ensemble may look to the untrained eye like spontaneous events without much order or organization. Nonetheless, an urban professional is aware of basic principles that need to be observed to enable the continued vibrancy of those places. There is a fundamental concern with the extent to which human behaviors are influenced by socioeconomic, cultural, legal, and corporate frameworks that may vary from country to country. In the absence of universal rules, how can professionals help to create and encourage vibrant main streets and city centers?

This chapter analyzes four walk-only commercial precincts in the Ibero-American world. Common to these streets is the fact that walking has priority over other modes of transport. A comparative framework was developed to study: the symbiotic relationship between walking and activities in the adjacent urban fabric, the overall success of these streets and the existence (or not) of professional management organizations, and the quality of the physical schemes to minimize potential conflicts among street users. The argument is that the study of governance practices is important to understand whether similar phenomena in distinct contexts have been dealt with differently and have produced relatively unique outcomes in terms of improved public spaces, a reinvigorated built environment, and more robust governance networks, especially at the neighborhood and city levels.

---

1. Whyte (1988), Zacharias (2001), and Paumier (2004).

With a few exceptions, everyone walks, everyone shops, and everyone lives somewhere.[2] That somewhere varies throughout the world. This chapter examines how commercial pedestrian precincts have been used to improve cities. Retailing and commercial activities are important in cities and they are likely to remain so in the future. The history of commercial pedestrian precincts (i.e., pedestrian malls) in the US is convoluted; during the 1960s and early 1970s many pedestrian malls were built and most of them were abandoned, adapted, or demolished in subsequent decades, with only a few successful ones remaining in operation nowadays.[3] Lincoln Road Mall in Miami Beach, Florida, and Third Street Promenade in Santa Monica, California, are good examples of early malls that have been partially rebuilt in recent years.[4]

Probably the most adopted typology in US main streets is that of a thoroughfare with wide sidewalks, on-street parking, and calmed traffic—a compromised hybrid version between the fully enclosed pedestrian mall and the street for vehicular and foot traffic. Despite this format, many private shopping malls do have walk-only precincts. The assumption is that they create an environment conducive to shopping and to entertainment (i.e., a designed "there," often in the middle of outlying big box stores). The issue is that, quite often, these shopping malls drain people and economic activity out of older downtown areas, many of which may have benefited from public efforts aimed at revitalizing their cores.

Downtown revitalization organizations and local authorities have an important role in devising mechanisms to revive and maintain vibrant downtowns.[5] Many of those rules and principles have been identified in the literature and applied to cities across the world.[6] This chapter examines some of the general principles in face of the 2008–2009 global financial crisis. It is assumed that many of the old principles of urbanity (e.g., centers; human scale; a safe, healthy, and attractive built environment) that have endured for centuries in cities throughout the world will remain.[7]

In recent decades, many European cities have embarked in urban revitalization operations and have attempted to increase walkability, despite

---

2. Untermann (1984) and Solnit (2000).

3. Gibbs (2012).

4. Shulman (2009) and Pojani (2008).

5. Vargas and Castilho (2015).

6. Speck (2012).

7. Montgomery (1998).

being organically a lot more walkable than their North American counterparts.[8] Can planners, architects, and designers learn from interventions in those older agglomerations? As the saying goes, "Design counts! Great streets do not just happen."[9] This chapter reviews several pertinent features of commercial pedestrian precincts currently in operation. The methods consisted of literature reviews on walking, urban design and pedestrian malls, commercial urbanism, as well as mainly qualitative analysis based on study visits to the selected streets and semi-structured interviews with urban professionals during the last decade and a half.[10]

Although it is common to find literature on single case study streets, this chapter presents a comparative analysis of common themes to this particular type of street arrangement, with emphasis on Latin America. Although "it is usually not possible to compare neighborhoods on the basis of their spatial pattern, walkability or morphological characteristics,"[11] it is important to remember that "the subject of commercial culture begs for worldwide comparison because . . . consumption as a global ideal [is] the most universal ideal in human history."[12] The ultimate aim is to arrive at a set of planning implications helpful to both scholars and practitioners.

The walk-only commercial precincts reviewed in this chapter are the Rua Direita, Rua Barão de Itapetininga, and Rua de São Bento in São Paulo, Brazil; Calle de Francisco Madero in Mexico City, Mexico; Las Ramblas in Barcelona, Spain; and the Rua de Santa Catarina in Porto, Portugal (see Figure 3.1 on page 62). These streets were selected based on the author's prior analysis and on available data and literature. The motivation was reinforced by the author's knowledge of the evolution of recent shopping districts and walk-only streets in various parts of the world, including Portugal, Spain, Brazil, Mexico, the UK, and China.

The chapter is divided into four main sections. Following this introduction, the first section is a brief review of three main literature strands. The second section introduces the case studies. The third section is a comparative analysis of nine themes identified by the author as critical to the vibrancy of commercial pedestrian precincts. The fourth section gives some concluding remarks and discusses implications for practice.

---

8. Castillo-Manzano, Lopez-Valpuesta, and Asencio-Flores (2014).

9. Jacobs (1993, 314).

10. Zagatto (2012), García (2015), Redón (2015), and Delgado (2016).

11. Talen (2002, 258).

12. Cochran (1999, 17–18).

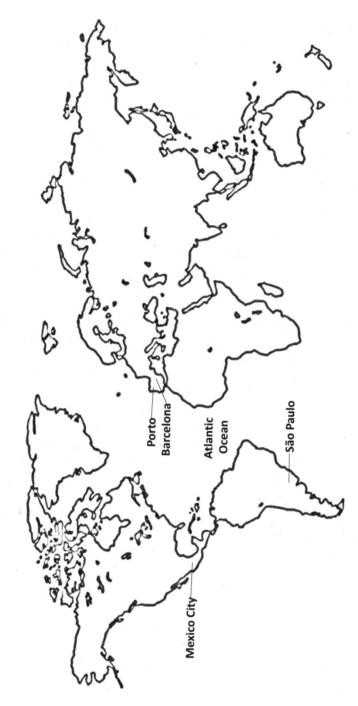

Porto

Barcelona

Atlantic
Ocean

São Paulo

Mexico City

Figure 3.1. Location of the Ibero-American walk-only commercial precincts.

Analytical Mechanism

This section is a review of these main literature strands: downtown revitalization, shopping, and walking environments. Downtown revitalization involves a set of articulations among various stakeholders aimed at accomplishing common goals.[13] Shared visions, collaborations, and joint implementation agendas are important to ameliorating urban problems in central city areas. The 21st-century analytical framework for downtown revitalization comprises three dimensions of analysis: urban restructuring, neoliberal policies, and social milieu (see Figure 3.2). Public policies for downtown revitalization tend to be twofold: placemarketing and placemaking.[14] A city's size, place within the urban hierarchy, urban morphology, socioeconomic structure, civic community, and political regimes tend to impact the type, extent, and effectiveness of governance mechanisms. The downtowns of global Latin American cities have undergone transformative experiences relatively similar to those of the global north, with a slight time lag and with a higher presence of the informal sector.[15]

Latin American global downtowns (see Table 3.1 for basic socioeconomic indicators) have been influenced by two important trends: entrepreneurship

Table 3.1. Comparison of the Latin American global cities[16]

	São Paulo	Mexico City
Current population in the city (millions)	10.4	8.6
Current population in the metropolitan area (millions)	19.2	19.2
Central area density (people per km²)	10,370	12,880
Percent of GDP produced by each city	11.9	21.5
Percent of the country's population residing in each city	5.8	8.4
GDP per capita (US$)	12,020	18,320
Average annual growth of GVA 1993–2010	3.2	2.9
Income inequality (Gini index)	61	56
Murder rate (homicides per 100,000 inhabitants)	13.2	21.0
Annual CO_2 emissions (kg per capita)	1,120	5,860

13. Robertson (1997) and Rotenberg (2011).

14. Castello (2010) and Sepe (2013).

15. Herzog (2006) and Roy (2012).

16. LSE, "Urban Age Cities Compared" (2011).

and design management. The entrepreneurship trend strongly dominates the private sector in the political economy of the city. In addition, international organizations, such as the Inter-American Development Bank (IDB) and the World Bank (WB), have influenced the development and urban agenda of many neighborhoods in these large cities, such as the IDB-funded program in downtown São Paulo.[17] This has led to the importation of models and practices from the global north, which increasingly tend to force the recipients of their financial assistance to follow stringent business criteria. On the other hand, the design management trend places more emphasis on the traditional design and architectonic management of the built environment. This trend ascertains a belief in the capacity of professional expertise to inform public policy through the making of plans and their strict implementation (e.g., the *Programa Parcial de Desarollo Urbano* and the *Plan Integral de Manejo del Centro* for downtown Mexico City). These plans cover many intervention areas ranging from housing to public spaces, monuments, transportation, and community economic development.

Entrepreneurship is associated with placemarketing practices, while design management is more related to placemaking strategies, and one could almost retrace their ancestry to two different Ibero-American urban-istic traditions. The Portuguese city-building archetype in the New World has been distinguished from the Spanish.[18] The Portuguese followed barely no urbanistic rules besides choosing locations close to rivers, elevations for safety, adaptation to the existing terrain, and the existence of a main street (i.e., *Rua Direita da cadeia para a ponte*), which has resulted in high levels of organicity and spontaneous development.[19] The Spanish model was based on a well-established set of formal rules (i.e., Law of the Indies, *Plaza Mayor*, key institutions located around it, gridiron street pattern) utilized by Spanish conquistadores in their city-building enterprises in cities like Mexico City, Guadalajara, Buenos Aires, and Caracas.[20]

Shopping and consumption are among the most important activities in cities.[21] They occur in a multitude of formats spread throughout the city. The traditional hierarchical relationship of core and periphery has sub-

---

17. Leite (2009) and Viana and Fonseca (2011).

18. Smith (1955).

19. Smith (1955, 9).

20. Scarpaci (2004).

21. Urry (1995), Robertson (1997), Chung et al. (2002), and Kunzmann (2011).

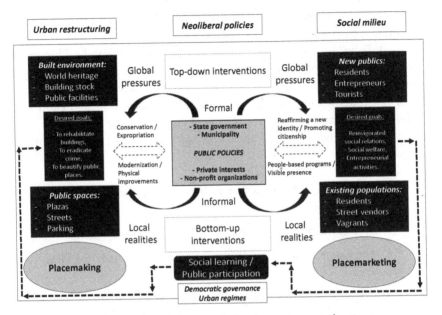

Figure 3.2. Analytical framework for downtown revitalization.

stantially disappeared with the building of suburbs.[22] In many cases, shopping malls have contributed to emptying out retail activities from central locations and onto more car-accessible peripheries. While people may have adapted to this new reality, many consolidated urban areas have experienced urban decline due to a hollowing-out of other urban activities.

During the 1960s and 1970s, pedestrian malls were built in many US cities, in part to attempt to reverse this situation. In Southern European cities, walk-only streets were implemented to create more livable and pleasant centers, often in conjunction with urban revitalization programs. German cities built this type of precinct during the war reconstruction efforts.[23] British and Nordic cities also took advantage of this technique to create more livable cities.[24] In addition, São Paulo and other Latin American

22. Dear and Flusty (1998).

23. Monheim (1992).

24. Karrholm (2008).

cities, such as Santiago and Buenos Aires, also have had pedestrian streets for quite a number of decades.

Walking is a quintessential human activity. Walkability has been defined as "the extent the built environment supports and encourages walking by providing for pedestrian comfort and safety, connecting people with varied destinations within a reasonable amount of time and effort and offering visual interest in journeys throughout the network."[25]

On the other hand, a walkable network has several of the following attributes:

- Connectivity of path network, both locally and in the larger urban setting

- Linkages with other modes: bus, streetcar, subway, train

- Fine-grained and varied land use patterns, especially for local serving uses

- Safety, both from traffic and social crime

- Quality of path, including width, paving, landscaping, signage, and lighting

- Path context, including street design, visual interest of the built environment, transparency, spatial definition, landscape, and overall explorability.[26]

The subjective characteristics of the urban street environment included imageability, enclosure, human scale, transparency, and complexity.[27] The main reason behind these scholars' study was the need to "arm researchers with operational definitions they can use to measure the street environment and test for significant associations with walking behavior." Although those researchers studied commercial streets, they did not study walk-only commercial precincts. On the other hand, it has been concluded that there is a hierarchy of walking needs and that "given a safe and comfortable setting people look for usefulness, sense of belonging and pleasurability as additional and distinct needs to enhance their walking experience."[28]

---

25. Southworth (2005, 247–248).

26. Southworth (2005, 249).

27. Ewing and Handy (2009, 65).

28. Mehta (2008, 217).

Usually, commercial pedestrian streets combine shopping and walking. The main reason for the building of pedestrian malls in the US was the competition from suburban shopping malls.[29] Municipalities and downtown organizations decided to recreate the shopping mall environment by pedestrianizing some of their main streets.[30] However, it has been argued that in the United States, this practice was, for the most part, a "failed experiment."[31] The success of a pedestrian area appears to depend, to a certain degree, on its proximity to employment centers. It has also been observed that pedestrian malls have been successful mainly in college towns and that other pedestrian malls are "exceptions to the rule or the result of extraordinary public-private partnerships."[32]

European cities, which grew according to organic patterns and were undamaged by (or rebuilt subsequently to) wars and or natural catastrophes, are usually more vibrant and livable than the cities built after the automobile became the main design element.[33] In those older cities, the urban fabric creates more intimate and human-scale living arrangements; shopping can be easily accomplished without reliance on automobiles;[34] and walking occurs with minimum effort. Those cities have rich urban environments capable of making walking a very pleasant and social activity. European cities, such as Barcelona and Porto, among many others, have maintained much of their urban fabric and walking appeal over recent decades. North American Sunbelt cities, such as Phoenix, Los Angeles, and Las Vegas, have grown very rapidly, which resulted in a combination of extensive low-density suburban areas, populated by housing subdivisions and shopping malls.[35]

A very important question is whether businesses and real estate properties located in walkable areas command higher rents, sales volumes, and consequently higher returns on investments than other properties. Some of the most recent research seems to confirm it to a certain extent.[36] For instance, the rents of stores on a pedestrian-only precinct in Hong Kong

---

29. Logemann (2009).

30. Soni and Soni (2016).

31. Gibbs (2012).

32. Gibbs (2012, 46).

33. Newman and Kenworthy (1999) and Gospodini (2004).

34. Crawford (2000).

35. Dear and Flusty (1998).

36. Leinberger (2008), Litman (2011), and Sohn, Moudon, and Lee (2012).

were compared to a control precinct on a regular street to conclude that, on the pedestrian precinct, rents were about 17 percent higher.[37]

Overview of the Case Studies

Despite cities' endemic characteristics, many cities and urban places have similar features and planning solutions that transcend geospatial, sociocultural, and legal country-specific contexts. The case studies presented here are or have been considered, in a not-too-distant past, successful examples of walk-only commercial precincts. Each one of them has its own history and was built according to specific legal, socioeconomic, and geographical contexts. Given recent changes in lifestyle habits, family composition, demographics, cultural influences, and spending patterns, one or more of their characteristics may need to be rethought in order to help maintain and improve the urban livability of their respective city centers.

In historical and spatial contexts, all four case studies have polycentric urban arrangements. Their scales, as well as their integration into large metropolitan areas, influence their urban structures, urban dynamics, built environments, transportation flows, and footfall volumes. The case studies vary in size, nature, and location but they all share one common feature, the visible manifestation that vulnerable city users should benefit from having parts of city streets closed off to cars. These walk-only precincts seem to increase safety and comfort levels for all, in addition to contributing toward more humane, democratic, vibrant, and economically sustainable communities.[38]

São Paulo, Brazil

São Paulo is one of the largest metropolises in Latin America. It is a global city and an important financial center. The city has evolved from the formal historic district settled by the Portuguese in 1553 to the Avenida Paulista created at the turn of the 20th century, and to the more recent centralities in the Faria Lima and Berrini Avenues.[39] Downtown São Paulo comprises two halves on either side of the Vale do Anhangabaú—known as the old

---

37. Yiu (2011).

38. Lo (2009) and Sinnett et al. (2011).

39. Frúgoli (2000) and Vasconcellos (2005).

Figure 3.3. *Largo do Patriarca*, São Paulo.

and the new centers—and both had many of their streets pedestrianized in the 1970s. These halves coincide with the neighborhoods of Sé and República in an area of approximately 1.7 square miles, which represents only approximately 0.5 percent of the whole city area. The resident population of these two districts was 60,263 people in 2000 (down from 93,964 in 1980) and 45,654 in 2011.[40] Until quite recently, it had specialized and popular retail stores, informal street traders, low-income households, and homeless individuals.

The daytime population increases several fold since the city center is served by 300 radial bus lines, three main bus stations, and multiple subway stations, and it also has many service jobs. Patriarca Square is the most central square in the downtown area (see Figure 3.3). In total, there are more than 4.4 miles of streets closed off to vehicular traffic. This was an initiative of then-mayor Olavo Setúbal. Although a successful strategy when it was implemented, over the years the large area without vehicular

---

40. LSE (2011).

access led to accessibility complaints and the municipality decided to open up a few streets in the second half of the 2000s.[41]

The center has a high concentration of governmental facilities and several financial institutions, including the São Paulo stock exchange.[42] A singular feature of the shopping structure is the presence of galleries, several stories high vertical shopping malls featuring small retail establishments open to inner courtyards with escalators (e.g., *Galeria do Rock*). Socially, these galleries are not Walter Benjamin's 19th-century arcades (i.e., *le passages*) and the Paulistanos most commonly found in the downtown area are not Parisians flaneurs. More than a century later, even though the construction techniques, materials (glass and iron roofs), and heights differ substantially, the weather-protected inner courtyards, escalators, and small stores still perform the same functions, and the population is eagerly engaged in communal social and economic activities.[43]

Mexico City, Mexico

Mexico City is also one of the largest metropolises in the world with its 19.2 million people in 2011.[44] The primate city comprises 16 *Delegaciones* in Distrito Federal (DF), 58 municipalities in the state of Mexico, and one municipality in the adjacent state of Hidalgo. Similarly to São Paulo, it has acute poverty levels (slums and a substantial informal economy). Mexico City's growth can be interpreted in three phases: The historic center, the growth of the suburbs, and the late-20th-century peri-urban megacity.

Mexico City's historic district is located on the ruins of Tenochtitlan, the ancient Aztec city of 1524. The city encapsulates the Law of the Indies with its *Plaza Mayor* and a gridiron urban pattern. The Zócalo, or Plaza de la Constitución, is not only the city's square but due to its large proportions—the second largest plaza in the world—literally the country's plaza, surrounded by ministry buildings, a 16th-century metropolitan cathedral, and the Templo Mayor Museum. This museum features buildings and artifacts of Aztec pre-Hispanic civilization. The historic center is one of the largest in the world and it was formally designated as a World Heritage site by

---

41. Leme and Ventura (2000).

42. Frúgoli (2000).

43. Vargas and Castilho (2015).

44. LSE (2011).

Figure 3.4. *Calle de Francisco Madero*, Mexico City.

UNESCO in 1987. The city center area known as "el Centro" occupies approximately 1 percent of the land and has a population of less than 200 thousand inhabitants. The population inside UNESCO's perimeter B was only 75,992 people in 2011.[45]

The city center has a high social, economic, symbolic, and cultural heritage value, including its substantial concentration of governmental buildings, palaces, churches, urban fabric, and many public spaces such as squares, parks, and the two recently pedestrianized streets, Francisco Madero and Regina (see Figure 3.4).[46] The southeastern area of the historic center has suffered from most of the same ailments that affect many downtowns in Latin America. The demolitions caused by the 1985 earthquake have aggravated the deterioration of the built environment.[47] Other urban problems

45. LSE (2011).

46. García (2015).

47. Inam (2005).

include decaying buildings, unemployment, social exclusion, insecurity, and congestion.[48]

Until the end of the 19th century, core urban functions were located in the city center proper. Only in the 20th century did the city expand, and the center saw many of its functions transferred to peripheral neighborhoods. The second growth phase corresponded to the linear corridor centered on Paseo de la Reforma, inspired by the monumental Champs-Élysées in Paris. The third spatial constellation corresponded to the expansion area beyond the Federal District borders in the 1900s.[49] If one were to read the city by its parks, the outward progression would be: Alameda, Chapultepec, and Xochimilco parks. The population growth was astounding, from 345 thousand inhabitants in 1900 to more than 18 million people approximately 100 years later. It has also been recognized that Mexico City is "the best planned city in the country, or if you like, the least badly planned."[50]

Barcelona, Spain

Besides its centuries-old and rich cultural heritage, the city's architectural jewels and its well-regarded urban design interventions, Barcelona gained international notoriety with the hosting of a series of mega-events in the 1990s and 2000s (i.e., the 1992 Olympic Games and the 2004 Forum of Cultures). Despite the city's modern transformations,[51] most of its retail activity is the result of family-based entrepreneurialism, which has resulted in neighborhoods anchored in a network of emblematic public markets linked through streets with specialized retail establishments. Part of the city's retail success can be attributed to the late arrival of postmodern commercial formats, including shopping malls and franchise and department stores.

In the center of Barcelona Las Ramblas is one of the world's most preeminent walking streets.[52] Its 0.74-mile-long central walking median bordered by rows of trees and lanes of traffic in each direction is the ideal place to stroll and enjoy the urban environment (see Figure 3.5). The adjacent built environment consists of six- and seven-story-high buildings with retail

48. Connolly (1999) and Walker (2013).

49. Davis (1994).

50. Garza (1999, 165).

51. Calavita and Ferrer (2000).

52. Jacobs (1993).

Figure 3.5. *Las Ramblas*, Barcelona. Courtesy of L'Associació d'Amics, Veïns i Comerciants de la Rambla.

and services on the ground floor. A centrality located approximately midway along Las Ramblas is the public market, Mercat S. Josep de Boqueria.

This example of municipal intervention in the retail sector is frequently promoted as a best practice in neighborhood retail planning. The pedestrian median is richly decorated with street lamps, fountains, public art, kiosks, and street furniture.[53] This street is included in the sample not because it is an exclusively walk-only precinct but because it enables unobstructed walking in a safe and comfortable environment, while enabling vehicular access at controlled speeds in the quite narrow lateral corridors.

Porto, Portugal

Porto is the second-largest city in Portugal and the capital of the northern region. It is known for its hard-working and industrious character. The city's location on the River Douro's margin has influenced its development uphill

---

53. Sepe (2013).

from the water. The historic district, and part of the downtown area, was designated as a World Heritage site by UNESCO in the mid-1990s. The city has only a few pedestrian areas that connect to public open spaces.[54] A significant number of those public spaces in the downtown area were renovated in conjunction with the event Porto 2001 European Capital of Culture. Many of the downtown streets had their sidewalks widened to create more comfortable walking conditions for the pedestrian. More recently, the new light rail system has improved mobility in the metro area despite having changed the urban dynamics in the city. It greatly increased accessibility to other neighborhoods, in addition to having altered the traditional pedestrian flows of people and centers of activity.

The closing off of the Rua de Santa Catarina to vehicular traffic goes back to the early 1990s (see Figure 3.6). This street benefits from its large concentration of stores and from being the center of a living neighborhood located very close to the downtown area. Its physical proportions in terms of length and width as well as the variety of retail stores on the street, including the public square at one end and the presence of a downtown shopping mall on the other end of the street, help to explain, in part, the success it has had during the last two decades. The compactness of the surrounding urban fabric, its good accessibility on foot and by public transportation, and the relatively high concentration of housing in the neighborhood as well as the proximity to a variety of other economic activities, including restaurants, bars, grocery stores, hotels, and a public market, all contribute toward its functionality and character.

Comparative Analysis of Themes

It has been established that places can be assessed by the degree that they perform their intended functions. Among some of the main assessment characteristics one finds access and linkages, comfort and identity, usability, economic activity, and sociability, among others.[55] This section of the chapter analyzes and compares nine main themes running across the four case studies (see Tables 3.2 and 3.3 on pages 76 and 77).

---

54. Fernandes (1989).

55. Paumier (2004).

Figure 3.6. *Rua de Santa Catarina*, Porto.

Location of the Streets

The four walk-only precincts in this study are located in the downtown area of a metropolitan main city. Urban morphologies, design plans, or both, have influenced their locations. In the case of Barcelona, Las Ramblas was built along the ancient city walls. Streets are by their very nature fluid spaces for people, goods, and intangibles to circulate in a myriad of ways.[56] Most city centers have a great concentration of activities that can

---

56. Ellin (2006).

Table 3.2. Comparison of the Latin American global downtowns[57]

	São Paulo	Mexico City
Population (creation date)	10.4 million people in the city; 19.2 million in the metropolitan area, 2011 (1976).	8.6 million people in the city; 19.2 million in the metropolitan area in 2011 (2010 and 2008, respectively).
Location and streets	Downtown (Rua Direita, Rua Barão de Itapetininga and Rua de São Bento).	Downtown (Calle de Francisco Madero and Calle Regina).
Proportion of the pedestrian precinct	An area with pedestrianized streets and plazas on both sides of the Vale do Anhangabaú; in total there are more than 2.7 miles of pedestrianized streets.	Approximately 0.43 miles and 0.4 miles, respectively.
Relationship between the streets and the surrounding areas /activities	Combination of government buildings, galleries, department stores, shops, shopping centers, restaurants, services, hotels, cultural centers, and performance venues.	Combination of a variety of shops and stores, art galleries, department stores, shopping centers, restaurants, services, hotels, churches.
Accessibility to the pedestrian precincts and movement in the street	Pedestrian bridge (Viaduto de Santa Ifigênia) connecting both sides of the downtown area, opening up of a few streets to vehicular traffic in recent years, subway stations.	Both streets are on a gridiron pattern; Calle del Francisco Madero is more centrally located and an integral part of a major axis, while Calle Regina is more secluded.
Conciliation between the needs of different street users	Cobblestones, concrete, and granite.	Cobblestones, concrete, and granite.

57. Author's fieldwork and selected references.

	São Paulo	Mexico City
Strategies to respond to competition from new and emerging centers	Surveillance on the precinct, recent removal of advertising from buildings, street furniture, *zeladores* (hospitality ambassadors).	Surveillance on the precinct, on foot police presence.
Funding of improvements and continued management and promotional activities	Municipality, Viva o Centro, and Aliança pelo Centro Histórico de São Paulo.	Municipality, and la Autoridad del Espacio Público, la Secretaría de Desarrollo Urbano y Vivienda, la Autoridad del Centro Histórico, and el Fideicomiso del Centro Histórico.
Perpetuate success and avoidance of decline	Popular retail; combination of governmental, historic, financial, services; entertainment and cultural buildings.	Popular retail; combination of governmental, historic, financial, services; entertainment and cultural buildings.

Table 3.3. Comparison of the second-tier Iberian cities[58]

	Barcelona	Porto
Population (creation date)	1.6 million in the city, 5 million in the metro area (1800s, renovation in the early 1970s).	237,584 in the city, 1.2 million in the metro area (late 1980s).
Location of the street(s)	Downtown (Las Ramblas).	Downtown (Rua de Santa Catarina).
Proportion of the pedestrian precinct	Linear pedestrian walkway area bordered by lanes of traffic in each direction, series of successive *ramblas*, approximately 0.7 miles in length.	Pedestrian-only linear street, 3-blocks long, approximately 0.4 miles.

continued on next page

58. Author's fieldwork and selected references.

Table 3.3. Continued.

	Barcelona	Porto
Relationship between the streets and the surrounding areas / activities	Existence of landmarks at both ends of the street (Columbus statue and Plaza de Catalunya), combination of independent, franchise, and brand name retail stores; public market; service activities.	Consolidated urban fabric, downtown shopping center on the pedestrian mall launched in 1996, department store, specialized retail, proximity to cultural venues.
Accessibility to the pedestrian precincts and movement in the street	No vehicular interruption or access to the pedestrian area, lateral on-street parking, subway stations	Nearby subway stations and bus stops, parking garages.
Conciliation between the needs of different street users	Tree-lined boulevard, use of different materials to delimit movement corridors, uniform signage, fountain, lights.	Granite and basalt cobblestones.
Strategies to respond to competition from new and emerging centers	Spontaneous activities (living statutes), design features, light poles, stalls, chairs, pigeons, designed and artistic pavements.	Cleanliness, safety, and attractiveness.
Funding of improvements and continued management and promotional activities	Municipality and L'Associació d'Amics, Veïns i Comerciants de la Rambla.	Municipality.
Perpetuate success and avoidance of decline	Grand scale, gentle slope, and framed deep vistas; no sense of crowding; orchestrated spontaneity.	Street width / composition and ensemble, retail establishments, and a downtown shopping center.

attract many people. The existence of possible conflicts among street users has led some city administrations to find answers to this problem, and in collaboration with individual merchants and their associations, many have created walk-only precincts. Such a street arrangement is an interruption in the regular flow of total traffic through a particular street. As a consequence, vehicular traffic may be diverted to surrounding streets. But the novelty, and the reduction in conflicts between users, facilitates the flow of walkers, and the newly created space is more likely to attract people who just want to enjoy the precinct without spending much money in the local economy.

A critical mass of activities may be able to maintain or increase the number of people attracted to the precincts. Those who invest in them expect a return; otherwise they will go somewhere else with fewer risks and higher returns. The center usually benefits from a concentration of rich architectural buildings, public spaces, and a high concentration of activities. People patronize those spaces differently depending on their demographic group, socioeconomic background, gender, marital status, and profession.

Public authorities are usually responsible for ensuring that public spaces remain public, clean, safe, and attractive; that vehicular traffic flows uninterruptedly; and, indirectly, that businesses are successful. They are receptive to contributions for improvements in the public realm, which also may benefit commercial establishments, but business owners are ultimately responsible for their own spaces. The separation between public and private realms is critical. When cities are successful, they grow, usually in outward ways, which can, if nothing is done, partially weaken their commercial and historical cores. The risk of new centralities may dislocate some economic activities to other areas of the city, as has happened in many of the case studies.

Proportion of the Pedestrian Precincts

Very few studies have examined the location of pedestrian areas and their relationships to the entirety of the agglomerations and to other centers and subcenters. Usually, commercial pedestrian precincts coincide with the core of a city as was argued previously. Suburban neighborhoods may not have the same density of patrimonial assets as those that can be easily found in downtowns. There can be commercial areas anchored in specific stores or in groups of stores. Successful walk-only precincts normally have a very diverse concentration of businesses.

The mix of activities influences the precincts physicality and character. Depending on the organicity and how a city evolved over time—or was deliberately planned—pedestrian precincts may coincide with or extend to public spaces such as squares and parks. A common occurrence is the partial appropriation of many of those public spaces by adjacent businesses. Quite often, this includes the payment of a specific fee, but such charge is in the mutual interest of both the municipality and of the businesses.

Pedestrian areas may also connect emblematic and touristic places in a city, which is likely to attract a high number of visitors.[59] It is the continuous flow of footfall that maintains the vibrancy and the economic success of the businesses located in the precinct. Pedestrians are also encouraged by short distances. In large cities, such as São Paulo, the option to extend the precinct to most of the streets in the downtown area has made it relatively difficult for people to reach certain destinations far away from the main access points.

A design feature common to several of the case studies is how the main thoroughfare connects two main points or centralities (e.g., Mexico City: Zócalo to Plaza de la República via Alameda Central and Palacio de Bellas Artes; Barcelona: the statue of Columbus and the Plaza de Catalunya). This represents an important planning principle that demonstrates the power of landmarks to define and terminate vistas.

Relationship with Surroundings

A vibrant walk-only precinct can only meet its purposes if it satisfies the needs of its users. It is in the interest of both businesses and local authorities to create and maintain quality public spaces. Those spaces are successful if they attract and entice patrons to remain there for a while, patrons who then also might end up visiting the stores and purchasing goods and services. In collaboration with the city's social services, homeless people can be helped in humane ways by downtown ambassadors. A combination of retail stores, restaurants, and other commercial establishments constitute the bulk of economic activity in those precincts. Those stores need to be serviced with goods; goods need to be stored and sold. Depending on the layout of the neighborhood blocks, the servicing can be commonly carried out through alleyways or through the front of the stores.

---

59. Scarpaci (2004).

Retail businesses will typically be located on the ground floor and in some cases will occupy the upper floors as well. Services such as law offices, medical, insurance, language schools, travel agencies, banks, post offices, internet cafés, beauty parlors, and personal grooming are traditionally located in these areas. Many and varied entertainment venues can also be easily found in central areas. Some of them attract large crowds ranging in size from several hundred to a few thousand people.

Improvements in the public space are usually reflected in gains for the adjacent built environment. Usually, commercial and entertainment districts do not have many housing units because of the inconvenience and nuisance created by loud entertainment activities and their attendees, difficulty with parking, high monthly rents, and small unit sizes.

Accessibility to the Pedestrian Precincts

Since residence in the commercial precinct tends to be low, usually people have to travel to get there. There are many ways to access it; while there, the main mode is usually walking. Plentiful parking will help ensure that patrons will find it convenient to reach the precinct. Affordable parking rates can also influence how long customers will stay in the precinct. Reaching it by foot is probably the easiest way to ensure that people will not be worried about having to extend the parking payment, in case of meters.

Among the most common design strategies capable of influencing the comfort and safety of the walking experience one finds the type and smoothness of pavements used, the marking of crosswalks, the existence of bulb-outs to decrease crossing distances.

Also very important is the regulation of logistics and delivery of goods and products. Most cities have regulations coordinating the servicing of economic activities located in the streets and access to parking garages. For instance, in the Rua de Santa Catarina in Porto, deliveries are to be made no later than 11 a.m. and only after 9 p.m. The simple existence of regulations is limited if there is lack of enforcement. An alternative to having delivery and service vehicles driving on pedestrianized areas is to establish a neighborhood logistics center and to attempt less intrusive deliveries.

Conciliation of Needs

Cities are used by everyone. Commercial precincts are mainly aimed at shoppers. Those are likely to constitute the main group in the area. Visitors are also attracted to special events, such as art walks, food and festive occasions, and other celebrations (e.g., end-of-the-year block parties). As one would expect, these spaces are appropriated differently depending on the needs of their users. Adjacent businesses are likely to benefit from high footfall and the celebration of community events. Business owners might even be among the event organizers in cooperation with public officials. The success of pedestrian areas can sometimes lead to unwanted activities, such as unsolicited attempts at selling goods and services.

Important conflicts that need to be avoided include reserved parking for store owners and employees and the time and frequency of deliveries, as well as minimum clearance for emergency services and cleaning crews. Vulnerable street users, such as blind and handicapped people, rely on physical markings and designed solutions to navigate their way through walk-only precincts. This type of precinct with well-delimited movement corridors and tactile mats enable disabled people to walk or ride wheelchairs in safe, convenient, and unobstructed ways. Pedestrians need to be protected when crossing the street, and São Paulo has recently promoted a successful safety campaign to reduce traffic accidents.

Strategies to Respond to the Competition

One of the main reasons why pedestrian malls are dismantled and streets reopened to vehicular traffic results from added competition from new shopping areas, with a larger variety of stores, centralized retail management, and better adapted to the needs of customers. Accessibility to the precincts is critical as is parking. The reason why modern shopping malls are so popular is because they are designed and planned with careful attention to details, an approach that cannot be easily found in the organicity of the downtown urban fabric. For some people, authenticity is one of a city's biggest advantages, which cannot be easily replicated elsewhere.

In the shopping mall, the threshold might involve appeals to differentiation and niche market segmentation. Certain pedestrian precincts are known for their expensive brand stores and signature designers. Establishments are likely to capitalize on the realism and vibrancy of those spaces. Urban authenticity and patrimonial value might be the main reasons behind the success of some of the most well-known commercial streets and precincts in the world, such as Rua Oscar Freire in São Paulo, Champs-Élysées in Paris, Montenapoleone in Milan, or Ginza in Tokyo.

The compactness of old historic districts with a high density of commercial activities and without the disruption caused by vehicular traffic makes walking in the downtown area a very pleasant way of experiencing the city, something that cannot be easily found anywhere else in the world. In most cases, the strategy might be to capitalize on the authenticity and urbanity of the downtown cores while reducing the threats posed by new centers. The local and regional authorities have an important role in implementing such strategies without curbing development opportunities excessively. In short, a "town center first" approach coupled with high levels of cleanliness, safety, and attractiveness, while leaving the rest to spontaneity, is a strategy attempted by some of the cities in the sample.

São Paulo's pedestrian streets have seen a steady number of patrons in the city center. The efforts of Viva o Centro and its neighborhood local actions (i.e., *ações locais*) were critical to the development of a growing awareness about the value of urban conservation and historic preservation. The Viva o Centro was created to aid with the revitalization of the downtown, which, over the years, had seen its pedestrianized streets become overcrowded and littered with rubbish, its pavements damaged by utility crews and service vehicles, and the presence of many informal street vendors (i.e., *camelôs*). Also, in Mexico City, a considerable number of street vendors have been relocated to shopping areas within buildings, while others have been resisting the entrepreneurial city with their struggle and rebel tactics.[60]

The Viva o Centro was modeled after the North American business improvement district (BID) concept, and it developed campaigns to attract residents to the center, to help revitalize the area, and to increase the area's levels of safety and cleanliness, services that continue today. The main difference was that financing was based on sponsorship and voluntary contributions and not on enforceable taxation, which may have limited the effectiveness of the organization.[61]

Funding of Improvements and Management

Funding (or the lack of it, to be more specific) is probably one of the most critical reasons why some of these commercial precincts may deteriorate in

---

60. Crossa (2009) and Walker (2013).

61. Frúgoli (2000).

appearance over time. Funding for professional management in shopping centers is part of operating budgets and it is covered, in part, by monthly rents, as well as by other financial mechanisms. As explained before, BIDs in the United States and TCMs in the United Kingdom have been relatively successful financial arrangements to pay for the activities of downtown management associations. In other cases, community development corporations have been used to help rehabilitate neighborhoods and to provide training and new skills for people in need.

Certain temporary events require a cover charge to enter a precinct. These funds help defray operating costs but usually are insufficient to pay for major capital improvements. Capital improvements, such as new pavements and street furniture, are likely to be funded in collaboration with other public authorities. One of the main differences between walk-only precincts and privatized retail environments such as festival malls and theme parks is that people want to have a pleasant experience without necessarily having to shop. The concentration of shopping and entertainment activities, and the professionalism of the enterprise, is in many cases not comparable to the experience found in a commercial pedestrian precinct. Partnerships and alliances are powerful mechanisms capable of generating public participation and additional resources.[62]

Perpetuation of Success

Urban professionals can sometimes become very attached to the places where they work or frustrated with sameness and stalled status quo that they may disengage from public causes. In certain contexts, they may attempt to preserve legacies passed on to them by their predecessors and they do it by enacting legislation and other regulations that limit the uses allowed in certain urban zones and buildings. In other cases, they may deregulate and allow patrimonial heritage to become irremediably lost. Urban regeneration programs can sometimes lead to gentrification processes,[63] with residents in central areas getting displaced to the suburbs where they may become "heavy car users or spatially marginalized pedestrians."[64]

---

62. Frieden and Sagalyn (1989).

63. Janoschka, Sequera, and Salinas (2014).

64. Ramos (2010, 93).

Retailers may initially oppose walk-only precincts, but in the majority of European cases, generally, businesses appreciate the additional patronage created by these pedestrian areas. Pedestrian streets tend to attract international brands, which often increases competition and may displace independent family-owned businesses. In democratic societies, the broader public sphere plays an important role in balancing the preservation and upkeep of patrimonial assets and local entrepreneurship.

In a highly globalized world, it is becoming increasingly difficult to prevent international trends, technologies, and ideologies from dominating local and regional agendas and from shaping the urban landscapes of cities. Cities are shaped by a myriad of decisions, sometimes beyond the control of public officials. Yet their livability depends, to a large extent, on the degree to which appropriate visions and models can be devised and implemented in coordinated ways. In brief, do not over plan, but be aware that consumers will definitely know the difference between authentic and genuine places and their built environments and the recreation of structures and places in faux, yet hyperreal, themed environments.[65]

Conclusion and Implications

Walk-only precincts have been used to create more enjoyable public places in cities for several decades, if not centuries.[66] In the 21st century, the human needs to experience urban vibrancy, to gather collectively in open public spaces, and to socialize remain the same. One of the big differences in relation to earlier urban development stages is that, over the years, cities have become less pedestrian friendly, mainly as a consequence of an increase in automobile usage. The nature of walking cities has evolved and as a consequence, progressive authorities have taken on the responsibility for creating walk-only precincts.

The main purpose of this chapter was to identify how professionals with responsibility over the design, planning, engineering, and management of commercial pedestrian areas can help to create and encourage more vibrant main streets and city centers. The increase in urban living, with all its demands, requires a transition to a low-carbon society. Pedestrian areas

---

65. Castello (2010).

66. Loukaitou-Sideris and Banerjee (1998).

have the potential to make urban living a more interesting, authentic, and pleasant experience. They can bring back the socializing and communal realms, partly stolen by modern transport and information revolutions, and by the pervasiveness of mobile technologies.

Professionals interested in improving urban vibrancy have much to learn from past experiences in cities throughout the world. Shopping mall and theme park designers have successfully applied CU principles to their developments in the past, often in ways that have weakened downtowns and central areas of cities. But design and urbanism principles have also been used in the planning of Mexico City's historic district, among others. Its concept was the result of a deliberate planning and architectural intervention, which made use of a CU model to articulate the whole design approach.

More than subscribing to a particular model, it is suggested that the application of individual planning and urbanistic principles ought to augment endogenous assets, values, and intangibles capable of strengthening the foundations of authenticity and urbanity proper to each cultural practice. Building pedestrian streets may be expensive in terms of initial capital costs; however, such investments will likely last a considerable time.[67] Keeping those areas attractive and fully performing their functions requires professional practice and a combination of leadership, common vision, resources, and continued management. Due to a lack of reliable and comparable data sets, further research is needed on the economic impact of these pedestrian precincts on retail rents, profitability levels, and on how individual contributions and common pool revenues can be leveraged to promote future actions.[68]

In terms of planning implications, it is important to learn from each other's revitalization attempts. For instance, it is risky to overdo revitalization without first testing the design concept. São Paulo's pedestrianized area is the most extensive of the four case studies, and the number of closed streets had to be reduced recently given its accessibility difficulties. Second, certain streets are more conducive to pedestrianization schemes than others; neighborhoods with high density, small blocks, good under- and above-ground linkages and parking, and relatively narrow streets seem to be ideal candidates. Third, even when streets can be closed off to automobile traffic, they still need to be serviced and remain "open" to service crews and emergency vehicles.

---

67. Hass-Klau (2015).

68. Yiu (2011).

Fourth, these implications are based on the four case studies and do not constitute an endorsement of the creation of pedestrian malls in other cities.

Finally, downtown professionals should not blindly emulate walk-only commercial precincts, but they need to know that under certain conditions, this type of revitalization solution can create vibrant public spaces for everybody. The pedestrian precincts from two different continents reviewed in this chapter show that, given the proper location, design, and management solutions, commercial pedestrian precincts are successful and advantageous to cities, to the point where the phenomenon has been called: "Pedestrianisation for the masses."[69] More than using walk-only commercial streets to stimulate shopping and consumption, the promotion of a walking culture to the survival of livable cities will lead to and ensure more vibrant, democratic, and socially cohesive cities.[70]

---

69. Rowe (2011, 187).

70. Beatley (2004).

PART II

UNITED STATES

4

Revitalization and Homelessness

Introduction

City centers undergo cycles of growth, decline, and revitalization, but not everyone benefits equally.[1] The main research question discussed in this chapter is, to what extent has the city of Phoenix (see Figure 4.1) attempted to resolve its homelessness? Using Phoenix as a case study, this chapter utilizes an eclectic array of data sources from personal interviews, focus group meetings, media sources, public reports, and technical studies to identify how institutional and civic leaders and citizens have responded to the presence of homeless individuals in the city. The argument is that the process of revitalizing urban areas ought to include efforts to eradicate homelessness. Land constitutes the support for the revitalization process;[2] however, people—with their hopes and dreams—are the real assets of the city.[3] Furthermore, there will not be a livable downtown until everyone benefits from the revitalization process. In the framework of the just city this might seem like a utopian goal. But, nonetheless, its practical realization does provide a direction in which to strive. This chapter presents seven recommendations for addressing homelessness in contexts of downtown revitalization.

This chapter is organized in six sections. The first provides the theoretical background and characterizes the poverty debate in the United States and in Arizona. The second characterizes the homelessness situation in the Phoenix metropolitan area before the global financial crisis. The third explains the

---

1. Harvey (1992), Bright (2000), Fainstein (2006), and Marcuse (2007).

2. Birch (2006).

3. Spencer (2005).

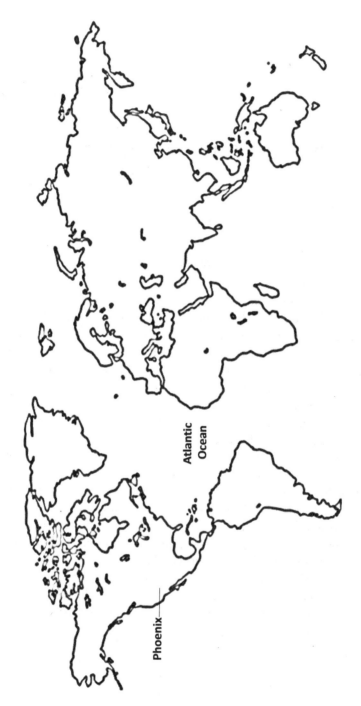

Atlantic
Ocean

Phoenix

Figure 4.1. Location of Phoenix.

evolution of downtown revitalization in Phoenix and how certain critical projects have helped to build a 21st-century new city. The fourth discusses the three main types of responses customarily deployed to deal with home-lessness problems in the context of major urban revitalization efforts. These include the solidary city, the NIMBY city, and the city of fear. The fifth presents a set of implications for downtown revitalization. And finally, the sixth presents some concluding comments on the need to pursue solidarity in the framework of the just city, not simply based on compassion but on civic creativity and institutional capacity-building.

Theoretical Background on Homelessness in the United States

The theoretical debate on poverty and homelessness in the United States has been evolving for several decades.[4] A comprehensive framework to understand the overlaps between government and individual responsibility in dealing with the needs of homeless individuals is provided in Table 4.1.Only win-win solutions combining individual and government responsibility for the welfare of the homeless seem to help solve the long-term root causes of homelessness and not simply alleviate its symptoms.[5] Poverty is a somewhat silent and hidden social problem, with the exception of the homeless people we tend to see in central city areas and in the poor neighborhoods of cities.[6] The United States is seen throughout the world as a land of opportunities, but these are not yet available to everybody. In fact, statistics indicate that about 36 million people still live below the poverty line.[7] In 2005, Hurricane

Table 4.1. Perspectives on poverty and homelessness[8]

| | | Personal Responsibility | |
		Yes	No
Government	Yes	Educators	Liberals
Responsibility	No	Conservatives	

4. See for example Wilson (1987), Hoch and Slayton (1989), Collin (1992), Jencks (1994), Takahashi (1996), and DeVerteuil (2006).

5. APA (2003).

6. Boston and Ross (2001) and Barrett, Price-Spratlen, and Kanan (2003).

7. Ladner (2006).

8. Adapted from Kyle (2005).

Katrina in New Orleans showed very clearly that some Southern states are hampered by serious problems of urban poverty. Various federal administrations have attempted to end chronic homelessness with little success.

Homelessness in the United States is a serious problem and a very difficult one to quantify and eradicate. On an average day it is estimated that about 750,000 homeless people sleep on the streets and in shelters.[9] However, the total number might be between 2.3 to 3.5 million people who experience some form of homelessness.[10] The increase in homelessness among single adults and families seems to be a byproduct of the following changes: the elimination of voluntary commitment, the eviction of patients from mental hospitals, the advent of crack, the increases in long-term joblessness, the political restrictions on the creation of flophouses, the spread of single motherhood, and the erosion of welfare recipients' purchasing power.[11] And the most common reasons for continued homelessness in the US in the 2000s were, among others, the lack of health care, domestic violence, the existence of mental illness, and substance abuse.

The McKinney-Vento Homeless Assistance Act was the first major federal legislative response to homelessness in the US. This major act was signed by President Reagan in 1987. The legislation created several programs that have helped hundreds of thousands of Americans recover their stability through emergency shelters, transitional housing, job training, primary health care, education, and some permanent housing.[12] One of the main problems with this legislation seems to be the focus on homelessness symptoms and not on its root causes. Among the most relevant institutional arrangements to end homelessness at the national level, one finds the US Interagency Council on Homelessness. This program has been charged with the creation of a 10-year plan to end chronic homelessness. Several other more recent innovations include the Homeless Management Information System (HMIS), the support of intergovernmental and intercommunity collaborations, as well as the development of other technical assistance packages to state and local initiatives.

Finally, it is important to mention the HUD Continuum of Care, which aims at providing a wide range of integrated housing solutions for

---

9. HUD (2007).

10. NCH and NLCHP (2006).

11. Jencks (1994).

12. HUD (2005).

homeless people. One of the main shortcomings of these programs is that they are relatively expensive to run and do not seem to be solving the root causes of homelessness. More recently, the housing-first approach endorsed by many nonprofits and official organizations includes providing houses and apartments to homeless individuals, instead of simply housing them at shelters and enabling access to social services.

The Injustices of Fast-Paced Development in Phoenix

Phoenix is located in the Sonoran Desert of the Southwest region of the United States. Phoenix, the state capital, was the fifth largest city in the country in 2007 with 1.4 million people in about 1,700 square miles. The Phoenix metropolitan area had approximately 3.7 million inhabitants in the same year. With some lapses, Arizona has intermittently been the nation's fastest growing state in terms of population. The state grew 3.6 percent during the year ended on July 1, 2006. In fact, "growth" and "Phoenix" have been synonymous for many years over various decades. The metropolitan population has grown more than 45 percent in the period from 1996 to 2006 alone. The metropolitan area is 9,995 square miles, an area almost twice the size of Los Angeles County. The urbanized area of Phoenix's metropolitan area comprises twenty-five cities and towns, three Indian communities, and Maricopa County. Traditionally, the economy of the state has been characterized by the five Cs: copper, cattle, cotton, citrus, and climate. More recently two other Cs have been added to this list: construction and computers. Phoenix is an impressive metropolis only made possible by a very elaborate irrigation and water delivery system, the stamina of its leadership, the sharp rise of its population, and the vision and risk-taking approaches of its entrepreneurs.[13]

Phoenix developed mostly after World War II. Military personnel migrated there due to the availability of jobs in the state's military bases. Many stayed because of the pleasant life and relatively cheap living. These characteristics also attracted many retirees when the real estate industry discovered the state in the 1960s with the construction of retirement communities like Sun City, a Del Webb development. The region started attracting many partial-year residents, known as snowbirds, who wanted to escape the winter rigors of the Midwest and New England states. The most

---

13. Luckingham (1989).

recent wave of migrants is constituted mostly by a Hispanic labor force to work in the booming construction and tourism industry.

In terms of urban development, Phoenix was relatively compact until World War II. Until then, downtown Phoenix aggregated most of the urban functions.[14] Like many other cities, Phoenix also developed a streetcar system. Central Avenue evolved over the years as the "spine" of the metropolis. The first signs of decentralization occurred when financial activities started moving north on Central Avenue. The appearance of automobiles and shopping malls in suburban locations also influenced the decline of the central city.[15] Flat desert land allowed almost limitless urban developments and imaginations, including Frank Lloyd Wright's Broadacre utopian city. However, the growth of the suburbs, continuous land annexations, and the boom of retirement communities weakened downtown Phoenix's urban supremacy.

In this context, the Phoenix airport, Sky Harbor, has played a pivotal role in urban development over the years. Its expansion in the 1960s and 1970s led to the relocation of many families to a booming suburb on the west side of the city: Maryvale.[16] The damming of the Rio Salado in Tempe in the early 1990s allowed the reinforcement of a centrality in the eastern part of the valley. The growth of the metropolitan area during the last 50 years has been quite impressive: From little more than 100 thousand people in 1950 to 1.4 million in 2000.[17] The projections for the future of Phoenix are no less ambitious.[18] The region is expected to grow to more than 5 million inhabitants by 2030. It is expected that most of the population growth will happen on the fringes of the metropolitan area, mainly in Buckeye and Queen Creek.

Of course, this fast-paced development brings not only many opportunities but also a high number of urban problems. The opportunities allow citizens to maximize their individual pursuits, no matter what they are.[19] Among the many opportunities, one finds wealth creation through jobs in almost all sectors of the economy, particularly in those sectors associated with the construction and tourism industries.[20] However, it is also well known

---

14. Gober (2006).

15. Beauregard (2003b).

16. Collins (2005).

17. Gammage and Fink (2004) and Heim (2001).

18. Guathakurta and Stimson (2007).

19. Kotkin (2005).

20. Gammage (2003).

that "when we pursue what we want as an individual, we don't necessarily get what we want as a community."[21] Among the main problems associated with fast-paced urban growth in Arizona, one encounters the following: downtown and urban decline; loss of desert, agricultural land, open space, and fauna and flora; air pollution and the brown cloud; noise pollution; traffic congestion; urban heat island; lack of affordable housing; and socially unjust developments and practices.

General poverty decreased in Arizona by 11.5 percent during the 1990s. It is estimated that there were approximately 12,000 homeless people in the state in 2006, but this number could have been as high as 25,000, and these numbers included chronically ill, veterans, sexual offenders, and drug addicts.[22] About a thousand homeless people gathered in the downtown area, mainly in the capitol mall district because of the high concentration of service providers.[23] That spatial concentration dates to the early 1980s when *Newsweek* magazine ran a story about a "tent city" in Phoenix, which led valley officials to unite and devise a solution for the homeless problem in 1984. The first response was the creation of a "temporary" shelter with 400 beds for homeless people called Central Arizona Shelter Services.[24] Almost 25 years later, the shelter is still there, now in a new Human Services Campus and with more dignifying conditions.[25]

Downtown Revitalization: Building a 21st-Century City

Like many other downtowns throughout the US, the revitalization of downtown Phoenix started in the 1970s with the construction of the Civic Plaza, which comprises the Convention Center and the Symphony Hall.[26] This was followed by the creation of a redevelopment area in 1979. The Arizona Center shopping center, as well as several museums, the ballpark, and the sports arena were all built to capitalize on the central location and help revitalize the downtown area.[27] These two latter developments were built

21. Lincoln Institute of Land Policy (2003).

22. AZDES (2006).

23. Peck (2004) and Larsen, Poortinga, and Hurdle (2004).

24. Brinegar (2003).

25. "Homeless Campus" (2003).

26. Frieden and Sagalyn (1989) and Robertson (1995).

27. Hackworth (1999).

with public support.[28] Instrumental in this process has been the creation of a business improvement district (BID) called Copper Square. If the initial objective of this new organization was to create a "clean and safe" downtown, now it is getting more involved in the promotion of redevelopment opportunities in the downtown area. The Phoenix Convention Center was also greatly expanded recently.

The most impressive attempt at revitalizing the downtown area is the construction of a new campus of the Arizona State University in downtown Phoenix. When fully completed, the campus is expected to serve an estimated 15,000 students and 2,000 staff and faculty.[29] This development was accompanied by a new biomedical campus also in downtown Phoenix based on the Translational Genomics Research Institute (TGen), the College of Medicine, and the bioscience high school.[30] There have also been several revitalization projects developed for the capitol mall district. Finally, the city of Phoenix has also conducted a form-based project aimed at revamping its regulatory environment.

In addition to these urban projects, the Phoenix light rail system has completely revamped the downtown area. The Phoenix light rail project comprised the initial construction of 20 miles of light rail connecting three cities in the core of the metro area: Phoenix, Tempe, and Mesa. This light rail system was developed not as an alternative to the freeway system but as one more option for commuters in the central part of the metropolitan area.[31] The merit of this new transportation system is reflected in the redevelopment opportunities that it provides.[32] The station areas are seen as major opportunities for infill development, and the three cities have developed transit-oriented development (TOD) ordinances to facilitate and encourage redevelopment opportunities.

One of the most immediate results of this set of projects has been the building of several loft developments in the downtown district. In 2005, there were "more than 1,700 residential units just opening, planned or starting construction soon. And the biggest fuel to the fire [was] the Arizona State University Downtown Phoenix Campus."[33] However, most of these housing

28. Collins and Grineski (2007).

29. ASU (2004).

30. Kearney (2006).

31. ULI (2001).

32. Fulton, Weaver, and Waits (2004).

33. Richardson and Stearns (2005).

units targeted a high-income clientele and were not very affordable for the middle class. So, the critical question of this revitalization was who could afford those units when prices range from $300,000 to $900,000 for small two-bedroom condos. And the city plan called for as many as 10,000 units in the next decade.[34]

One of the main design principles of ASU as the "New American University" has been community embeddedness.[35] With that in mind, in 2005 a team of faculty and students from the College of Design engaged in a studio exercise to revitalize the capitol mall district.[36] This is the area with the highest concentration of homeless people and service providers in the city. It is an area with a high concentration of state buildings, a small housing enclave, many surface parking lots, and light industry buildings and warehouses.[37] This project was a follow up to a major studio conducted in 1996, which led to the construction of the Human Services Campus in 2005.[38] In our studio project, among different suggestions, we identified the need to develop a network of satellite campuses throughout the metropolitan area.[39] The most recent phase of this plan included the "flag walk" project along the capitol mall's main thoroughfare in anticipation of the 2012 Arizona centennial celebration. This symbolic project seemed to be galvanizing supporters behind the idea of revitalizing the entire capitol mall district. The most important aspect behind the revitalization of downtown Phoenix in the second half of the 2000s was a critical mass of revitalization projects.[40]

Downtown Revitalization: Consequences and Responses

Downtown revitalization involves choices and priorities and (intended and unintended) consequences in terms of public policies and the minimization of potentially negative unequal impacts. The revitalization process in Phoenix started in the 1970s with the construction of the civic square. The subsequent construction of sports stadiums led to the demolition of several

---

34. Slater (2006).

35. Crow (2002).

36. College of Design (2005).

37. Newtown (2006).

38. McIntosh (1997).

39. Balsas (2006).

40. Richardson and Pancrazio (2007).

single-occupancy room hotels (SORs) in the downtown area.[41] The area known as the skid row or deuce was left only with two small SOR hotels by 2005. Unfortunately, not too many SORs were built since then; a notable exception being the Campaign Place. Also, the YMCA on First Avenue just north of Van Buren Street remains an option for low-income residents.

But the fast-paced urban growth in Phoenix is producing mainly unaffordable homes. In fact, this lack of affordable housing is easily observed by looking at median sales prices and family incomes. From 2000 to 2006, the median sales price of homes in Arizona increased by 74 percent, but during the same period, median family income increased by only 15 percent.[42] The downtown area is to a certain extent a reflex of this trend, with several exceptions identified later in the chapter. During the period 2000–2004, home values in Maricopa County increased by 25.7 percent as compared to only a 4.1 percent increase in median household income.[43]

In a nutshell, I identified three main types of direct responses to homelessness in Arizona, and in Phoenix in particular. Some of them are directly related and or influenced by the downtown revitalization process; others are more general. They include solidarity, NIMBYism, and urban fear.

The Solidary State and City

This first response is characterized by intergovernmental and public-private partnerships at the state and city levels. In 2003, the Maricopa Association of Governments (MAG), a regional planning entity representing cities and towns in the Phoenix metropolitan area, crafted its 10-year plan to end homelessness.[44] This plan more than anything else recognized the homelessness problem in Phoenix and expressed the collective wishes of the people in the metro area to end homelessness. In 2004, the governor of Arizona created a Governor's Interagency and Community Council on Homelessness.[45] This was a demonstration that the state government cared about homeless people not only in the valley but throughout the state. This interagency council was responsible for overseeing several continuums of care programs in the

---

41. Groth (1994).

42. AZDH (2006, 1).

43. AZDH (2006, 2).

44. MAG (2003).

45. ICCH (2004, 2005).

state, as well as implementing the federally mandated Homeless Management Information Systems (HMIS) in Arizona. The Continuum of Care Regional Committee on Homelessness (CCRCH) hosted by MAG is very active in getting federal funds to implement many of the programs devised in the Maricopa Plan to End Homelessness.

At the county and city levels, one of the most symbolic examples of solidarity has been the partnership led and nurtured by community advocate Martin Shultz to study, plan, fund, build, and manage a new state-of-the art Human Services Campus on the capitol mall district. This $24-million facility congregates five agencies and service providers: the Central Arizona Shelter Services (CASS), the Maricopa County Healthcare for the Homeless, NOVA Safe Haven, St. Joseph the Worker, and St. Vincent de Paul. These were all organizations already located in the capitol mall district but without proper operating conditions. The new Human Services Campus allows for more integrated social services.

The CASS shelter did not increase the number of beds considerably, but it now has space to provide a more complete array of services. The individualized case management approach each individual receives is very critical to the rehabilitation of homeless individuals. If homeless individuals do not follow their particular counseling, they will not be able to receive the advantage of services provided by CASS. It is important to emphasize not only the medical help homeless people receive at CASS but also the social and work opportunities they are introduced to at the Human Services Campus. The dental clinic is a state-of-the-art facility where dentists volunteer to work on patients. A different but equally effective partnership is one where ASU nursing students volunteer to provide health services to homeless individuals.

Another strand of solidarity is the one generated by the many religious and charity organizations in the Valley of the Sun. Religious organizations of many different denominations provide services to homeless people. They open their doors to the homeless during hot summer days, they provide them with breakfast and several meals a day, and exemplary among them is the partnership between Grace Lutheran Church and ASU's School of Nursing, where students volunteer to provide care to homeless and poor Hispanic people.[46]

At the city level, there are several partnerships among city departments that aim at providing an integrative package of social services to the home-

46. Thompson (2006) and Bowers (2007).

less. Also, the City of Phoenix has worked with several housing developers to facilitate assembling and developing some affordable housing projects. These include the Legacy Bungalows project developed by developer Reid Butler on the capitol mall and, more recently, the construction of a HOPE VI affordable housing project with 550 mixed-income rental units called Matthew Henson, just south of the capitol mall district.

The NIMBY City

Siting of homeless facilities evokes fears and doubts about what that will do to a certain neighborhood.[47] That includes the physical presence of the facility itself and all the homeless people they will potentially attract to the area, not to mention some of the activities that exploit and might take advantage of the fragile nature of those who find themselves in a homeless situation. These include but are not restricted to prostitution, drug activities, and crime, among others. Of course, these were all arguments put forward by the Capitol Mall Association when Maricopa County and homeless advocates started debating the location of a new Human Services Campus in Phoenix. Conversations with capitol mall residents over the last two and half years have shown that these fears are real, and some of the residents have found homeless people sleeping on their front porches and observed suspicious behaviors in the neighborhood, in addition to litter on the streets.[48] Ultimately, the residents fear that their property values might depreciate and in general they are not very supportive of any expansions to current facilities or even the opening of new ones, as was the case with a new women-only shelter also built on the capitol mall by the Phoenix Rescue Mission.

During a visit to the Human Services Campus, a CASS manager revealed that those fears were motivated more by the idea of having a shelter in the neighborhood than by the concrete evidence of an increase in the number of homeless people in the area and any other illicit activities. In fact, the rationale for developing a campus was the need to contain homeless individuals within the campus precinct.[49] In addition, CASS has run a program devised to minimize the potentially negative impacts of the homeless presence in the area, which included asking homeless volunteers

---

47. Takahashi and Dear (1997), Takahashi and Gaber (1998), and Oakley (2002).
48. Dubasik (2006).
49. Lee and Price-Spratlen (2004).

to regularly clean up debris and litter around the campus area, paying for increased lighting in the neighborhood and working with the police to monitor and deter crime and other illicit activities.[50]

Another important aspect in the NIMBY discussion is about who voices those opinions and when they settled in the neighborhood. In other words: Did the residents arrive to the neighborhood before the homeless and before the opening of the temporary CASS facility, or were they just gentrifiers who bought their properties for very low prices at the peak of the downtown decline?[51] The answer seems to be mixed. Local media has reported on the latter, with some properties having tripled or quadrupled in value during the 1990s and early 2000s.

Finally, planning literature has demonstrated that businesses can be very hostile to the presence of homeless individuals in central business districts. They are normally concerned that the homeless will scare off potential customers (and visitors), causing a loss of profit and giving a negative image to the downtown area.[52] This seems to be the case associated with a passive approach to homelessness in urban areas. More progressive business communities have adopted a proactive stance in which they work together with city administrations and charitable organizations to help homeless people find shelter or any other services they may need.[53] In the Phoenix case, the Phoenix Downtown Partnership, the organization in charge of the Copper Square business improvement district, has trained many of its street ambassadors to identify homeless people and to help them receive, in partnership with local and state organizations, the services they need. According to the International Downtown Association,[54] this approach appeared to be quite prevalent in cities throughout the United States during the early 2000s.

In fact, the situation in Phoenix was somewhat different because the Human Services Campus is located on the edge of the formal downtown and homeless people have traditionally congregated (or been pushed away) to that western part of the inner city. The campus seems to provide a way to contain homeless people within a circumscribed area, out of sight of visitors to the main entertainment venues in downtown Phoenix.

---

50. Holleran (2006) and Wall (2006).

51. Fraser (2004).

52. Weinstein and Clower (2004).

53. Smith (2006).

54. IDA (2000).

The City of Fear

The final response to the homeless situation in urban areas has to do with what various scholars have coined "urban fear."[55] This is basically the criminalization of being homeless in today's American society.[56] While some authors frame this response in terms of an infringement and the denial of some basic human rights and civil liberties,[57] others contend that only an orderly society governed by strictly enforceable laws can be truly inclusive and prosper in the long term. Among the answers on this front, we find anticamping, no drinking in public spaces, closed park ordinances,[58] and a more recent institutional innovation called homeless municipal court.[59] Table 4.2 shows a set of laws prohibiting certain conduct. In Phoenix they have all been implemented with different degrees of austerity.

The Phoenix City Council voted in December 2004 to ban camping in all city parks in order to preserve the parks as "family places." The measure was aimed at keeping homeless people from areas where children and others

Table 4.2. Prohibited conduct chart[60]

Sanitation	Urination/defecation in public
Begging	Begging in public places citywide. Begging in particular public places. "Aggressive" panhandling.
Sleeping	Sleeping in public citywide.
Camping	Camping in public citywide.
Sitting/lying down	Sitting or lying down in particular public places.
Loitering	Loitering/loafing in particular public places.
Vagrancy	Obstruction of sidewalks / public places. Closure of particular public places.

55. Ellin (1997) and Zukin (2003).

56. NCH and NLCHP (2006).

57. Hopkins and Nackerud (1999).

58. Law (2001) and Mitchell (2003).

59. Nelson (2005).

60. NCH and NLCHP (2006, 141).

Figure 4.2. Woodland Parkway in Phoenix.

tend to gather (see Figure 4.2). Even though few homeless caused trouble, "many people are intimidated by the homeless and won't use the park."[61] One of the problems with this type of approach is that homeless people will be squeezed into other areas where they may be more invisible and might be victims of crimes and drug and sexual abuse.[62] While the police may or may not have manpower to cover every single location where homeless people might want to spend the night, the BID street ambassadors have managed to spot many recidivists, create a database, and contact the police to have them taken to court.

Finally, the homeless municipal court seems to be a remissive opportunity for those who either may not be aware of the support services available to them or deliberately chose not to obey existing laws. In addition, the sense of urban fear created by the installation of CCTV networks,[63] frequent patrolling of urban areas by ground and helicopter rides, and the design of anti-homeless street furniture has confirmed the presence of urban fear.

Some institutional stakeholders argue that the presence of homeless people in downtown areas equals the broken window syndrome, which has

---

61. NCH and NLCHP (2006, 40).

62. Harter et al. (2005).

63. Monahan (2006).

been conceptualized as follows: in a dilapidated neighborhood, once a house gets a broken window, others are likely to follow in what becomes a spiral of decline for the entire neighborhood.[64] The same rationale would apply to homeless: once we see one in a central location, others might follow and the image of a "spectacular city" might be distorted in the minds of visitors and tourists.[65] Although this broken window theory is well known among urban revitalization practitioners and scholars, it is contended that simply criminalizing homelessness without further understanding the reasons why homeless are on the streets does not provide robust evidence that home-lessness will be ended anytime soon.

When it comes to poverty and homelessness alleviation, as demonstrated in the first part of this chapter, one of the most appropriate theories seems to emphasize the overlap between government and individual responsibility in eradicating homelessness. Only win-win solutions combining individual and government responsibility for the welfare of the homeless will help resolve the long-term root causes of homelessness rather than simply alle-viating its symptoms.[66]

Downtown Revitalization: Implications

Following successful coaching by the president of Cornell University, a scholar and administrator with more than 30 honorary doctorates from institutions throughout the world, Arizona State University's president Dr. Michael Crow has devised an agenda for what he conceptualized as the "New American University." This university model has these eight design imperatives: leveraging place, transforming society, academic enterprise, use-inspired research, focus on the individual, intellectual fusion, global engagement, and social embeddedness.[67] An extension of the New American University agenda gave rise to an art exhibit at the university museum where local artists developed pieces capable of spurring the citizenry's imagination about a New American City.

---

64. Kelling and Coles (1996).

65. Gibson (2004).

66. Wright, Rubin, and Devine (1998).

67. Crow (2002).

If taken separately by themselves, these observations may not mean much. However, if put in the context of the fast-paced and sprawl-oriented urban development experienced in Phoenix during the past three decades or so, it does represent a major shift in direction toward the creation of a New American downtown in a 21st-century city.[68] A downtown revitalized with the help of many stakeholders, but most importantly the help of a state university. It has been argued very eloquently that universities are the new city planners.[69] These "university city planners" have helped to reduce complexity, so that individual residents, investors, and others could maximize their own opportunities. Is this approach different from traditional "Urban Growth Machine"[70] and "regime governance"[71] conceptualizations?

This approach was anchored in sustainability concepts in their more traditional formulations of economic efficiency, environmental responsiveness, and social justice.[72] It has been argued that sustainability hides more than it reveals.[73] Nonetheless, it is up to planners to articulate, in cooperation with civil society, what sustainability can reveal. Civic creativity and institutional capacity-building,[74] more than the institutionalization of fear, seem to be powerful drivers in the achievement of a new downtown culture.

In 2007 it was argued that the downtown areas of the two main Portuguese cities of Lisbon and Porto had paid too much attention to the physicality of revitalization processes and neglected their social and economic components.[75] The reason for this might have been the embedded institutional governance processes and the fact that Portugal has received EU funds to revitalize downtown public spaces. The Phoenix story presents itself differently, Phoenix is not Lisbon or Porto, or Portland for that matter, but it has spasmodically risen from the ashes every once in a while, this time with what one would hope a very strong social consciousness. Studies such as "Can We Make the Cities We Want?," "New Directions in Planning

---

68. Ford (2003) and Ellin (2006).

69. Campbell (2005), Perry and Wiewel (2005), and Rodin (2005).

70. Logan and Molotch (1987).

71. Stone (1989).

72. Portney (2003).

73. See Peter Marcuse's influential article "Sustainability Is Not Enough" (1998).

74. Landry (2000) and Cars, Healey, and Magalhães (2002).

75. Balsas (2007).

Theory," and Planning and the Just City provide us with some intellectual directions in this scholarly debate.[76] The Phoenix cause is just one example of how that can be done if we stoke the creative furnace that resides deep inside each individual.[77]

At the dawn of the 21st century, we have seen major technological revolutions shaping society and the cities we live in. From the "world is flat"[78] approach to the "world is spiky."[79] From the identification of the human genome to the idea that cities have their own DNA,[80] which can actually be mapped, computed, and improved with the help of cellular automata technologies. For the less technology inclined, good advocacy planning, community-building, and the pursuit of just and solidary cities seem to be within our reach.[81] It is true that a world of possibilities seems to be just within reach, but we cannot ignore the 36 million Americans who still live in poverty. For those located in urban areas, where most homeless tend to be found, the following recommendations based on the Phoenix experience seem adequate. What follows is necessarily an incomplete list of implications for addressing homelessness problems in contexts of urban revitalization, but it is intended to serve as a point of departure and not arrival.

Cities ought not to hide homelessness: Advocates of the broken window theory would most likely say otherwise.[82] Out of sight is not necessarily out of heart![83] The series of partnerships identified under the solidary city and state response shows that cities have a lot to gain by proactively dealing with the needs of their most vulnerable citizens. Cities should also capitalize and celebrate their accomplishments in eradicating homelessness. Progress measured in the form of milestones offers moments of reflection, which can then also help to build momentum. The Human Services Campus in Phoenix is just one example of one of those milestones. The press can either be a foe or an ally. It is important to involve the press at key steps during the process of building partnerships.

---

76. Fainstein (1999, 2000, and 2006).

77. Florida (2005a).

78. Friedman (2005).

79. Florida (2006).

80. Silva (2004).

81. Krumholz (1999), Friedmann (2000), and Ross and Leigh (2000).

82. Brinegar (2000).

83. Fiedler, Schuurman, and Hyndman (2006).

Cities should invite and embrace new volunteers: Helping to eradicate poverty and homelessness in the US will require the help of everyone.[84] No one ought to be excluded from this process, and the challenge seems to be in captivating those who protest the most against the location of new homeless facilities without doing much to help resolve current problems. A main contempt here seems to be associated with the old motto put forward by a Brazilian priest: "If I give bread to a poor person, they call me a saint; if I ask why that person is hungry, they call me a communist."

Cities must dedicate a percentage of their public funds to help fight homelessness and create affordable housing: It has been proven that it might be cheaper to provide homes to homeless individuals rather than keep building more shelters to accommodate them in segregated locations. The housing-first model provides only one option in the fight against homelessness. In the case of the chronically ill homeless, there is still need for shelters with integrated services, as well as a continuum of care system of service delivery.[85] Finding funding for a wide range of housing options (i.e., transitional, supportive, affordable, and market rate) is not easy; thus, dedicating a certain percentage of public funds to the creation of more housing choices seems to be a way to complement other public, private, and volunteer sources.[86]

Cities can foster "social business enterprises": Building on the approach of the 2006 Nobel Peace Prize–winner Muhammad Yunus and his work with the Grameen Bank's micro-lending programs, the idea of creating social business enterprises and generating wealth out of social and economic difficulties is increasing not only at the international level but also at state and local levels. Many charities and philanthropic foundations have developed and guided their action programs according to the motto "helping others to help themselves." In the Phoenix case, the daycare and job centers seem to be fully anchored in this philosophy. Tonatierra, a community-based organization comprised of Native American representatives, has also tried to establish a trade center called the Indigenous International Trade Center in downtown Phoenix as a way to preserve its rich ethnic and cultural heritage.

Cities must promote nonexclusionary urban design practices: In urban areas, design practices tend to cater to the needs of the most affluent citizens and city users—usually those who pay taxes or spend money in a certain key

---

84. Hoffman (2003).

85. Culhane and Metraux (2008).

86. Ahrentzen (2001) and Walker and Seasons (2002).

strategic location. Much progress has been made in terms of implementing the Americans with Disabilities Act (ADA) and promoting universal design practices. Unfortunately, some street furniture in downtown Phoenix was designed to directly exclude homeless from sleeping on benches. In other cities, spikes are put on walls and rails to prevent individuals from even sitting and enjoying public spaces.[87] Universal design seems to be more concerned with the accessibility and mobility of disabled people. This debate ought to go beyond physical movement to also include the characteristics of places as places to remain and not simply to move through.[88] The full potential of universal design is in addressing the needs of all human beings.

Cities should foster local and regional collaborations: Spatial equity is required to effectively deal with homelessness issues. This includes the celebration and implementation of vertical and horizontal collaborations. Vertical collaborations include arrangements between agencies at different levels of government: local, regional, state, and federal. And horizontal collaborations involve arrangements among different agencies and organizations at a given level. The regional continuum of care promoted by the Maricopa Association of Governments is a sound example of these different collaborations. Also, several religious organizations have developed fruitful collaborations between congregations located in the city of Phoenix and their counterparts in suburban cities.

Cities also ought to develop a network of human services campuses: Finally, urban development in the Phoenix metro area is definitely polycentric.[89] The number of homeless in the downtown area is just a small fraction of the homeless population in the valley. The location and construction of the human services campus in the capitol mall district was justified in terms of its centrality and proximity to existing service providers. Nonetheless, there is anecdotal evidence of suburban service providers dropping off homeless people in downtown Phoenix so that they could get appropriate medical services. A network of campuses with specific complementary services could help alleviate potential overcrowding and help create spatial equity in terms of service delivery and the maximization of economies of scale. The argument of raising funds, which some will immediately voice, can be solved with a housing linkage policy, a reversed Boston-style approach, where value

87. Hume (2005).

88. Loukaitou-Sideris and Banerjee (1998), Greed (2003), and Mitchell (2003).

89. Kirby (2005).

gains from downtown/suburban developments can be redirected to solving the problems of affordable housing and homelessness in areas of need.[90] A network of campuses, which could be modeled on the successes of the downtown campus, ought to help alleviate downtown NIMBY symptoms without causing them elsewhere.

Conclusion

This chapter has built upon earlier research on commercial urbanism in Portugal and on the use of business improvements districts and main street programs in the US and their British counterparts, the town center management schemes. After more than ten years in the US, I found myself in Phoenix researching the revitalization of the capitol mall district and studying how revitalization processes affect the lives of some of the city's most vulnerable citizens—those without a place they can call home.

In a very popular documentary about urban growth in Phoenix, sponsored by the Lincoln Institute of Land Policy, there is a very powerful argument that says: "When we pursue what we want as individuals, we do not necessarily get what we want as a community!" In fact, as the urbanist Vernon Swaback argues in that documentary, this is one of "the most fundamental paradoxes of our contemporary urbanization processes." In a distinguished planning lecture at ASU years ago, Columbia University professor emeritus Peter Marcuse (2007) itemized a four-pronged approach to creating a solidary and just city, which could lead to the eradication of urban poverty and homelessness:

- Think about the bottom third of our society

- Expose the inequalities associated with the way we currently build cities

- Propose and prioritize solutions and the allocation of resources accordingly

- And implement those solutions politically through democratic processes

---

90. Keating (1986) and Krumholz (1999).

These just city theories are echoed in the work of many planning schol-ars and practitioners in the US and elsewhere.[91] They might be difficult to define and even might constitute the perfect utopia for some. However, their practical realization provides a direction to strive for. In this vein, political economy approaches seem to be critical to understanding contemporary urbanization phenomena and to provide a framework and course of action to pursue more just and solidary cities. The Phoenix example of a New American downtown constituted one possible testing ground for this theory. Its full potential might have been partially realized with the celebration of the Arizona centennial celebration in 2012: not necessarily as a propaganda project, as I have referred to some of these mega-events elsewhere,[92] but as a truly valuable, inimitable, resourceful, organizationally capable, and sus-tainable (VIROS) event that builds civic creativity and fosters institutional capacity-building in the context of solidary and just cities.[93]

---

91. Fainstein (2000, 2006) and Marcuse (2007).

92. Balsas (2004a).

93. Landry (2000), Sandercock (2004), and Cars, Healey, and Magalhães (2002).

5

Commercial Innovations

Introduction

The relationship between commercial activities and the growth of cities can be traced to time immemorial.[1] This relationship has resulted in different commercial formats and has been either spontaneous or planned depending on people's needs, production and distribution technologies, storage and sales techniques, and the innovation capacity of companies.[2] The Phoenix metropolitan area is an interesting case study due to its rapid and recent evolution in the construction of multiple traditional, modern, and postmodern retail formats,[3] as well as its urban and suburban transformations as a consequence of the 2008–2009 global financial crisis. This chapter seeks to analyze the characteristics of four commercial formats in the Phoenix metropolitan area and to discuss a set of four lessons learned for the future of commercial urbanism (CU) in the Western world: local-global, material-immaterial, essential-dispensable, and authentic-illusory.

This chapter is organized into five main sections. The first discusses the fundamental distinctions between urban planning and commercial urbanism in Europe and the US. The second characterizes the urban evolution of the Phoenix metropolitan area. The third summarizes the four commercial

---

1. Chung et al. (2002).

2. Balsas (2003) and DeLisle (2005).

3. Cachinho (2006).

formats. The fourth discusses the four centers according to year, location, concept, accessibility, functions, organization and types of interior spaces, stores, pedestrian centrality, types of management, and main lessons in terms of innovation and levels of success. The fifth is a conclusive synthesis of the four main dilemmas underlying these new commercial formats.

Urban Planning or Commercial Urbanism?

European cities have grown and evolved over many centuries. This organic growth created a type of city where the traditional formats of the public market and the retail store gave way to the big department stores, suburban centers, and peripheral shopping centers.[4] In many European countries the appearance of these new commercial formats in expansion areas led to the decline of the traditional formats located in city centers.[5] In other cases, a healthy coexistence between the various formats was observed, mostly due to public interventions aimed at preserving endogenous cultures and practices.[6] Some of these interventions are seen by various authors as limitations to the functioning of markets. However, other authors defend said practices as a justification for the preservation of lifestyles, cultural dynamics, and the maintenance of pleasant cities.[7]

In the United States, where cities appeared only more recently, commercial formats have evolved relatively faster than in Europe.[8] For some authors the positive effects are visible in the access to a very diversified range of products by a relatively high number of consumers.[9] For other authors, these new commercial formats generate uniformity and homogeneity in cities, which is seen as a detriment to urban habitability.[10]

The fundamental point is the need to manage commercial activities as influencers of quality of urban life.[11] Commercial urbanism in European

---

4. Gaspar (1987).

5. Balsas (2003).

6. Vargas and Castilho (2006).

7. Balsas (2002), Balsas (2003), and Carrizo and Gardon (2003).

8. Robertson (1997), Crawford (2002), and Wall (2005).

9. Balsas (2001).

10. Goss (1993) and Halebsky (2004).

11. Vargas and Castilho (2006).

countries for the most part is implemented according to collective societal needs. In the United States, a logic of economic efficiency that privileges the individual over the collective has led to the creation of typified and easily reproduced commercial formats.

Furthermore, in Europe there are high levels of public participation capable of generating gains for society as a whole, while in the US, new commercial formats are proposed by investors and consumed by citizens without much attention to the indirect effects of those enterprises.[12] In Europe, commercial urbanism is also more rooted in local cultures than in the United States. Therefore, the planning of commercial activities is seen as a system of rules that allows the functioning of a global economy with relatively strong local variations depending on the contexts of urban and regional growth or decline.[13]

Regarding the commercial urbanism of airport terminals, it has been stated that these sites are highly privileged as shopping places because their users have average incomes three to five times higher as well as much higher passenger volumes than those traditionally found in any given regional shopping center—around 88 million per year in contrast to around 8 to 12 million annual visitors to a regional shopping center.[14] Similarly, according to the same author, turnover in the airport shops can be up to six times higher than in the traditional retail formats in urban settings. In addition to retailing, car rental and parking are two major sources of revenue at airports, especially at North American airports.[15]

Finally, a recent wave of revitalization of public markets and weekly farmers' markets in many European countries and the United States is contributing to the commercial gentrification of many city center districts.[16]

Phoenix, Arizona

The Phoenix metropolitan area is a paradigmatic example of low-density growth with expansive features, based on polynucleated centers, single-family

---

12. Scharoun (2012).

13. Mappin and Allmendinger (2000), Loukaitou-Sideris (2002), and Balsas (2003).

14. Kasarda (2008, 52).

15. Graham (2009).

16. Gonzalez and Waley (2012) and Mallard (2016).

housing, and a high car dependence. The rise of the Phoenix metropolitan area dates back to the turn of the 20th century, and its urban evolution was relatively slow until World War II.[17] In the center of the city one would find different types of retail establishments, the most important public buildings, bank headquarters, and other types of services usually found in central locations.[18]

Over the years, the city grew based on a rectilinear-orthogonal gridiron pattern. The first shopping mall outside of the historic area (i.e., Park Central) was built on Phoenix's Central Avenue, which led to the expansion of the city and its financial and service area outside of the traditional center. This road structure gave rise to the maximization of commercial locations at the city's main road intersections. Due to high levels of car accessibility, the commercial L-shaped square format at the four corners of many intersections is used in the planning of commercial areas more as an element of economic development and less as an urban design feature.[19]

The urban growth of the city of Phoenix after World War II was almost explosive, increasing from around 100 thousand inhabitants in 1950 to 1.4 million in the year 2010. The growth of the metropolitan area was even more impressive: from about 330 thousand to 3.8 million inhabitants in 2010.[20] The reasons for this very rapid urban growth comprised the existence of urbanized land, the efficient distribution of water, a mild climate for about eight months of the year, the existence of jobs, and a constant flow of immigrants.[21]

It is clear that this urban growth has had some not-so-positive consequences, such as destruction of the Sonoran Desert, the extinction of some fauna and flora, and all the impacts related to intense urban growth in a very short time: environmental pollution, sprawl development, and traffic congestion during peak hours, among others.[22]

In terms of urban planning, the city of Phoenix has used commercial centers simultaneously as landmarks of the urban landscapes and as subcenters to anchor the expansion of suburban areas. The urban village model was used

---

17. Gammage (2003).

18. Sertich (1980).

19. Collins (2005).

20. Wu et al. (2011).

21. Collins (2005).

22. Gober (2006) and Ross (2011).

to create autonomous centers that would meet the employment and daily needs of residents in the new suburbs. The first shopping centers functioned relatively well for the supply of daily necessities, but the construction of shopping malls in more peripheral locations led to the decline of the older and more central retail formats. Examples of these two situations are the Old Maryvale Center in west Phoenix and the Paradise Village shopping mall in the northern part of Phoenix.[23]

As the city of Phoenix grew, new shopping malls were built in the suburbs.[24] This phenomenon influenced the decline of downtown Phoenix, which was very visible until a few years ago. The abandoned and vacant buildings in central areas resulted in relative impoverishment and decay.[25] Residents in the immediate vicinity of the center also saw their commercial offers significantly reduced. This phenomenon became known as "food deserts."

The construction of a series of urban revitalization projects in the city center—including a convention center, sports complexes, hotels, the recent construction of a new university campus of Arizona State University (ASU), a series of housing and commercial developments, as well as a new public market in the city center—have contributed to the revitalization of the city center.[26]

On the other hand, the growth of the number of new commercial centers with different typologies in many municipalities throughout the metropolitan area was very intense.[27] Suburban jurisdictions such as Scottsdale, Gilbert, Mesa, and Chandler on the east side, and Surprise, Glendale, Buckeye, and Avondale on the west side have built many different commercial formats since the 1990s.[28] These new commercial developments were built in close proximity to highways and ring roads throughout the metropolitan area.[29]

The geography of shopping centers in the Phoenix metropolitan area includes the following developments in order of opening and in a centrifugal direction from the center to the periphery: Park Central in Phoenix; Spectrum

---

23. Sertich (1980).

24. Garreau (1992).

25. Schmandt (1995).

26. Gober (2006) and Ehrenhalt (2012).

27. Hackworth (2007) and ÓhUallacháin and Leslie (2013).

28. Romero (2004) and Johnson (2008).

29. Arizona Town Hall (2009).

Mall (initially called the Chris-Town Mall) and Phoenix Metro Center, both in Phoenix; Fiesta Mall in the city of Mesa; Fashion Square in downtown Scottsdale; Phoenix Desert Sky Mall as well as the new shopping centers of Towne Center and Desert Ridge on the northern outskirts of Phoenix, and the Chandler Mall in the city of Chandler; and the latest Outlet Mall Center located in a Native American reservation at the base of South Mountain. Many of these regional-scale shopping centers receive around 100 million visits per year.[30] It is interesting to note the redevelopment of some dead malls that have only recently been converted to other functions, such as the Los Arcos Mall in South Scottsdale, now a new technology campus of Arizona State University called Sky Song.

The Phoenix metropolitan area was severely affected by the global financial crisis, which has led to a recentering of urban development in the city of Phoenix and the more central area of the metropolis. The construction of a new light rail line in 2008 has helped to recenter new housing and commercial developments according to new patterns and typologies. For example, the increase in the number of transit-oriented developments (TOD) in areas surrounding the light rail stations, including Phoenix's Central Avenue, Van Buren Avenue, and Apache Avenue in Tempe was truly remarkable.

Another major change in the urban structure of Phoenix was the demolition of a central plaza located between Jefferson and Washington Avenues and the construction of a new development called Cityscape. This change led to the creation of a much more modern and dynamic civic space in the area adjacent to the newly built downtown campus of Arizona State University. The Cityscape development built in the late 2000s is a mixed-use complex with retail, entertainment, hospitality, and two office towers. On the other hand, the new downtown campus included the renovation of existing buildings for classrooms and the construction of new dormitories, which were expected to increase the resident population in the city center by about 15,000 people.

The expansion and refurbishment of the Phoenix Convention Center was also very important for the refocusing of service activities in the downtown area. These rehabilitation works have contributed greatly to the increase in the number of hotels in the central area with brand new hotels having opened recently, including the Sheraton, Westin, Palomar, Hilton

---

30. Magahern (2004, 20).

Resort, and the Renaissance; the latter two hotels are located in recently renovated historic buildings.

The revitalization of two neighborhoods in downtown Phoenix—the arts district and the warehouse district—contributed to the increased visibility of commercial and recreational activities in the central area. The former includes Central Avenue, Roosevelt Street, and Grand Avenue, and the latter includes the area south of the sports complexes (i.e., Talking Sticks Resort Arena and Chase Field).

Finally, in addition to these new urban planning interventions, there were also new housing and commercial development complexes built in 2014 and 2015 in central areas of the adjacent city of Tempe, not necessarily located along the light rail line but with important locational advantages, such as the expansion areas along the Salado River, the southeastern side of Papago Park, and even in downtown Tempe. In the mid-2010s, the relative market slowdown in the metropolitan area, as well as the higher prices and rents in relatively high-income areas, was quite evident in areas like Paradise Valley and North Scottsdale. In addition to these developments, the percentage of vacant commercial spaces has remained high since the start of the global financial crisis.

Four Commercial Formats

The commercial formats chosen for a more detailed analysis were all constructed or renovated in the 2000s and are, respectively: Phoenix's public market, the Phoenix lifestyle center called Kierland Commons, the commercial center called Tempe Marketplace in the city of Tempe, and finally the shopping mall at Terminal Four of Phoenix's Sky Harbor International Airport. Although these commercial spaces have relatively different characteristics, they all have a common purpose: the trading of goods and services to consumers with different characteristics.

Public Market

This public market is located in downtown Phoenix (see Figure 5.1 on page 120), a few blocks north from the city's old civic center. Unlike the emblematic supply markets in European cities such as Barcelona, Lisbon, Vienna, and so on, public markets in North American cities have declined and many have long since disappeared. Honorable exceptions are the public markets

Figure 5.1. Phoenix's public market. Courtesy of H. Cachinho.

in Seattle and downtown Los Angeles.[31] The public market in Phoenix was initially held once a week on Saturdays, later on also held on Wednesdays, and more recently it has been relocated to a permanent location.[32]

In this public market one finds agricultural products, vegetables, jams, pieces of art, clothes, and so forth. The main emphasis is on organic products. The quality and the personalized service during the act of buying and selling is also very important. The presence of musical bands in the marketplace has been used to captivate people and to create an atmosphere of well-being, relaxation, and conviviality. The market is managed by a nonprofit organization (i.e., Community Food Connections). The rather limited number of people who patronize this retail facility conditions its future expansion.

---

31. PPS (1996).

32. Burwell (2007).

Figure 5.2. Kierland Commons.

Kierland Commons

This shopping center represents a relative break with the commercial typologies built in the metropolitan area in previous decades (see Figure 5.2). These typologies were mostly centered on three or four anchor stores, completely covered and air-conditioned common areas, surrounded by vast car parking lots. Kierland Commons is a different format due to its main street concept, with a square and a fountain in the center of the development, on-street parking and parking lots behind the shops, ample pedestrian walkways next to the stores and, above all, a mix of commercial, residential, and service functions.

Tempe Marketplace

This shopping center built in 2007 illustrates the tendency that cities in the center of the metropolitan area have to carry out urban infill strategies. This

Figure 5.3. Tempe Marketplace.

shopping center was built in a relatively abandoned area but with a very good location near two main highways, the ring roads 101 and 202. The commercial concept included the combination of two types of commercial spaces, the traditional urban commercial square with the shops open to the parking lots and a pedestrian district with specialized commerce, restaurants, and cinemas. This commercial format uses public art in different locations within the center and a multiple set of events to attract consumers (see Figure 5.3).

Sky Harbor International Airport

Phoenix Sky Harbor International Airport had more than 40 million passengers in 2011.[33] The commercial spaces at the airport offer consumers an opportunity to make an impulse purchase before departing Phoenix. This space functions almost as a "last" opportunity to acquire a souvenir illustrative of

33. Allett (2012).

Figure 5.4. Sky Harbor International Airport.

the local culture. This format is very different from the other three formats in this chapter in that people usually do not travel to the airport to shop, unless they work or volunteer there. In these cases, they do not incur additional expenses for parking; on the other hand, they may even benefit from discounts at certain stores.[34] All three terminals at the airport have shops and services, but terminal four is the one with the highest concentration of commercial establishments (figure 5.4). At present, terminal three is undergoing expansion and the remodeling is planned to be completed by 2020.

Comparative Study

The construction, and in certain cases the renovation, of the commercial formats is very recent. Terminal four at Sky Harbor was renovated in 2004.[35]

---

34. MJ (2008).

35. Sunnucks (2004).

With the exception of the shopping center in Scottsdale, the location of
the remaining three commercial spaces is in the center of the Phoenix
metropolitan area. The public market shows a return to the city center, a
tendency also evidenced in other North American cities.[36]

Deliberate planning and urban revitalization interventions are partly
responsible for the emergence of the public market and other urban revitalization projects in downtown Phoenix. In terms of commercial models,
the establishment of the public market in downtown Phoenix shows an
appreciation for the public dimensions of urban life, including an attempt
at creating more livable spaces for those who prefer to live in the city center,
even if those spaces are still relatively different from the more vibrant cities
of the Northeastern US and Southern Europe.

The conceptual models of the other three commercial formats are relatively new to Phoenix. The location of the lifestyle center in north Phoenix
in a location bordering the city of Scottsdale seems to take advantage of
commercial land uses in the vicinity of Scottsdale airport and its financial
and business area.[37] The brand stores attract a clientele with high purchasing
power. Tempe Marketplace, with its mix of franchise chains and lesser-known
stores and restaurants, attracts a more eclectic group of consumers, including
many students and staff from Arizona State University in Tempe. Finally,
the airport's shops attract people flying somewhere else or people who have
accompanied travelers and enjoy an impulse purchase.

Good accessibility to these commercial formats appears as an added
value and as one of the aspects that influence not only its location but
also its future viability as commercial investments. Unfortunately, the heavy
dependence on cars in the state of Arizona, and in Phoenix in particular,
made it more convenient to locate Kierland Commons and Tempe Marketplace near major highways and freeways. Congestion during rush hour
on highways near downtown Phoenix can be interpreted as a limitation to
the successful revitalization of the downtown area.

However, construction of a light rail line connecting the cities of Mesa,
Tempe, and Phoenix seems to guarantee alternative, relatively quick, convenient, and direct journeys in the center of the metropolitan area. Since this
light rail line already has a direct connection to Sky Harbor International
Airport, consumers are able to reach the airport by simply taking public

36. Stearns (2004).

37. Leinberger (2008) and Yan and Eckman (2009).

transport. This accessibility improvement is likely to change the character of this commercial format, enabling it to become more diverse and appealing not just for those already en route but also for those who want to use it as a space of commerce and leisure.

Kierland Commons is the only format of the four that combines residential with commercial and service functions. The ludic and leisure aspects are a common feature of all ventures, albeit with different nuances.[38] Restaurants can be found at Kierland Commons, Tempe Marketplace, and in the various terminals at Sky Harbor Airport. The presence of movie theaters at Tempe Marketplace attracts a large clientele who will watch movies and then decide to visit the shops, restaurants, and bars located in the shopping mall. The presence of art galleries and museums is also a constant in three of these spaces, including at the airport.

There is the same percentage (36%) of clothing and footwear establishments at Kierland Commons and Tempe Marketplace. As far as restaurants and bars are concerned, the public market and the airport have relatively higher percentages (40–50%) than the other two developments, with only 21 to 23 percent of the establishments. It is also worth mentioning the great concentration of establishments dedicated to the sale of products for the home, personal health, and beauty at the Tempe Marketplace with 44 percent of the total stores. This high percentage is the result of a combination of two different types of establishments—the smaller stores located in the pedestrian zone (with areas of around 2,152 square feet) and larger stores, such as big-box stores (e.g., 134,548–172,222 square feet), with ample parking in their vicinities. Finally, it is important to emphasize the location and differentiated number of restaurants in the airport terminal before and after passing through the security and identification services. In 2015 boarding areas (A, B, C, and D) had 36 restaurants unlike the common area of terminal four, which featured 11.

The internal organization of the commercial developments is relatively different. The public market in downtown Phoenix started with temporary tents at a central downtown location. This improvised character tended to attract consumers with a pioneering spirit who looked for a different assortment of goods and experiences not easily found in the supermarkets of the suburbs. Scottsdale's case study, with its city streets in a privately owned precinct, is an innovative example of blending urban functions with gains,

---

38. Kunzmann (2011).

in this particular case, primarily for the owner of the shopping center, and indirectly, for the cities of Phoenix and Scottsdale.

The Tempe Marketplace combines areas for both cars and pedestrians. The architects used decorative and other elements such as fire and water. Fountains and fireplaces can be found in the pedestrian district, as well as the emblematic palm trees, which, because they are very slender, do not provide much shade to passersby. Finally, the commercial areas of the airport are made with high-quality, expensive materials. This detail partially shows the architects' intention to leave a good impression on the minds of all those who utilize the airport on their way to other places.[39]

Another characteristic of these commercial formats is their differentiated walking centrality. Using the Walkscore metric it is easy to see that both Tempe Marketplace and Sky Harbor International Airport have a walking score typical of areas that are heavily dependent on automobile transportation, while Kierland Commons is considered to be walkable. Finally, the location of the public market in the downtown area reveals a high pedestrian score to the point of even being designated as a pedestrian paradise. The management of these commercial formats ranges from a public-private partnership in the case of the public market, to private ownership and management in the Scottsdale and Tempe cases, to highly professionalized public management by the City of Phoenix in the airport's case.

In terms of lessons learned we can conclude that the public market is a first attempt to eliminate the existence of "food deserts" in Phoenix. The future success of this commercial space depends on the success of the remaining urban revitalization projects in the city center.[40] The Discovery Triangle is a new multipurpose community development initiative aimed at implementing a new territorial infill development strategy—given its close proximity to downtown Phoenix and downtown Tempe as well as to the two ASU campuses and Sky Harbor International Airport;[41] and addressing the shortage of supermarkets that provide fresh food and vegetables to low-income populations through a bus service, which entails the use of a refurbished mass transit bus (i.e., *busmobile)* to distribute and sell food to residents in impoverished areas of the inner-ring suburbs of Phoenix.

It is easy to realize that the public market commercial concept has been relatively successful to the point where a new similar market, the Uptown

39. Kasarda and Lindsay (2011).

40. Stone (2007).

41. Talen (2011).

Farmers Market, now takes place a few miles north from the original public market location, on the parking lot of a mega-church (North Phoenix Baptist Church), in the area known as North Phoenix, on the same Central Avenue alignment, just north of Camelback Avenue. This public market with more than 60 tents and street vendors began in 2014 and, like the Phoenix public market, is also held on Saturday mornings.

Kierland Commons in Scottsdale is seen as a breakthrough in the regional context of existing commercial spaces, and its success to date seems to show that well-planned commercial open spaces as well as the blending of various functions is beneficial to retailing. The success of this shopping center led, in large part, to the recent construction of the Scottsdale Quarter in an adjacent location just across the street from Kierland Commons. This commercial enterprise opened to the public in 2009 and it represents an attempt to capitalize on the subcentrality created by Kierland Resort and Spa and Kierland Commons. This new venture consists of 27.9 acres, 365,973 square feet of retail and restaurants, and 204,514 square feet of offices. Its mixed-use, office, and housing typology is groundbreaking for the area and its sophisticated architecture, landscaping, and natural desert beauty tend to appeal to a mid-to-high-end clientele. The adjacent housing development, Crescent Scottsdale Quarter, comprises 2.47 acres and includes luxury housing units.

The subcentrality created by Kierland Commons and Scottsdale Quarter embodies the urbanistic model proposed in *The Option of Urbanism* where the author identifies the concept of the "favored quarter"—relatively broader and more encompassing in scope but nonetheless evidenced by its high concentrations of commercial offerings, infrastructure, and good accessibility.[42]

Tempe Marketplace is seen as an innovation capable of combining a traditional shopping center's appeal with pedestrian leisure and recreational spaces. Its initial success is related to the proximity to the adjacent highways and the central location in the metropolitan area. The airport has a unique market niche that does not create much competition with other commercial formats, with the exception of the touristic destination known as Old Town Scottsdale. The success of this format is linked to the time available for shopping and the authenticity of local and state cultural artifacts and souvenirs.[43]

---

42. Leinberger (2008, 35–37).

43. Rowley and Slack (1999) and Berry (2007).

Conclusion

The main objective of this chapter was to review the characteristics of four commercial formats in the Phoenix metropolitan area. These four case studies represent different concepts and recent innovations in Phoenix's commercial landscape. At the beginning of the 21st century, the success of commercial activities seems to be based on their ability to create unique shopping and entertainment experiences and the feelings that ensue in consumers.[44]

Some authors argue that commercial activities have reached such a degree of specialization that they manipulate the sensations of citizens, in an almost endless spiral of consumption, with less positive consequences for some societal groups.[45] While there are issues underlying the capitalist model that has fueled this spiral, the human mind appears to have equally unique capabilities that, up to a certain point, seem to ensure constant adaptation to various adverse situations. In the context of this small incursion into Phoenix's commercial spaces there are four dilemmas that merit some considerations: local-global, material-immaterial, essential-dispensable, authentic-illusory.

The dilemma between the local and the global scale appears today as something that confuses and at the same time amazes local consumers accustomed to buying objects produced thousands of miles away.[46] Examples of this dilemma are the tuna cans sold by the tinsmith himself with a special Washington seasoning, or the steak sauce with prune flavor made by the seller himself in Texas. But there are also the dreamcatchers made in countries of the Far East and sold to tourists in many shops in the various terminals of the Sky Harbor International Airport as examples of authentic regional arts and crafts. Similar examples can be found in the stores of the other two malls, for example, the wide assortment of wines, beers, and alcoholic beverages from virtually the entire world that we can find at the Bevmo store or the various products at the World Market at Tempe Marketplace.

The dilemma between material and immaterial realities can be seen in the products that we take home and purchase with money (or more often with debit or credit cards) and the events that we "experience" during our shopping activities. These sensations are intensified by designers who apply previously tested formulas to make consumers spend more time in shopping malls and more money on shopping.

---

44. Kowinski (1985), Pine and Gilmore (1999), and Rigby (2011).

45. Barber (2007) and Bolin et al. (2013).

46. Santos (2013).

The third dilemma concerns the distinction between what is essential and what is dispensable. In the category of essential we find products and experiences that allow our physical and spiritual existence. Maslow's pyramid of needs allows a hierarchization of human needs and our physical and psychological tolerances in a continuum that goes from the most tangible to dispensable. It is clear that in the four commercial formats analyzed in this chapter, we find not only essential products but also many other goods and services that are dispensable given their lack of emotional value or possible future uses.

Finally, the last dilemma concerns the values of authenticity and the illusory or imaginary.[47] The Phoenix metropolitan area, like many other North American cities and metropolises, has an eclectic and relatively new culture where what is authentic is sometimes a source of pride and in other cases a reason for misunderstanding and disdain. Cultural aspects related to the Southwest, the Sonoran Desert, and cowboys are examples of the former motives, while mistreatment of Native Americans of this part of the US constitutes an example of the latter.

The relationships between cities and their commercial areas have evolved differently and according to distinct regulatory systems[48] depending on the legal norms and cultural values of the various eras.[49] In the United States, the shopping mall in its multiple nuances has reached technical levels equated with a commercial "science."[50] What seems to be missing from this "science" is the reason for the purchase,[51] the legitimation of unethical business practices, and the demonstration of increasing levels of respect for local cultures far and near, as well as the resolution of the four dilemmas identified previously. The 2008–2009 global financial crisis has led to a slowdown and refocusing of urban development in more central areas of the Phoenix metropolitan area, as well as to greater awareness of issues related to the environment, sustainability, and urban resilience.[52] The concept of solidary economy that has been popularized in Brazil and in other countries with alternative visions of responsible citizenship appears to provide some further answers.[53]

---

47. Schmookler (1993) and Pile (2005).

48. Guy (2007).

49. Smiley (2002) and Salgueiro and Cachinho (2007).

50. Goss (1993) and Barber (2007).

51. Sandel (2012).

52. Meunier (2012) and Sheridan (2015).

53. Valencia (2002) and Gaiger (2004).

6

Redesigning for Walkability

Introduction

The existence of safe, attractive, and comfortable walking environments is critical to the vibrancy of downtowns in global cities.[1] This policy goal is a significant departure from the traditional transportation planning approach that has catered mostly to the needs of drivers. Many cities such as London, Copenhagen, and Melbourne have managed to reduce the number of cars in city center areas without losing their urban character.[2]

The City of New York and the NYS Department of Transportation (DOT) have engaged in a long-term commitment to redesign the public spaces in the core of Manhattan,[3] particularly the public squares along Broadway from Forty-Seventh to Twenty-Third Streets: Times Square, Herald Square (HS), and Madison Square (MS). This ongoing program was to be completed in 2015 and included the creation of pleasant public spaces, such as pedestrian precincts, plazas, and bike lanes. Urban sustainability is one of the main theoretical compasses orienting the improvements program. Urban sustainability can be approached from multiple viewpoints, such as reductions in car dependence, easing of vehicular congestion, better mobility, safety and comfort for pedestrians (mainly shoppers and tourists), and better integration of multiple modes of transportation (i.e., walking, bicycling,

---

1. Peterson and McDonogh (2011).

2. NYCDOT and Gehl Architects (2012).

3. Miller (2007).

subway, and transit).[4] Although this program emphasizes pedestrian comfort, it is hoped that it will also create value from livability, attractiveness, and real estate perspectives.

Within this context, most published research in North America has examined central cities from safety and traffic engineering standpoints. This chapter examines the motivations, designs, and expectations behind the recent walkability improvements to Times Square. The emphasis is on understanding the significance of the design proposals for the rebranding and community design of this global city's core.[5] Their expected impacts from both management's and users' perspectives are reviewed. Furthermore, the chapter also discusses walking and safety levels prior to and after the initial improvements, the intended pedestrian behaviors, and the image rebranding as a direct consequence of the reconstruction.[6]

The argument is that although one could not find substantial organized protests to the redesign of Times Square, the creation of an almost exhilarating "theme park" setting in the core of Manhattan is as much an example of American neoliberalism as it is a demonstration of liberty and a human desire made so by marketing campaigns, which increasingly broadcast Times Square and American-inspired globalization to the rest of the world. The research methods involved extensive literature reviews and reviews of official planning and design documents. The key findings enable an up-to-date analysis of the overall impact of the improvements on the vibrancy of Times Square. The findings are relevant to those interested in the creation and promotion of vibrant, safe, attractive, and comfortable districts in global downtowns.

Following this introduction, this chapter is organized into five sections. First is the analytical framework. The second is an overview of Times Square. The third utilizes a set of six challenges to analyze three different phases in the reconstruction of Times Square. The goal is to uncover the square's potential and to discuss whether walkability is utilized as a fundamental right or as a tool to facilitate capitalistic accumulation. The fourth identifies the stakeholders' motivations and design solutions. The fifth analyzes the expected community design impacts both from management's and users' perspectives. The sixth presents a synthesis of the major findings.

---

4. Carmona (2001) and Banister (2005).

5. Kotler, Haiderr, and Rein (1993) and Greenberg (2003).

6. Zavattaro (2013).

Analytical Framework

The central areas of global cities are subjected to a unique set of forces.[7] Decades of intense real estate markets have contributed to an expensive built environment. Most global cities are characterized by very high densities. These built-up areas have resulted from major investments by many private entrepreneurs. Tall high rises are a result of land speculation, developmental pressures, tight credit markets, and stringent regulatory regimes. Also, commercial areas are shaped by a history of multiple regulations created to reinforce certain activities and to stir development according to investment strategies mostly by an array of corporate interests. The outcomes of this intense real estate development are expected not only to benefit private investors but also contribute toward more functional and dynamic neighborhoods.[8] Public authorities have added responsibilities in this intense environment. They are responsible not only for setting norms and standards but also for enforcing existing regulations in order to reduce conflicts among city users. This includes enabling not only the safety, cleanliness, and vibrancy of public spaces but also the creation of fluid accessibility and mobility for all street users as well as attractive and competitive city environments.[9]

Transportation planning had historically emphasized vehicular accessibility.[10] Even with quite high transit ridership, a considerable proportion of road transportation has been dedicated to accommodating moving vehicles, while parking was restricted to limited surface lots and garages. High-density global cities are characterized by extremely high numbers of both pedestrians and automobiles. Also, the potential for conflict is relatively high as a result of either crossing the street or due to insufficient sidewalk width to accommodate a high number of passersby.[11] Retail development as well as other commercial establishments, such as cafés, restaurants, entertainment venues, banks, offices, among others, tend to increase the number of people in certain streets segments.[12] Intense window shopping creates irregular flows

---

7. Sassen (2001).

8. Hack and Sagalyn (2011).

9. Carmona, Magalhães, and Hammond (2008).

10. Banister (2005).

11. Ehrenfeucht and Loukaitou-Sideris (2010).

12. Lloyd and Clark (2001).

of movement, which impact those whose main goal is to walk quickly to their destinations.[13]

Busy public spaces are usually good for businesses but unsavory from the perspective of place vibrancy and the creation of everyday places. Intense places—influenced by a myriad of activities, signs, lights, and publicity and regulated by multiple city departments—tend to result in unkempt and trivial places, which can be below their potential. This conclusion is easily reachable by studying the evolution of such places.[14] They have evolved according to dominant influences of each era, often performing critical functions as part of larger networks and systematic routines, while slowly abandoning concerns with quality, cleanliness, and attractiveness. These undesirable outcomes lead to needed interventions, which basically aim to reverse processes of decline. The revitalization of central neighborhoods is accompanied by improvements to their public spaces, changes in land occupation and real estate markets, and by governance restructuring with the active participation and leadership of private-sector representatives.

Table 6.1 synthesizes the dimensions of a typical urban design process applied to a sustainable urban transportation planning process. The emphasis is not only on place-shaping processes but also on the levels of awareness required to influence design outcomes. A typical design process entails knowing place-shaping intentions and a self-conscious positionality, which in the case of streets and public spaces has to conform to specific standards and traffic engineering methods. Appropriate widths, calibers, cross-sections, and respect for industry standards dictate the likely design options. Redesigns are intended to influence future behaviors through knowledge of universal or near-universal proportions and harmonies.[15] Originality is usually required to foster distinctiveness.[16]

The typical transportation planning process aims to achieve sustainable mobility. The planning principles of sustainable transportation comprise environmental diversity, self-sufficiency, and stewardship. PlaNYC was seen as New York City's blueprint for "going green"—a broad-scope directive

---

13. Alfonzo (2005).

14. Ehrenhalt (2012).

15. Roger Evans Associates (2007).

16. Bunnell (2002).

Table 6.1. Sustainable urban transportation design process[17]

	Self-conscious design	Unself-conscious design
Knowing place-shaping	Design process Goal: safer transportation planning. Principles: futurity, carrying capacity, distinctiveness.	Development process Goal: sustainable mobility. Principles: environmental diversity, self-sufficiency, stewardship.
Unknowing place-shaping	Management process Goal: governance leadership. Principles: the polluter pays, precautionary, resource efficiency.	Space in use Goal: making livable places. Principles: participation, equity, human needs.

intended to promote a sustainable and resilient future, bringing jobs and opportunities to New Yorkers.[18]

A myriad of new design practices and interpretations have recently been conceptualized. These range from tactical urbanism, DIY urban design, guerrilla urbanism, and pop-up spaces.[19] Despite having a relatively temporary and tactical character, these methods are relevant in the initial stages of a redesign and reconstruction project. However, it is important not to lose sight of the need for structural and relatively permanent modifications to iconic public spaces. Sustainability goals and principles have the capacity to help professionals think about the long-term implications of their designs.[20]

The management process of sustainable transportation planning comprises broad governance leadership. Political motivations are usually key in urban redesigns because elected officials have the responsibility to resolve problems and, usually, they also control the funding streams for those improvements. Common sustainability principles include polluter pays, precautionary, and resource efficiency.[21]

---

17. Self-elaboration with generic adaptation from Carmona (2001, 2014).

18. Jabareen (2013).

19. Hou (2011), Lydon and Garcia (2015), and Schwartz (2015).

20. Gehl (2010) and Dalsgaard (2012).

21. Low and Smith (2006).

Overview of Times Square

New York City is a major global city of 8.5 million people. New York City is located in a megalopolis of about 118 million people (see Figure 6.1). It is structured in five boroughs, Manhattan, Brooklyn, Bronx, Queens, and Staten Island. The city covers an area of almost 309 square miles with a density of about 4,038 people per square mile. The New York tristate region attempts to manage the forces of globalization without a well-organized system of regional governance.[22] Manhattan has a gridiron pattern imposed uniformly on the island in 1811 in response to public health problems and the need for planned development (i.e., the commissioner's plan). There are approximately 1.6 million residents living in Manhattan. Journeys to work in transit and walking mode share for NYC in the period 2008–2010 equaled 68.3 percent with that number being only 8.2 percent for the whole country during the same period.[23] Despite these figures, traffic congestion had been rampant and there was need for additional road investments.

One of the major planning challenges facing New York City is its chaotic and unjust transportation system. A congestion pricing proposal for Manhattan failed to launch in 2008 mostly due to the opposition or indifference of suburban and state interests.[24] Most legislators who voted down the proposal were responding to voters and drivers in the suburbs who opposed this measure as a tax on them.[25] The Department of City Planning (DCP) has advanced specific innovations such as traffic calming, bicycle lanes, and greenways. However, until recently, policy was mostly determined by the city's Department of Transportation (NYCDOT), which was mainly interested in moving as many cars through the city streets as quickly as possible.

For years, civic and community groups have demanded that the city policy be balanced and serve the needs of the people who walk from transit stops and stations to places of work, commerce, and entertainment and who would bike, not of the small minority who drive to work and to watch a Broadway show.[26] This situation finally changed during Mayor Bloomberg's

---

22. Vogel et al. (2010).

23. Russo (2012).

24. Vogel et al. (2010).

25. Schaller (2010).

26. Angotti (2008).

Figure 6.1. Location of New York City.

second term in office. He created pedestrian plazas, cycling infrastructure (i.e., lanes, bike parking, and a shared bicycle scheme), bus rapid transit lanes, and other measures allocating more street space to pedestrians.[27]

The Times Square evolution is relatively well covered in such seminal books as *The Culture of Cities*,[28] *Times Square Roulette*,[29] *Where the Ball Drops*,[30] *The Devil's Playground*,[31] and *Money Jungle*,[32] among others. This literature is extensive and covers many nuances of the history, character, economy, and regulation of the area from its initial inception prior to the 1811 commissioner's plan until recently. The boundaries of the district are usually defined from Fortieth to Fifty-Third Streets and from the Avenue of the Americas to Eighth Avenue. Broadway runs transversally to the avenues' alignment and intersects Seventh Avenue at Forty-Fourth Street. The area is perceived as almost exclusively commercial due to its more than 30 theaters, many hotels, and the extremely high number of retail and service establishments. But the district also has almost 20,000 inhabitants in addition to its about 200 thousand daily workers.[33]

The district is affectionately called the "crossroads of the world" given its concentration of commercial activities and proximity to CUNY, NYC's public library, Bryant Park, and several transportation hubs. The combination of a critical mass of entertainment with service-sector jobs, high-profile mass media headquarters, as well as many retail offerings contribute to the area's unique identity.[34] This has been augmented over the years by regularly held events, such as the New Year's Eve celebration, the Macy's parade, and a myriad of smaller scale but quite well-attended events. The many neon signs and LCD screens in the area contribute to its immense allure.

During the 1970s and 1980s, Times Square included a substantial amount of vice and prostitution. The 1990s saw the rejuvenation of the area with skyscrapers that have attracted new tenants, hotels, and residential buildings, in great part because of special tax incentives.[35] The Times Square

---

27. Millard (2014) and Sadik-Khan and Solomonow (2016).

28. Zukin (1995).

29. Sagalyn (2001).

30. Makagon (2004).

31. Traub (2004).

32. Chesluk 2008).

33. Times Square Alliance (2012).

34. Chesluk (2008).

35. Roost (1998) and Hack and Sagalyn (2011).

clean-up campaign initiated by Mayor Giuliani was hotly contested. Proponents argued that it made the neighborhood cleaner and safer;[36] opponents criticized the resulting homogenization and "Disneyfication" of the neighborhood as well as the replacement of old businesses by upscale venues and tourist attractions.[37] Times Square is a place known around the world and immediately recognizable for the role it plays in popular social and media culture. Over the years, it has stood as a symbol of American modernism.

It has been argued that "this neon-encrusted 'X' is regulated by design guidelines that call for a requisite number of *Lutses* (*Light Units in Times Square*) and controlled by urban designers who have planned its spontaneous unplannedness."[38] Times Square has benefited from large tax breaks that favored developers and tenants. It has been estimated that the redevelopment has entailed more than $1 billion in "unnecessary" property tax abatements and other benefits like zoning changes that allowed for taller towers than would otherwise be permitted.[39] Also, during the 1960s the zoning code in New York created privately owned public spaces, or POPS.[40] There are now more than 500 of these plazas, arcades, and atriums—spaces that often nobody wanted, least of all developers who built them in exchange for valuable zoning concessions.[41]

From a public works perspective, Times Square infrastructure was dramatically outdated and in need of extensive repair. Even though the number of fatalities has been decreasing in NYC as demonstrated in Table 6.2, Broadway has had one of Manhattan's worst safety records for many years. It averaged 137 percent more pedestrian crashes than other avenues in the area.

Table 6.2. Pedestrian safety in New York City through the decades[42]

Decades	NYC pedestrian fatalities (average per year)	Pedestrian fatalities (per 100,000 residents per year)	% pedestrians
1910–1919	381	7.3	70
1960–1969	434	5.5	60
2000–2009	167	2.0	51

36. Roberts (2009).

37. Eeckhout (2001).

38. Boyer (2003, 430).

39. Bagli (2010).

40. Nemeth (2009).

41. Miller (2007).

Times Square was consistently ranked among New York City's most dangerous intersections. It basically referred to two triangles formed by the intersection of Seventh Avenue (running north-south) and Broadway (running diagonally across the grid of New York City). Even though pedestrians greatly outnumbered cars, 89 percent of the right-of-way in Times Square was taken up by busy through streets dedicated to moving motor vehicles. Times Square has 4.5 times as many people as vehicles in about 11 percent of the right-of-way (i.e., the sidewalk), which was used to accommodate not only pedestrian movement but also newsstands, street lights, vendors, and many other activities.[43] A considerable part of Times Square's public space has been redesigned to accommodate the increasing number of people who patronize the district.

Uncovering Urban Design Challenges: Walkable Places

As in all urban redesign projects there are always challenges that condition realities, processes, and outcomes. It is possible to identify six challenges at the heart of participatory urban design processes: bureaucratization, self-interest, multiculturalism, privatization, design aesthetic, and mistrust.[44] Table 6.3 shows the evolution of participatory urban design challenges in Times Square. The planning and design process for Times Square was part of Michael Bloomberg's 2007 PlaNYC Sustainable Streets.[45] World Class Streets was an initiative implemented to conceptualize and bring about a radically new approach to mobility and motorization.[46] The goal was to use planning and design processes to accomplish alternative results. Bureaucratization in the form of existing long-held traffic standards, which favored automobiles at the expense of all other modes of transport, characterized reality prior to the intervention. The test phase was marked by experimentation, which allowed stakeholders to reach a different transport paradigm where both redesigned and regulated spaces now favor pedestrian mobility.

The self-interest challenge can be observed in the change from drivers' staying power in their overall goal to have privileged rights to the

42. Russo (2012).

43. NYCDOT (2010).

44. Hou (2011).

45. NYCDOT (2008).

46. NYCDOT and Gehl Architects (2012).

streets to a new urban regime in city hall, which increasingly tended to favor walkability. Green Light for Midtown was the program that led to the creation of permanent plazas along Broadway.[47] But the goal has been continued by current NYC mayor Bill de Blasio with the Zero Vision Safety Plan.[48] Overall the idea was to create safer transportation planning with fewer collisions, injuries, and fatalities. Multiculturalism is critical to a city that values different cultures and groups instead of treating everyone as a uniform category. In fact, New York is one of the most diverse cities in the world. About 60 percent of the population are people of color, and over a third are foreign-born, representing every nation on earth.[49] The test phase entailed the regaining of street space and the reconstructed phase is

Table 6.3. Evolution of participatory urban design challenges in Times Square[50]

	Pre-improvements phase (–2009)	Test phase (2009)	Final design phase (2011–2015)
Bureaucratization	Vehicular standards.	Experimentation.	Regulation.
Self-interest	Drivers' staying power.	Urban regime.	Reconstruction and urban regime.
Multiculturalism	Serendipitous use of crowded sidewalks.	Regain street space.	World-class space.
Privatization	Emphasis on cleanliness and redevelopment.	Appropriation of right-of-way.	Cloaked captivity.
Design aesthetic	Minimal emphasis on the quality of the space.	Spontaneity.	Simplicity and finality of solutions.
Mistrust	Dissimulated role of street ambassadors.	Cautious appropriation of the right-of-way.	Control of uses on the redesigned spaces.

47. NYCDOT (2010).

48. Viola et al. (2015).

49. Angotti (2008).

50. Self-elaboration with generic adaptation from Hou (2011).

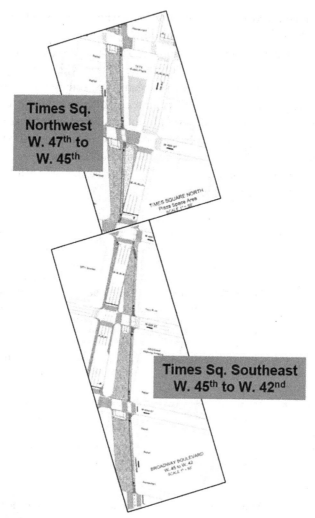

Figure 6.2. Map of the Times Square improvements. Source: NYCDOT (2010).

leading to the creation of world-class space that will help to serve multiple and varied publics (see Figure 6.2).

Times Square is the product of intense forces, all attempting to benefit positively from the integration and interaction of loosely coordinated actions and strategies within a carefully crafted regulatory framework. Footloose capital in search of higher returns on investment is careful to minimize risks by locating in well-tested settings within a critical mass of world-class spaces.

The privatization challenge was observed in the change of emphasis from mainly cleanliness and redevelopment provided by the business improvement district—Times Square Alliance—to full appropriation of the central space and capture of value for the district.[51] Manhattan espouses the paradigm of a global city but also of a very dense and walkable borough. It has been argued that "the market has rediscovered walkable urbanism" in North America.[52] This rediscovery has been translated into extra amenities in master-planned communities in suburban locations but also in redesigned walkable spaces in urban settings.[53]

City neighborhoods are usually endowed with limited public spaces. Many of these public spaces are nonetheless subjected to regulations that forbid certain practices, such as camping, drinking alcoholic beverages, and playing loud music.[54] However, the right of access to those public spaces is guaranteed by the US Constitution and its amendments.

The Times Square redesign has been perceived by some as possibly infringing on those rights.[55] Cloaked captivity represents loss of self-possession and agency; captive individuals are usually no longer in charge of their own fate. In a way, they stop owning themselves and their condition becomes one of existential alienation.[56] The centrality of the area, together with the privatization of wall space for advertising purposes through electronic monitorization and connectivity, raises personal privacy concerns as well.

In terms of design aesthetics, the district prior to the current reconstruction was characterized by relatively poor quality and disorganized space. During the test phase the emphasis was put on promoting public spontaneity through the utilization of inexpensive materials ranging from planters, beach lawn chairs, esplanade tables and umbrellas, and gallons of paint to designate the new pedestrian areas. The design aesthetics of the new squares are relatively simple with the requirement to create pedestrian plazas for collective activities and corridor channels for passersby (see Figure 6.3 on page 144).

---

51. Gross (2013).

52. Leinberger (2008, 86).

53. Lovasi et al. (2013).

54. Mitchell (2003) and Blomley (2007).

55. Low and Smith (2006).

56. Barber (2007).

Figure 6.3. Times Square walk-only squares during the day.

Regulations are endemic to creating mistrust by those negatively affected by them. Examples of mistrust experienced by Times Square users in the pre-improvements phase resulted from the dissimulated role of street ambassadors who removed homeless individuals from the district as a result of partnerships with NYPD and several housing nonprofits in the city. The test phase generated feelings of cautious appropriations of the right-of-way due to the public's incredulity with the radicalism of the transformation. Finally, the reconstruction phase is likely to strengthen the need for control of the public space in order to keep the area safe for residents, workers, and tourists.

Stakeholders' Motivations and Designs

There were six main categories of motivations in the redesigning of Times Square. The first category can be broadly defined as urban vibrancy where the main motivation was to increase the number and variety of people and activities in Times Square. While Times Square represents only 0.1 percent of New York City's land area, 5 percent of the city's jobs are located there and the district generates about 10 percent of the city's economic output.[57] In the early 2000s, Times Square contributed $1.1 billion in annual taxes to New York City and $1.3 billion in annual taxes to New York State.[58] The redevelopment of Forty-Second Street began a major process of improvements that brought new investment, businesses, workers, and visitors to the district.[59] The number of tourists has grown from 31 million in the mid-2000s to a record-breaking 56.4 million tourists according to 2015 Times Square Alliance estimates. The number of people walking along Broadway and Seventh Avenue in Times Square increased by 11 percent, and pedestrian volume also increased by 6 percent in Herald Square. In absolute numbers the increase was from 350,000 people a day in 2009 to as high as 480,000 a day in 2014.[60]

The second motivation was safety in the form of reductions in pedestrian-vehicular crashes. Green Light for Midtown was a major city initiative to improve mobility and safety.[61] This program began implementation in May 2009. It discontinued vehicular traffic on Broadway, with new pedestrian areas on Broadway in Times Square (Forty-Seventh and Forty-Second Streets) and Herald Square (Thirty-Fifth and Thirty-Third Streets). The project was made based on a feasibility analysis that indicated improved traffic flow on Sixth and Seventh Avenue and improved traffic on Broadway. Injuries to motorists and passengers decreased by 63 percent while pedestrian injuries decreased by approximately 35 percent.[62]

The third category of motivations was pleasantness. Prior to the improvements, according to Design Trust for Public Space the area was characterized by three main challenges:

- Pedlock (i.e., severe pedestrian overcrowding) impeding movement on sidewalks, which created a public safety hazard by forcing people into the street

---

57. Times Square Alliance (2012).

58. HRA (2007).

59. Fainstein and Stokes (1998).

60. Bagli (2015).

61. NYCDOT (2010).

62. NYCDOT (2010).

- Fierce competition between multiple users for very limited space

- Ugly and cluttered ground plane ("streetscape schlock")[63]

It is expected that more pleasant and comfortable public spaces are likely to increase permanence in Times Square. The district was perceived as a central fluid place, mainly due to its continuous vehicular traffic. The exiguous sidewalks and small size of its median refuge islands were unlikely to influence permanence decisions positively. The redesigned plaza has contributed to about 80 percent fewer pedestrians walking in the roadway in Times Square. About 74 percent of pedestrians surveyed by the Times Square Alliance agreed that Times Square had improved dramatically over the last year.[64]

The fourth category of motivations pertains to functionality and the need to improve the logistical conditions for filming crews and event organizers in the district. Extension power cords—together with other camera, sound, and light cords and cables for filming and reporting in the district—created many walking hazards. The fifth category is branding and the need to strengthen and rebrand Times Square and NYC's global image. New York City's economy was greatly impacted by 9/11 and, over the years, the city has attempted to reenergize its image with multiple campaigns, ranging from Quality of Life, I♥NY, Green City, World Class City, and Global City to Resilient City, especially after Hurricane Sandy's 2011 catastrophe.[65]

The sixth motivation was obviously very important as well, which was to increase commercial activity in the form of sales volumes and increase the number of tourists, workers, and residents in the area. Nearly half (42%) of New York residents surveyed in Times Square mentioned that they do more shopping in the area since the changes took place, 70 percent of theatergoers recognized that the plazas have had a positive effect on their experience, and 26 percent of Times Square employees reported leaving their offices for lunch more often.[66] It was based on these findings that Mayor Bloomberg decided to make the redesign changes permanent. The assessed real estate value of the district has also increased from 2 billion dollars in 1992 to 5.6 billion in 2012.[67]

---

63. Design Trust for Public Space (2003).

64. NYCDOT (2010).

65. Greenberg (2003) and Greenberg and Fox (2013).

66. NYCDOT (2010).

67. Times Square Alliance (2012).

In addition to the more visible Times Square plazas, NYC also has a Public Plaza Program for other potential plaza locations and a "Street Seats" program for parking space, both run by NYCDOT. The goal of the pilot parklet/pop-up café program is to provide seasonal outdoor public seating in the parking lane as an amenity to pedestrians at places where sidewalk seating is not available and to build well-designed public open spaces that invite people to stay.

It is believed that this reconstruction is perhaps the largest ground-up redesign of Times Square in generations. Among its most important goals are enjoyment and the need to provide safe and secure public spaces.[68] Crime Prevention through Environmental Design (CPTED) techniques were fully utilized in the conception of the new squares. The permanent pedestrian plaza along Broadway between Forty-Second and Forty-Third Streets is 3,333.2 square yards of newly redesigned pedestrian space featuring distinctive pavers; planned seating; the area's permanent electrical, sound, and broadcasting connections for the numerous public events in the plaza; pedestrian way-finding signage and LED lighting; in addition to replaced utilities and electrical components, sewers, and water mains. The area between Forty-Third and Forty-Seventh Street has 1,554.7 square yards of permanent plaza space. The plaza's redesign project was conceptualized by the architecture firm Snohetta.[69]

Duffy Square was also reconstructed and a new TKTS booth was installed as a viewing platform for experiencing the full scope of the surrounding neon signs.[70] In addition, a ground-level map made out of steel and granite highlighting Broadway's theater district has been installed in Duffy Square.[71] This map serves as a way-finder for visitors to Times Square, allowing them to visualize the density of the world's largest theater district.

Future Expectations

Public spaces are utilized for multiple purposes. As expected, they are directly influenced by the activities in the surrounding built environment. Although it is plausible to criticize the role of markets and of commerce (i.e., shopping) in shaping societal behaviors, it is well known that retail activities,

---

68. Carmona, Magalhães, and Hammond (2008).

69. NYC (2013).

70. Townsend (2004) and Nevárez (2009).

71. NYC (2013).

restaurants, and coffee shops (conceptualized as third places) contribute to the livability and vibrancy of urban public spaces. Regularly held events in public spaces have the capacity to increase sociability practices and social capital. This is critical to the stability of democratic systems, which are based on engaged citizenship values. It is argued that higher levels of democratic citizenship result from active engagements in all four types of processes: design, development, making of city spaces, and management. The desirable outcome is for an engaged citizen designer.[72] On the other hand, there is also a need to fully uphold First Amendment rights in public spaces in cities.[73]

The essence of Times Square has been profoundly altered from a place of ephemerality to a place of temporary permanence. The new pedestrian precinct reminds everyone of the characteristics of European plazas. In fact, it is argued that Copenhagen served as the model for the Times Square improvements. Walkability advocates hope that reconstructed Times Square will now inspire other cities in the US and abroad to create their own walkable public spaces.

But this intervention has also faced some criticisms, including from motorists and taxi drivers who viewed the Broadway closures as obstacles and delays in their itineraries. Others have questioned the shared bicycle scheme and the number of bicycle lanes through Manhattan as an unviable traffic alteration in the long run, and the commercialization and privatization of the public realm due to its promotional partnership with a major financial institution.

In addition, neighborhoods in the other boroughs (e.g., Brooklyn) have resented the money spent in Times Square as additional improvements made to what is perhaps one of the most expensive neighborhoods on the planet, which was also likely to do quite well despite the added improvements. Nonetheless, the municipality went ahead with its plan, and based on before and after studies of pedestrian crashes, vehicular speeds, and traffic flows it concluded that the redesigns would bring placemaking advantages to the crossroads of the world. With this intent, seven directions for the future of community design were used to study these urban transformations from both the management's and the users' perspectives: new tools and technologies, expanding participation, citizenship and empowerment, asset-based approach, collaboration, public space activism, and nonprofit practice.[74]

72. Hou (2011).

73. Marcuse (2014).

74. Hou (2011).

Table 6.4 presents two different perspectives on the community design of Times Square: a management's and a user's. New tools and technologies offer two different possibilities. In the past, the publicity and luminous ads created a strong and dynamic visual effect, which detracted from the poor quality of the street environment. The fact that billboards are mandatory on buildings in the square propitiates their use not only for advertising but also for community purposes. It has been suggested that such billboards can be used for innovative purposes to the benefit of the community, similar to community airtime in television concessions.[75] Such a practice would expand participation possibilities not only for the stakeholders but also for community organizations. In the past, many events and installations have

Table 6.4. Two perspectives on the community design of Times Square[76]

	Management's perspective	Users' perspective
New tools and technologies	Advertisement and safety.	Everyday use, private and community purposes.
Expanding participation	Immersive environment for advertisement.	Community participation and sites of dissent.
Citizenship and empowerment	Attract and retain consumers in Times Square.	Multiple activities besides shopping and patronizing the businesses in Times Square.
Asset-based approach	Combination of permanence (built environment) and flux (streets and squares).	Centrality and proximity to multiple facilities.
Collaboration	Partnerships between public and private entities.	Spontaneous interactions between individuals and groups of people.
Public space activism	Scripted and controlled activities.	Improvised and free utilization of the squares.
Nonprofit practice	Exceptional and punctual activities.	First Amendment rights to spaces.

75. Hack (2011).

76. Self-elaboration with generic adaptation from Hou (2011).

Figure 6.4. Times Square at night.

utilized the horizontal dimension of Times Square, but there is equal potential to utilize the vertical dimension through the immersive environment for
advertisement and community participation (see Figure 6.4).

In terms of citizenship and empowerment, we can distinguish a (private) management's perspective that is mostly interested in attracting and
retaining consumers in Times Square, while from a user's perspective the
main aim might be to experience multiple activities, besides shopping and
patronizing the numerous businesses in the district. In addition, an asset-
based approach to public spaces can take advantage of the many resources
in or near the area to bolster the image and functionality of Times Square
and its surroundings. This includes a combination of permanence in the
built environment (i.e., entertainment, cultural, business) with enjoyment
of spaces of flux, such as streets and squares, coupled with the district's
centrality and proximity to the many transport facilities nearby (i.e., Grand
Central Station, Port Authority Bus Terminal, Penn Station, etc.).

In terms of collaboration, it is important to emphasize the many
possibilities for partnerships between public and private entities in the area,

as well as spontaneous interactions between individuals and loosely affiliated groups of people. In terms of public space activism, management is in charge of supervising most activities in the district. Management's preference might be toward scripted and controlled activities, while many users might favor an improvised and free utilization of the pavements.

Furthermore, it is important to recall that, perhaps, the most important motivation for the reconstruction of Times Square was the upgrade of the district and its emphasis on attracting and retaining consumers. Commercial success might not be synonymous with nonprofit practices in the area. These might have an exceptional and punctual nature from a management perspective. However, as Marcuse (2014) reminds us, First Amendment rights should enable citizens to utilize the public space consistently with full citizenship rights of freedom of speech, gathering, and of assembly.

This is quite pertinent in a context of increased conspicuous consumption. It is known that consumerism is characterized by a lack of sensitivity toward the true needs of people and that big corporations can be soulless agents of unrestricted consumerism, invading people's lives and depriving them of their inner soul.[77] The preservation of First Amendment rights is likely to ameliorate and redeem such usurpations and cloaked captivity.

Finally, one could question the long-term viability of this reconstruction given that the US has had a troubled history of pedestrian malls and that NYC is a winter city conditioned by harsh winter climatic patterns.[78] Paradigmatic examples include State Street in Chicago, which was transformed into a pedestrian transit–only mall in the 1980s, only to be reopened to automobile traffic years later. Furthermore, the harsh Northeast winters are not conducive to spending time outdoors and that is why many winter cities have put their hopes in underground shopping malls and above-ground connected skyway systems linking the commercial areas of most buildings in shopping districts.[79] Despite these arguments and given the drastic historic inversion in US vehicle miles traveled (VMT) during the great recession, the country seems to have finally realized the value of walkability toward the improvement of one's quality of life.[80]

---

77. Barber (2007) and Viteritti (2010).

78. Robertson (1994).

79. El-Geneidy, Kastelberger, and Abdelhamid (2011).

80. Wachs (2013).

Conclusion

Times Square is one of the most iconic places in the world.[81] The incremental approach to placemaking was critical to redesigning its public space. The temporary closings provided the data needed to make more substantial investments in new pavements and utility systems. The redesigns led to changes in the bus network and in the number of taxi cab pick-up and drop-off points in Times Square. However, the main goal was to correct a problem of pedestrian level of service: there were way too many pedestrians on too little pedestrian space. The pedestrians were already there spilling over from the sidewalks and the extra space was visibly necessary.[82]

Leadership at the top, clear and guiding vision from conceptualization to implementation, measurement of performance, openness to input from stakeholders, quick project delivery, and relatively low costs were some of the main success factors in the reconstruction. New York's high level of transit ridership and numerous intersections per square mile, consequences of pre-automotive expansion, are characteristics of "New York exceptionalism," which may also be partly responsible for its success.[83]

The rediscovery of walkable urbanism by the market raises equity issues that can only be resolved with more participation not less.[84] Across the world, politicians embrace environmental causes in certain cases almost exclusively to raise their own popularity. Public appearances on earth day or bike-to-work day and other similar one-day events might help to raise political profiles, but they do very little for the long-term betterment of the mobility conditions of those who are disproportionally burdened by current transportation systems.[85] One cannot forget that social justice prerogatives still constitute the core of a more sustainable and equal society and that a neoliberal political economy system dominated by growth motives at the expense of everyone else is unlikely to produce acceptable results.[86]

The closing of Broadway at certain locations was accomplished in its pilot phase using inexpensive materials and guerrilla-type strategies, typical of

---

81. Carmona, Magalhães, and Hammond (2008).

82. Hass-Klau (2015).

83. Speck (2012).

84. Hou (2011) and Rosan (2012).

85. Weis (2013).

86. Balsas (2017a).

tactical urbanism interventions.[87] The argument is that although one could not easily find organized protests to such tactics, they tended to resemble business intelligence covert operations associated with regime changes. The limited democratic scrutiny of such occurrences is often done as a subterfuge to unpalatable modifications. The creation of an almost exhilarating "theme park" setting in the core of Manhattan is as much an example of American neoliberalism (i.e., surrounded by visual immersion in some of the most well-recognized American brands) as it is a demonstration of liberty (i.e., the right to be orderly and safe in a public space) and a human desire made so by marketing campaigns, which increasingly broadcast Times Square and American-inspired globalization to the rest of the world.[88]

Since the most recent informal assessments of Times Square point toward mixed results (see Figure 6.5), one could question whether this transformation will lead from the world's greatest metropolis to a generic

Figure 6.5. Times Square in 2017.

---

87. Lydon and Garcia (2015).

88. Eisenschitzs (2010) and Bennett and Koudelova (2001).

tourist trap. Furthermore, it has also been argued that "the same reason that retailers and advertisers lust after a Times Square location is the same reason that others now find it unbearable: the crowds."[89] Although certain elements are under the control of urbanists and designers, others are not.[90] The very harsh winter weather patterns in New York City might be a natural way to ameliorate the excessive crowding effects, at least four months of the year or so.

Nonetheless, the key findings from this research enable an up-to-date analysis of the overall impact of the improvements to the vibrancy of Times Square. In summary these are:

- The need to maintain and augment a world-class status

- Localized street improvements as part of a more comprehensive public spaces redesign program

- Real vibrancy gains in terms of safety and comfort for the district

- Demonstrative potential for the creation of walkable cities elsewhere

---

89. Bagli (2015).

90. Borgers and Timmermans (2005) and Torrens (2012).

PART III

PORTUGAL

7

Tourism and Consumption

Introduction

The tourism sector in Europe has changed in recent decades due to alterations in societal habits, lifestyle preferences, family and household composition, travel behaviors, access to and utilization of online information about touristic destinations, and travel options. This chapter answers the research question of whether cities can augment their endogenous tourism potential while reducing their volatility to outside forces by devising and implementing a tourism planning strategy, as part of their urban revitalization and community economic development.

The need for new (scholarly) maps "to comprehend the new glocal identity through micro-urbanism and micro-transnationalism, through the glocal cultural division of work between metropolis and metropolization" has been defended for Portugal in its partial role as Europe's west coast.[1] Moreover and since a lack of research on small towns has been identified,[2] this chapter focuses its analyses on the case of a traditional "sun and sea" tourism city in central Portugal: Figueira da Foz (see Figure 7.1 on page 158). It is argued that over the last 50 years Figueira da Foz has had to reinvent its tourism branding and position itself numerous times through a myriad of city marketing and infrastructure development strategies in order to circumvent territorial and societal hurdles.

---

1. Seixas (2014, 85).

2. Mayer and Knox (2010) and James, Thompson-Fawcett, and Hansen (2016).

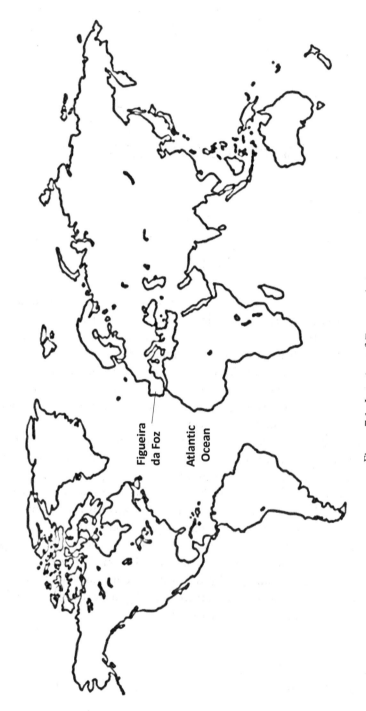

Figueira da Foz

Atlantic Ocean

Figure 7.1. Location of Figueira da Foz.

The research methods comprised reviews of specialized literature and of tourism and urban plans, interviews with various stakeholders, and *in loco* analysis of natural assets, cultural and patrimonial facilities, and attendance of diverse events such as festivals, performances, and championships. One of the key findings is that tourism reinvention beyond consumption-oriented planning is necessary to withstand major socioeconomic and territorial transformations.

This chapter is organized into six sections. Following this introduction, the first section is the analytical mechanism in three sub-areas: tourism planning, consumption, and city marketing. The second provides an overview of tourism in Portugal. The third introduces the case study of Figueira da Foz. The fourth discusses a set of four tourism myths and attempts to dispel those preconceived ideas with various types of evidence from the case study. The fifth proposes a three-stage best practice of urban management aimed at enabling a coherent and effective strategic planning process. Finally, the last section makes some concluding remarks.

Analytical Mechanism

Tourism Planning

Tourism comprises mostly leisure activities undertaken as part of one's own free time. Tourism activities are increasingly taking place in cities as well as rural and coastal areas. Tourism ranges from visits to unique natural environments to patrimonial heritage and a whole myriad of events and festivals.[3] Worldwide, the tourism sector has been growing exponentially mostly due to the liberalization of air travel, interest in visiting and learning more about other cultures, the growth and improvement of lodging facilities, and the increasing professionalization of the industry.[4]

According to the World Tourism Organization, "tourism has experienced continued expansion and diversification to become one of the largest and fastest-growing economic sectors in the world."[5] According to the same source, "international tourism now represents 7% of the world's exports in

---

3. Bradley and Hall (2006) and Getz and Page (2016).

4. Judd and Fainstein (1999).

5. World Tourism Organization (WTO 2016, 2).

goods and services, up from 6% in 2014, as tourism has grown faster than
world trade over the past four years." Tourism is an economic activity with
"few barriers to entry and the potential for large returns to investment."[6]
International tourist arrivals worldwide are expected to increase by 3.3 percent
a year between 2010 and 2030 to reach 1.8 billion by 2030.[7]

Besides direct impacts in terms of employment, professional qualification, and wealth creation, tourism activities also have indirect impacts
in terms of urban image and attempts at reducing territorial imbalances.
The tourism industry ought to be analyzed from both demand and supply
sides.[8] Tourism has suffered considerable locational changes with preference
for more exotic destinations due to the liberalization of aviation markets,
higher purchase power, and growing exigencies of tourists. Some of these
changes could create a potential spiral of decline for older and mature
tourism destinations. Henceforth, it is important to strengthen public intervention in order to identify and create new products, market destinations
more effectively, attract new tourists, expand the length of their stays, and
foster positive images.

Tourism planning has therefore emerged due to the need to enhance
tourism activities and to augment existing and future tourism assets and
amenities.[9] Tourism planning methodologies are for the most part based on
broader urban and regional planning theories and approaches.[10] Tourism
planning activities include the identification of activity types (e.g., natural
resources and patrimonial heritage) and their anticipated impacts (i.e., positive and negative, direct and indirect, etc.).

There is also a relationship between regional planning, infrastructure
development, and the growth of tourism activities. Two preeminent forms
of tourism include gastronomic and culinary activities as well as conferences
and congresses. In the former, visitors travel to destinations to savor culinary
dishes and gastronomic recipes not easily found anywhere else on earth.[11]
The latter comprises extending trips to conferences and congresses to also
visit their host cities and regions.[12]

---

6. Judd and Fainstein (1999, 2).

7. WTO (2016).

8. Van Leeuwen and Nijkamp (2009).

9. Hall and Lew (2009).

10. Costa (2001b) and Oliveira (2015).

11. Hall and Sharples (2003).

12. Marques and Santos (2013).

Consumption

Various consumption theories have been put forward by multiple scholars over the last two decades or so. Consumption has become quite prevalent to the point of influencing all members of society not only through the acquisition of goods and services but also through the symbolic meanings that consumed objects become imbued with during the various stages of the consumption process.[13] On the other hand, the role of consumption in a postmodern world has also been analyzed. Among various subjects, processes of cultural change, social practices, and the aestheticization of everyday life have been discussed within the claim that the postmodernism era has brought forward a global disorder where multiple cultures are mutually impacted by consumptive occurrences.[14]

Mass consumption of goods and services has been a direct outcome of industrialization and automation practices and the mass distribution of goods via imbricate networks of retail and wholesale facilities. New shopping practices have influenced different purchasing habits. The spectacularization of postmodern shopping rituals, which go beyond the simple acts of acquisition to even constituting the basis of an experiential and performative economy, has also been identified.[15] One of the latest phases in consumption studies is that of green and ecological products.[16] This tendency has gained special attention in small town sustainability, where these four emerging sensibilities have been identified: local, organic, and slow food; environmentalism; entrepreneurship, and creativity.[17]

Tourism is a cultural phenomenon and as tourism expands into more peripheral areas, it is important to question whether tourism consumes places.[18] The answer might depend on the scale and the exact level of peripherality. At the personal level, we ought to recognize that tourism is comprised of spaces of orchestrated consumption. In certain cases, tourists' gaze at various landscapes as if they could understand themselves by looking at their own reflections on those landscapes.[19] From a regional perspective, as is the case

---

13. Baudrillard (1998).

14. Featherstone (2007).

15. Cachinho (2006).

16. Santos (2013).

17. Mayer and Knox (2010, 1545).

18. Hall (2013).

19. Urry (2011).

of Portugal on Europe's west coast, tourism may contribute to a theming of the economy by providing value-added mutual production-consumption augmentations.

In this context, a fourth circuit of capital has been defended. It is particularly focused on "the production of the system of needs" based on the work of Baudrillard, which follows Marx's first circuit of capital (industrial) and the second circuit of consumption; Lefebvre's and Harvey's second circuit related to real estate and urban growth; while Harvey's third circuit of investment was in the new scientific and professional reproduction of the workforce.[20] Furthermore, "the production of the system of needs" closes the circuits, "transforming any production into consumption and any consumption into production (in a complex mixture of practices, representations of space and space representation)."[21]

City Marketing

City marketing attempts to attract investment, industry, and tourism to various territorial jurisdictions, such as cities, states, whole nations, and trading blocks.[22] The main objective of city marketing is to retain existing visitors and to attract new ones. In addition, city marketing campaigns also attempt to maintain and expand existing businesses, to create new businesses, to capture external investment, to attract new residents and qualified labor, as well as more visitors. In city marketing, "places are sold as products not only to potential tourists but also to other consumers."[23] City marketing strategies range from mega-events, festivals and concerts, trade shows, regional fairs and expositions to place branding and charming campaigns.

Competition among places has increased greatly in the last decades as a direct consequence of globalization tendencies, which have also impacted the mobility of capital and labor. Nonetheless, city marketing aims to increase the habitability, livability, attractiveness, and competitiveness of places. City marketing requires the evaluation of places based on the quality of life they offer.[24] It also requires a strong strategic management of the image of a city.

20. Seixas (2014, 83).

21. Seixas (2014, 84).

22. Kotler, Haiderr, and Rein (1993).

23. Ashworth and Voogd (1994, 8).

24. Kotler, Haiderr, and Rein (1993).

Characteristics of city images include dynamism, innovation, pleasantness, and sophistication. The criteria to accomplish said image includes honesty and credibility, attractiveness and differentiation, and simple and direct messages. City marketing campaigns include slogans, various positionings, visual symbols, events, and promotions.

City marketing is also referred to as placemarketing and place branding. Placemarketing ought to be complemented with placemaking operations aimed at conserving important cultural patrimony in cities as well as at revitalizing some of their most critical neighborhoods.[25] This dual intervention in the social and urban fabric of places might have led certain authors to rethink the theory and practice of place branding.[26] These authors have concluded that place branding is important because it provides strategic guidance for place development, a basis for stakeholder cooperation, and the maximization of positive place experience, and so on.[27]

Finally, a study of municipalities as public relations and marketing firms has concluded that cities sell themselves using these six tactics: "branding, media relations, in-house publications, use of outside people or organizations as PR surrogates, aesthetic and affective appeal, and built environment via sustainability."[28] These various theoretical findings are applied to the analysis of the case study later in the chapter, but first it is important to provide an account of the evolution of the tourism sector in Portugal.

Tourism in Portugal

Tourism in Southern Europe is very much influenced by national tourism policies,[29] local and regional cultures, natural and patrimonial heritage assets, market potential, the socioeconomic characteristics and affordability of the destinations, events and festivals, tourism infrastructure, safety and security conditions, and weather patterns. The Mediterranean region has various distinct but complementary tourism subregions. The Algarve, the Costa del Sol, southern France, and the main sites of the Italian and Greek

25. Castello (2007).

26. Kavaratzis, Warnaby, and Ashworth (2015).

27. Ashworth, Kavaratzis, and Warnaby (2015, 4).

28. Zavattaro (2013, x).

29. Turismo de Portugal (2017).

classical civilizations are good examples of traditional tourism subregions in the Mediterranean. The region benefits from temperate weather patterns, ancient civilizational histories, and relatively proximate distances between destinations.[30]

Portugal was considered an undiscovered part of Europe before the 1960s.[31] Portuguese tourism has since then been dominated by the centrality of the country's two largest metropolitan areas of Lisbon and Porto, the southern region of Algarve, and the islands of Madeira and Azores.[32] While the country's first significant tourism developments were domestic in scope and based around thermal spas (e.g., Curia, Luso) in central Portugal, the country's first deliberate tourism promotion strategy was the establishment of the *Sociedade de Propaganda* in 1906. This entity was responsible for "overseas promotion and for bringing about improvements in the basic tourism infrastructure."[33]

After the political revolution of 1974 and the restoration of democracy, Portugal started a deliberate strategy for tourism, with an autonomous ministry, regional plans, regional tourism boards, and collaborations with municipalities.[34] More recently, there has also been a strong emphasis on qualifying tourism specialists through vocational and higher educational training.[35] At the regional level, tourism boards perform a critical role in disseminating information about tourist attractions, activities, and events such as organized tours, cultural festivals, and sports.[36] Municipalities, often in collaboration with central agencies, have helped to renovate monuments and other patrimonial heritage, although the needs seem to be higher than their small municipal budgets allow.[37]

International agencies, on the other hand, have impacted the country's tourism markets directly and indirectly through the formal recognition of world heritage sites (e.g., Porto's historic district) and immaterial cultures (e.g., Alentejo's traditional singing and Fado music) in the case of UNESCO,

---

30. Leontidou (1990).

31. Lewis and Williams (1998).

32. Cavaco (2005) and Vaz et al. (2011).

33. Lewis and Williams (1998, 146).

34. Oliveira (2015).

35. Costa (2001a).

36. Eusébio (2006).

37. Fortuna (2016).

and the organization of cultural and sports mega-events such as the Lisbon, Porto, and Guimarães European Capital of Culture in 1994, 2001, and 2012, respectively, and the 2004 European Soccer Championship. The cultural mega-events were cosponsored by the European Union and the central government, and the championship was attributed by the Union of European Football Associations (UEFA). The EXPO'98 World's Fair in Lisbon constituted a turning point in the consolidation of the country's tourism strategy. The construction of the pavilions for the World's Fair as well as the stadiums for the EURO2004 championship demonstrated the country's capacity to design, project, and build the needed infrastructure for the mega-events.[38]

The positive publicity and city marketing attention garnered during the various mega-events during the last two decades or so has contributed greatly to place Portugal on the country marketing map in an era of increasing global competition among nations.[39] Tourism has been a very important economic opportunity for Portugal. It contributed 8.5 percent of the gross domestic product in 1999. The transaction volume was in the order of 4.825 million Euros and the number of foreign tourists comprised 11.6 million visitors.[40] More recent data from 2015 revealed that tourism represented 11.5 million Euros, 15.4 percent of the country's total exports, and employed 280 thousand people.[41] The future orientations for the tourism sector in Portugal have been centered on qualifying the sector and its human resources, diversifying tourism offerings and markets, and promoting social and territorial cohesion to help correct regional unbalances.

Case Study: Figueira da Foz

Figueira da Foz is a medium-size littoral city in central Portugal,[42] approximately 112.5 miles north of Lisbon and 75 miles south of Porto. The municipality's population was 62,125 inhabitants in 2011. Figueira da Foz is located in the district of Coimbra and is bordered by the districts of

38. Balsas (2018).

39. Seixas (2014).

40. Costa (2001a).

41. Turismo de Portugal (2017, 32).

42. Gomes and Veiga (2002), Câmara Municipal da Figueira da Foz (CMFF 2016).

Leiria and Aveiro to the south and north, respectively. The city of Figueira da Foz is strategically located on the north bank of the Mondego River, while the municipality covers both banks of the Mondego River estuary.[43] The city's three distinctive characteristics are: first, the Mondego River, which transverses the municipality; second, the Mountain of Boa Viagem, which provides magnificent views of the city at the bottom of the hill; and third, the Atlantic Ocean and its vast dunes.

The origins of the agglomeration date back to 1342 and the settlement was officially attributed the category of city in 1882.[44] The city has developed based on mercantile functions associated with its coastal location, and the deep-water seaport.[45] Fishing was always important throughout the history of the city as was salt production in the estuary's solar salterns. Before electric refrigeration became widely available, salt was utilized for conservation purposes. Salt from the large salterns complex located adjacent to the city was exported to other parts of the country and abroad. The city's harbor and its train and roadway connections have all facilitated the growth of industry. To this day, these transport facilities enable the importing of raw materials and the exporting of finished goods.

The city grew as a summer tourism destination even before World War II (see Figure 7.2).[46] Figueira da Foz was a privileged summer beach resort town for the well-educated, upper-income families from Coimbra and the interior Beira Alta region of the country (see Figure 7.3). Sea bathing and seaside leisure activities have always constituted the most important tourism activities in Figueira da Foz. The city's planning and development was influenced by the French resort towns of Arcachon, Biarritz, and Dieppe.[47] Furthermore, it was also a very affordable and convenient destination for Spanish tourists, mostly from cities in the border region of Castilla and Leon such as Salamanca, Burgos, and Valladolid, even after the Algarve beaches of Monte Gordo and Praia da Rocha overcame Figueira da Foz's primacy in the 1980s and 1990s.

Algarve's tourism boom occurred mostly after the end of the dictatorship regime in 1974. The socioeconomic transformations brought about by the Carnation Revolution (i.e., Revolução dos Cravos) increased income

43. Domingues (2006).

44. Gomes and Veiga (2002).

45. Cascão (1985).

46. Martins (2015).

47. Domingues (2006).

Figure 7.2. Figueira da Foz's Urbanization Plan of 1937. Courtesy of Faria da Costa.

Figure 7.3. City marketing poster advertising Figueira da Foz. Courtesy of Companhia dos Caminhos de Ferro Portugueses da Beira Alta.

levels, changed the welfare system, enabled more choice in vacation habits and routines, and enabled a boom in the construction sector in the most southern region of the country, where climatic conditions are warmer during the summer and the beaches facing the Atlantic Ocean have finer sand and more tepid and clearer water. Soon thereafter, tourists from Central Europe, mostly from England, Germany, and the Scandinavian countries, started flocking in hordes to Algarve.[48]

As a result, Figueira da Foz lost some of its prominence as a national tourism destination in the 1990s.[49] The city started utilizing economic development strategies to foster its year-round industrial sector with the construction of two large wood pulp factories in the southern part of the municipality and a glass factory adjacent to the Mondego River, among other more atomized and smaller-scale industrial developments throughout the rural countryside. The decline of the city's fishing industry due to the opening of global markets caused by advances in refrigeration, freezing, and packaging techniques has also contributed to the shrinking of the unqualified labor force in the municipality.

Nonetheless, the city modernized its harbor installations to also serve as a modern yacht club (see Figure 7.4). The extension of long piers to protect the harbor from silting and preventing the passage of deep cargo ships has caused sand deposition on the city's main beach, which increased the walking distance for tourists to reach the sea. In fact, now Figueira da Foz has the largest sandy beach in Europe, known affectionately as the Praia da Claridade. These dunes are bordered by a long boulevard that connects Figueira da Foz to the adjacent locality of Buarcos.

In the last two decades or so, Figueira da Foz has implemented various urban revitalization strategies to reinvent and regain its earlier prominence in the tourism sector,[50] including investing heavily in commercial urbanism,[51] city marketing operations based on market and tourism planning studies,[52] the construction of new high-end lodging and cultural facilities (e.g., the cultural performance center Centro de Artes e Espetáculos [CAE] was launched

---

48. Barreira, Cesário, and de Noronha (2017).

49. Alves et al. (2016).

50. Ferreira (2013).

51. Universidade Internacional da Figueira da Foz and Associação Comercial da Figueira da Foz (UIFF and ACIFF, 2002).

52. Roland Berger and Partner (1993).

Figure 7.4. Figueira da Foz's harbor.

in 2002 and is one of the largest performance venues in central Portugal), and the renovation and rehabilitation of existing pedestrian pavements and facilities (e.g., the city's emblematic centenary casino, a modernistic era *Grande Hotel* and swimming pool, and the city's coliseum) (see Figures 7.5 and 7.6 on page 170). In order to animate the vast beaches, the city has also constructed an artificial oasis with ponds, sidewalks, various sports fields, and other amenities.

These public investments contributed to a mini real estate bubble with an upsurge in construction during the 1990s and early 2000s resulting in the overdimensioning of tourism facilities, such as hotels and aparthotels and summer vacation homes, which led to unbalanced urbanization along the coast.[53] Although permanent population in the municipality experienced considerable growth between the 1981 and 2001, since 2001 it has remained mostly constant. The following two sections discuss four myths and three lessons learned from Figueira da Foz's territorial development likely to be helpful to cities experiencing similar situations elsewhere.

---

53. CMFF (2014a, 2014b) and Rodrigues (2016).

Figure 7.5. *Rua Cândido dos Reis* pedestrian precinct.

Figure 7.6. *Rua Bernardo Lopes* pedestrian precinct.

Discussion: Myths and Reality

As explained in Chapter 1, myths are preconceived ideas that get created and transmitted based mostly on partial information about a phenomenon or occurrence. Adequate research is needed to dispel these myths and to help public policy decision-makers, stakeholders, and investors remedy and prove that reality is in fact different from what popular media may convey and circulate through various means.

Myth 1: The Preference for the "Sun and Sea" Model

This myth is still quite prevalent due to the strong presence of popular tourism resorts in other parts of the country, such as Estoril, Troia, and Algarve. The "sun and sea" tourism model is relatively static, implying that tourists will spend most of their holidays at the beach. However, even when Figueira da Foz attempted to boost its "sun and sea" summer holidays model, the city always strove to diversify its offerings with tours to nearby regional attractions such as Coimbra, Conimbriga, and Fátima, for the 700-year-old University of Coimbra, the largest Roman settlement excavated in Portugal, and the religious sanctuary of Fátima, respectively. Figueira da Foz has also targeted more active tourism activities aimed at complementing traditional offerings with opportunities for ecological recreation and cultural erudition in the region's environmental amenities and many cultural assets.[54] This myth can be dispelled by recognizing that diversifying and segmenting tourism offerings are important planning strategies. These strategies can be easily accomplished through promotions aimed at the city's other natural and patrimonial heritages, including ecotourism and cultural opportunities, respectively.[55] Furthermore, local festivities and traditions unique to one's own culture, working thoughtfully through various economic, cultural, and gemination networks, creating exclusive and unique packages in the arts, culture, and entertainment, are also important planning strategies.

Myth 2: The Privileging of Coastal Areas

Coastal areas have unparalleled natural amenities.[56] These range from beaches, lagoons, forested areas, scenic mountains, agricultural fields, river estuaries,

---

54. Alcoforado, Cordeiro, and Ferreira (2013).

55. Zhang and Lei (2012).

56. Mega (2016).

salterns, nature preserves, and a rich patrimonial heritage typical of a traditional modus vivendi from bygone eras. Furthermore, the littoral municipalities between Setúbal in the south and Viana do Castelo in the north
concentrate a disproportionally high percentage of population in the country.
Coastal areas in Portugal suffer with disproportionately high imbalance in
terms of high and low tourism seasons, which requires the dimensioning of
infrastructure for peak demand, making it shamefully underused during the
rest of year. This territorial imbalance has been noted in that "the consumer
society has provoked serious environmental challenges in urban and rural
spaces," which have also contributed to the rapid rise of property markets
with very inflated housing prices for year-round residents.[57] This myth can
be dispelled by potentiating various other tourism offerings at multiple
geographical scales. This includes attractions, the need to create alternative
destinations as well as integrated packages that explore complementarities
and facilitate accessibility to environmentally protected fauna and flora,
keeping in mind the carrying capacity of natural and man-made systems.[58]

Myth 3: The Targeting of International Tourists

International markets are important. International tourism tends to demand
high levels of quality and professionalism and to generate considerable
profit margins. However, it is possible to target international and national
tourists simultaneously and to reach a balanced mix of tourists. Residents
and business owners ought to be involved in the conception of the tourism programs. It is important to attract various demographic groups and
to identify and create multiple niche markets.[59] Over the years, Figueira
da Foz has organized various sports tournaments, including surf championships, windsurf competitions, and the Mundialito de Praia (i.e., a beach
soccer tournament), which attracted international athletes and many visitors.
Simultaneously, the city also regularly organizes other radical sporting events,
such as sailing and paragliding, and summer music concerts and festivals,
which tend to attract tens of thousands of mostly national visitors. One
especially important annual event is organized by the student association of

---

57. Cunha and Cravidão (1997, 144).

58. Figueiredo (2008).

59. Clark (1994).

nearby University of Coimbra, which comprises a students' bullfight event at the Figueira da Foz's coliseum (i.e., a *Garraiada da Queima das Fitas*, young bull's fight of the academic festivities). Finally, Figueira da Foz also organizes the city's annual festivities at the end of June with traditional parish fairs and folk parades.

Myth 4: Seasonal Tourism Occurs Mostly During the Summer

Summer vacations have had an important role in Southern European and North American countries. However, more and more tourists are opting for new segmented holidays, which take advantage of periodical and year-long products and offerings. This includes for example spring festivals in Holland to visit blossoming tulip fields or the golden week in Japan to see the cherry blossoms; or even, for instance, the foliage season in the New England region of the United States. More and more business trips and congresses are complemented with extended short stays to visit and learn more about the host city region. A recent study has shown how cities in central Portugal have been taking advantage of conferences and congresses to expand tourism offerings.[60] Entertainment and periodic attractions serve to entice not only locals but also temporary visitors.

Finally, another appropriate strategy is to create habituation and regularity in the patronage of venues and events. Gastronomy is one of Figueira da Foz's most important tourism assets and attractions; traditional fish-based dishes can be eaten year-round there. Many of the perceived seasonal investments also function throughout the year, such as the modern marina and yacht club,[61] the salt heritage's ecomuseum,[62] sports training facilities in the adjacent village of Quiaios, the new thermal spa facilities in Bicanho, as well as multiuse trails throughout the municipality's nature preserves (e.g., Rota do Megalítico, Rota das Salinas, Rota das Lagoas) (see Figure 7.7 on page 174). The following section presents a set of best practices of urban management processes aimed at helping to reinvent the tourism destinies of places undergoing major regional transformations due to changes in the tourism sector.

---

60. Marques and Santos (2013).

61. Kortekaas (2004) and Kostopoulou (2013).

62. Davis (1999) and Wu, Xie, and Tsai (2015).

Figure 7.7. Rota das Salinas, salgado da Figueira.

Lessons for Other Cities: Best Practices of Urban Management

Best practices of urban management applied to tourism planning require a three-pronged approach: the first phase comprises establishing a strategic vision, the second phase entails the definition and implementation of the planning strategy, and the third phase is the monitorization and evaluation of the strategy.

Lesson 1: The Setting of a Vision

In the first phase, the strategic vision requires a rethinking of what the city wants to become on the five- to ten-year horizon. Such a vision ought to be consensual and participatory in the sense that it results from a consensual dialog of the highest number of stakeholders with interests in the city. Furthermore, the vision ought to be able to mobilize other stakeholders and integrate their ideas and projects. Figueira da Foz's latest strategic vision is centered on the goal "Figueira 2030: Sustainable Territory of the Atlantic."[63] This vision resulted from a broad strategic planning process that also articulated a planning strategy and implementation program.

Lesson 2: The Definition and Implementation of a Strategy

In the second phase, it is important to define a strategy centered on the following sixfold criteria: to establish specific and measurable objectives; to position the city in terms of local and global markets; to identify the cities' likely competitors and their key investments; to know the weaknesses and strengths of the local and regional supply; to locate the opportunities and threats caused or likely to be caused by external forces; and to analyze the five Ps of products, targeted publics, prices, promotions, and processes. Finally, it is important to phase the implementation of the tourism strategy in its short-, medium-, and long-range goals, actions, funding, and responsible partners. Figueira da Foz's most recent territorial development strategy ought to be centered on three pillars: first, the preservation of citizens' rights; second, public space; and third, economic activities.[64] Diversifying tourism and branding activities through multiscalar interventions is equally important.[65]

Lesson 3: The Monitorization and Evaluation of the Strategy

The third phase is the monitorization and evaluation of the strategy. In this phase it is important to realize that reality is in constant flux and that the strategy ought to be flexible in its conceptualization to account for unforeseen changes in terms of socioeconomic tendencies and market and societal fluctuations. It is also important to make periodic evaluations and adjustments to the strategy's main actions. Key performance indicators ought to have both quantitative and qualitative indicators. Among the former, it is important to collect and monitor statistics on the number of tourists, lodging, length of stays, attractions visited, and amounts of money spent. The qualitative indicators ought to be centered on such characteristics as quality of service, individual and group preferences, and opinions about the

---

63. CMFF (2014a, 11).

64. Cordeiro and Barros (2011).

65. Caldwell and Freire (2004).

various qualitative aspects of the visit. Finally, it is important to adjust the strategy to societal changes also happening outside of the targeted region.

Conclusion

This chapter attempted to answer the research question of whether cities can augment their endogenous tourism potential while reducing their volatility to outside forces by devising and implementing a tourism planning strategy, as part of their community economic development. This chapter analyzed the case of a traditional "sun and sea" tourism city in central Portugal: Figueira da Foz. It was argued that over the last 50 years Figueira da Foz has had to reinvent its tourism branding and positioning multiple times through a myriad of city marketing and infrastructure development strategies to circumvent territorial and societal hurdles. The field of tourism planning has evolved over various decades and tourism managers have acquired valuable knowledge and experience. Successful tourism destinations do not simply happen at random. They require hard work and diligent foresight usually based on a community-based vision and participatory strategy, implemented carefully and monitored regularly to account for unforeseen circumstances.

Tourism has been stated to have "an uneasy relationship" with development.[66] Successful cities are the hallmark of habitability (i.e., for residents and visitors), visibility (i.e., national and international), attractivity (i.e., to capture various types of flows), and competitiveness (i.e., to create wealth and prosperity). Tourism ought not to be considered a panacea in local and regional development strategies. However, it has been proved that tourism can give a substantial boost to local and regional economies.[67] On the other hand, city marketing requires a strategic and proactive attitude monitored regularly. With this chapter, it was demonstrated that the city of Figueira da Foz has natural, patrimonial, social, and political conditions to strengthen its role not only as a tourism destination but also as a growth engine in central Portugal.

---

66. Williams and Shaw (1998).

67. Williams and Shaw (1998) and Hall and Lew (2009).

8

Solid Waste Management

Introduction

Commerce involves exchanges and consumption. Commercial urbanism (CU) in contexts of urban revitalization has been used by public decision-makers to improve the urban livability of cities. The great majority of CU interventions in Portugal were carried out in city centers, which led, in part, to their direct improvement and beautification. Indirectly, many of the CU interventions, implemented mostly in partnership with the public sector, did not take into consideration the relationship between physical improvements to public spaces, increased levels of consumption, generation of solid waste, and associated environmental climate change pressures.

It is well known that retail development has traditionally not been contemplated in territorial management plans in Portugal, either at the local or regional levels. However, solid waste and effluent management programs at the regional level have been carried out by entities operating in metropolitan areas. These programs' goals are not only based on economic efficiency principles but also on the tenets of intermunicipal coordination and sustainable development.

Despite this, the implications of our continuous quest for sustainability,[1] the improvement of the urban environment of cities, our urban enjoyment, the improvement of commercial modernization of historic city centers and adjacent traditional neighborhoods, recent demographic changes in cities,

---

1. Soromenho-Marques (2003).

changes in lifestyle preferences, the growth in urban tourism opportunities, high consumption of ethnic goods and products with a certificate of origin, as well as the operationalization of waste recovery systems require more academic scrutiny and subsequent theoretical and applied discussion.

This chapter examines the relationships among these variables while attempting to understand the extent to which CU interventions in city centers have increased pressures on other rather peripheral and fragile areas, populated mostly by waste-sorting stations, wastewater treatment plants, and warehouses and logistic areas related to the collection, treatment, and disposal of domestic and commercial waste such as landfills. The chapter analyzes the relationship between merchants' participation rates in CU projects and waste-production generation in four regional jurisdictions (i.e., *distritos*) of the north-central coastal region of Portugal. Finally, a set of implications for future actions is proposed centered on the triad of reduction, recycling, and reuse; sustainable consumption; circular economy; and the implementation of a zero-waste city strategy.

Commercial Urbanism (CU)

Cities have a wide variety of attractions, functions, and services that enable individuals to satisfy a wide range of needs, desires, and aspirations. However, cities are heavily dependent on their hinterlands for energy, water, food, and other socioeconomic resources. On the other hand, cities also generate large amounts of solid waste. The capitalist economy, of which the United States is a paradigmatic example, is largely responsible for the increase of such waste. For example, in 2014, the US produced 258 million tons of municipal solid waste, which is about three times as much as was produced in the 1960s.[2]

I observed the important roles performed by the members of the cleaning brigades coordinated by the Times Square business improvement district (BID) during recurrent visits to Times Square in Manhattan as early as the mid-1990s. After an initial incredulity and fascination with the visual stimuli and the huge variety of neon signs and screens in the area, the presence of the street sweepers impressed me as something more than what is displayed to passersby on the screens and the high number of people who walk and drive through this central area of New York City:

2. APA (2017, 4).

the vast and rampant consumption levels of the most varied products and services in downtown Manhattan.

Retail is only one of the multiple economic areas critical to the functioning of cities. However, shopping occupies a central position in the urban metabolism of cities, since it serves as an interface between the entry of raw materials, the widespread use of many objects and goods, and processes of production, consumption, and disposal. As in other societal areas, retail innovations (e.g., shopping centers, outlet malls, and e-commerce) have been exported and adopted globally, while replicas of these various commercial formats have also served to increase consumption levels, in certain cases exponentially.

Commercial urbanism has been theorized in contexts of urban regeneration and improvement of central areas of cities in developed countries. These improvements have comprised mostly the physical upgrade of public spaces, such as squares, piazzas, and city streets, as well as the modernization of commercial establishments. One of the main objectives of CU has been to increase the habitability and livability of downtown areas through higher-quality public spaces and an increase in commercial activity (i.e., via increased volumes of traded goods and higher profits) for the owners and tenants of commercial establishments, while also meeting the needs of all who patronize those shopping areas in order to meet their various needs.[3]

Indirectly, CU and urban regeneration operations have also attempted to address the socioeconomic problems leading to the hollowing out of city centers and the consequent growth of peripheral areas. It is important to clarify that these problems are quite complex and go beyond the realm of commerce, also extending to the natural environment. Suburban lifestyles, greatly facilitated by the use of the automobile in commuting and the high use of energy-intensive household appliances (e.g., electronic equipment in kitchens, air conditioners, etc.), now shape everyday life in large cities as well as their expansions into rural areas.

Public policies to address many of these problems have been established in recent years, but, in general, with limited commitment and oversight by public decision-makers. CU has dealt primarily with retail and urban quality of life in downtown areas (i.e., physical improvements of public spaces, pedestrian zones, integrated waste collection and recycling systems, street animation campaigns, maintenance and cleaning, etc.), since it is much more complex to intervene in the rehabilitation of the urban fabric of the

---

3. Fernandes (2012).

consolidated city. On the other hand, it is also much easier for policymakers to promote, for example, waste management in new housing districts (with new wastewater systems and technical infrastructure galleries). Furthermore, the environment has also been improved through the implementation of Local Agendas 21 and a set of programs aimed at improving the environmental quality of specific neighborhoods (e.g., through the POLIS and POLIS XXI programs) in peripheral areas and waterfront districts.

Throughout, we find an emphasis on urban regeneration and on improving the quality of urban life. Furthermore, several broader national strategies, such as a national sustainable development strategy (ENDS), were conditioned by the most recent economic crisis and by austerity policies aimed at containing public debt expenditures. The nonimplementation of ENDS could also have been reflected in the area of solid waste management, which is now being tackled with political priorities aimed at strengthening the green, low-carbon, and circular economy and sustainable consumption.

The regeneration and rehabilitation of some central areas may also have contributed in part to the expulsion of residents from the historical areas of cities, mostly due to increases in housing rents. In addition to gentrification processes, the growing tourism markets in cities, various mega-events, and other ludic festivals might have also contributed to the commodification of the urban environments and associated lifestyles.

Moreover, public funds were also invested to minimize the apparent lack of competitiveness of some merchants in central areas, while the growth of urban waste was exported to landfills in the peripheries. Monetarily, the cost of removing waste is paid by all residents through their taxes, whether they consume excessive or small quantities, which in the end constitutes a severe social equity problem, with very serious environmental consequences.

Finally, recent attempts at implementing centralized retail management practices through city center governance structures, emulating similar practices in shopping centers, constitute one of the most important legacies of CU in Portugal. The collaboration partnerships proposed within the scope of CU projects (i.e., *Unidades de Acompanhamento e Coordenação*, UAC) were not very successful mostly because of the complexity of their operations, lack of consensus in the definition of intervention priorities, and lack of sustainable funds for their continued operations.[4] In this context, ensuring the resilience of commercial systems in times of great and profound socio-

---

4. DGAE (2010) and Guimarães (2017).

economic, cultural, and environmental change is important to maintain the habitability of cities in the 21st century, while achieving higher levels of urban sustainability.[5]

Production, Consumption, and Disposal

The vast majority of scholarly works on these themes deal with consumption as a purely acquisitive act or as a playful and entertaining experience.[6] However, it is necessary to take into account that consumption is only one of the three phases of the urban metabolism process in cities: production, consumption, and disposal.[7] Thus, in addition to cityscapes and mindscapes,[8] the increasing impact of consumption and waste production in cities may lead decision makers and researchers to question the creation of a new type of landscape, possibly called a wastescape, or geography of waste.[9]

The production of a substantial part of nonperishable goods consumed in the developed countries takes place in developing countries—in most cases thousands of miles away from the places where these same products are commercialized and consumed. The mass production is a consequence of economies of scale and large export volumes to reduce transaction and transportation costs. The benefit to developed countries arises from the relocation of production and the externalization of the harmful consequences associated with their production,[10] such as pollution and the exploitation of relatively low-cost labor.

One of the easily observable aspects in developed countries is the possibility of purchasing a wide range of products at relatively affordable prices, as well as the need to bear the disposal costs to take solid waste away from the public eye. The consumption habits of contemporary societies tend to result in excessive waste production, which is one of the main causes of the current environmental crisis.[11]

---

5. Cachinho and Salgueiro (2016).

6. Miles (2012).

7. Ferrão, Lorena, and Ribeiro (2016).

8. Cachinho (2006).

9. Correia and Vauléon (2005).

10. Sassen (2014).

11. Schmidt (2016).

Waste production is closely linked to the tangible acts of consumption,[12] which appears to lead the consumer-citizen to have a proactive complicity with the neoliberal city.[13] Packaging such as plastics, paperboard, and glass are materials commonly used in the preservation of food. Until recently and due to the relocation and distancing from production and consumption processes, these recyclable materials were not collected, reused, and reintegrated into the production chain. The realization of the intrinsic value of these materials has led most governments in the global north to set realistic targets to promote their recycling and reuse.

The capitalist model in developed countries has been responsible for environmentally unsustainable lifestyles, a phenomenon that becomes more complex every day due to current demographic trends. The world population is increasing, especially in developing countries, despite a slowdown in birth rates and increased life expectancy in developed countries. Thus, the "tragedy of the commons" conceptualized in the late 1960s maintains its relevance in the present crisis of the quest for a more sustainable planet.[14]

In this theory's most recent iterations, one finds a growing emphasis on the concepts of carrying capacity of the planet, the identification of ecological borders, and the fight against climate change. Climate change is the direct result of increased human activity now assessed mostly in terms of greenhouse gas (GHG) emissions, of which carbon emissions (CO_2) are one of the key metrics. The increase in GHG emissions has led to global warming with the consequent melting of the polar ice caps, extreme weather patterns, and sea-level rise. The severity of climate change phenomena appears to be increasing with costly economic damage, the destruction of infrastructure, and the loss of human lives.

Thus, from an environmental point of view the objective is to achieve a balance between the carbon released to the atmosphere as a result of anthropic processes and what is consumed organically due to natural occurrences. Current initiatives are trying to foster a transition to the so-called low-carbon society. Finally, sustainable urbanism based on smart growth, compact urban development, optimization of infrastructure in consolidated areas, reduction of energy consumption patterns, reduction in car trip frequencies and home to work travel distances, as well as higher levels of recycling, has been promoted by conscientious decision makers in order

---

12. Ekström (2014).

13. Miles (2012).

14. Hardin (1968).

to reduce the negative effects of consumption on the environment. In the area of consumption and subsequent waste generation, the targets are also quite ambitious, including the implementation of key strategies, such as sustainable consumption and the zero-waste city.

Solid Waste

It is necessary to recognize that the waste management sector generates employment; supports industrial activity; involves human, technological, and financial resources; and constitutes a business *filière* that can be combined with the defense and preservation of the environment.[15] Solid waste management in Portugal has gained increasing attention in the last two decades due to legislative acts and strict targets imposed by the European Union (EU). The main measures of urban solid waste management in the various European countries have been cataloged and a conclusion has been reached that there is a need to use systemic perspectives in the development of national programs to achieve the goals set forth by the EU.[16]

Nonetheless, it is sometimes hard to see what happens to solid waste when we put it out on the curb. Since we pay disproportionately less in garbage collection rates than the municipal solid waste management system costs to operate, we often forget the real costs, not to mention the environmental externalities. Thus, solid waste collection services provided by municipalities and other subcontractors have high costs both for collection, transport, sorting, and, in some cases, incineration and landfill disposal.

The ecological footprint is apparently felt less at the individual household level than at the commercial level, where small errors in large quantities can translate into substantial losses. Shopping centers and commercial areas designed for these functions are known to have common management schemes, including loading and unloading bays, usually at the service entrances of these commercial complexes. Certain shopping malls and hypermarkets have even created in-house systems to manage and reuse their own waste production and increase the energy efficiency of their own structures by compacting packaging, composting organic waste, and installing solar panels.[17] With the exception of the need to reuse food packaging for liquids in food (e.g., supermarkets and stores) and the HORECA (i.e.,

---

15. Ferreira (2002) and Davoudi (2009).

16. Pires, Martinho, and Chang (2011).

17. Fuller (1994) and Pitt (2005).

hotel, restaurant, and cafeteria) sectors, until recently solid waste separation and recycling practices in the Portuguese retail sector were not very common in shopping areas where most commercial establishments had to deal individually with disposal of their own solid waste.

The most recent advances in the management of solid urban waste in Portugal were driven by the transposition of European waste management directives and principles to the Portuguese legislation. The Packaging Directive (1994), the Landfill Directive (1999), as well as the Waste Framework Law created by Decree-Law 178/2006, and the codification of polluter-pays principles of product liability and proximity, and the principle of rectification at the source are important examples of legislative innovations.

The European instruments have also led to the creation of national plans for the management of municipal solid waste, such as the Strategic Plan for Urban Waste (PERSU I) (1997–2005). This plan led to the eradication of open dumps and the establishment of the current model of waste collection and treatment system with multimunicipal and intermunicipal collection models, allied to specific management practices. For its part, PERSU II (2007–2016) contemplated adjustments to the initial goals, while PERSU 2020 (2014–2020) established guidelines for prevention, awareness and mobilization of citizens, and the qualification and optimization of public management entities.[18] Two important targets include the need to achieve a reduction in per-inhabitant waste production of 10 percent by December 31, 2020, compared to 2012 levels; and an overall minimum increase of 50 percent relative to the preparation for the reuse and recycling of municipal waste.

The main objective of the PERSU 2020 currently in force is to meet the national backwardness in the goals that Portugal has committed to achieve, especially in recycling and valorization. The small reduction of solid municipal waste production in the country as of 2009 was largely due to the financial crisis. However, the trend has reversed from 2013 to 2014 with a 2.5 percent increase in garbage production and 3 percent in annual capitation.[19] The 453 kg/ha year of waste generated in 2014 placed Portugal below the EU average of almost 20 kg/ha year; while the amount of waste disposed of in landfills (222 kg/ha year in 2014) was much higher than the EU average (147 kg/ha year).[20]

---

18. Valente (2015).

19. Schmidt (2016).

20. INE (2016).

Management structures in Portugal continue to favor landfilling (49% of the total in 2014), while countries such as Germany, Belgium, Sweden, Denmark, and the Netherlands have achieved very low percentages of 1 percent and 2 percent of waste deposited in landfills. The recycling rate in Portugal remains low, only 25.8 percent, well below the EU average of 42 percent. In the EU as a whole, in 2013 Portugal was the third largest member state with waste management, only below Sweden and Romania.[21]

It is well known that the production of solid municipal waste varies according to localities, lifestyle habits, population, economic levels, and educational attainment. In addition, waste management activities involve many different agents at various administrative levels. Next, the chapter discusses a practical application in four districts of the north-central region of Portugal, and it provides some considerations regarding the implementation of a zero-waste city strategy.

Practical Application

The General Directorate of Economic Activities concluded that 38 percent of the historic centers, 45 percent of the cofinanced businesses, 50 percent of the total investment, and 54 percent of the total incentive for CU projects financed between 1997 and 2007 took place in only four districts of mainland Portugal: Aveiro, Braga, Porto, and Viana do Castelo.[22] Thus, it seems opportune to analyze if there was a relationship between the CU projects and the consumption and production of waste.

The methodology consisted in analyzing the participation rates in certain localities of each district to understand the extent to which CU projects, the public space improvements, and the modernization of the commercial establishments were directly related to increases in solid waste production. Since the sample contained a large number of agglomerations with quite diverse populations, it was decided to select for analysis only those agglomerations with the highest and lowest participation rates, as well as the four district cities. The period under review for the production of waste consisted of two dates, one prior (2002) and one subsequent (2014) to the implementation of commercial urbanism revitalization projects. The data on the production and destination of waste were obtained from the online digital database porbase.pt.

---

21. INE (2016).

22. DGAE (2010).

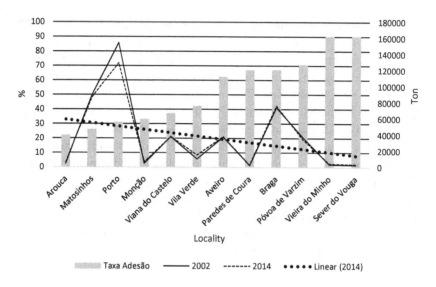

Figure 8.1. Participation rates in CU projects and solid waste production in 2002 and 2014.

Figure 8.1 shows the relationship between participation rates in CU projects and the production of urban waste in 2002 and 2014, respectively. With the exception of larger cities (i.e., Porto, Matosinhos, and Braga) it can be concluded that populations with higher participation rates had smaller waste production volumes. To a certain extent, this is corroborated by data for mainland Portugal showing that urban waste capitation in 2014 occurred in the metropolitan areas of Lisbon and Porto, in various municipalities located in the southern part of the country, and in some municipalities coinciding with district cities.[23]

Figure 8.2 shows the variation in the deposit of waste in landfills in the period under analysis. It is observed that the amount of waste sent to landfills tended to decrease from north to south. The localities south of Póvoa de Varzim registered reductions in the deposit of waste in municipal landfills. The most plausible explanation is the markedly more urban character of the localities on the Portuguese coastal strip between Braga to the north and Setúbal to the south. The size of the localities and their historical centers in the most northern part of the country as well as their more rural character may also partially explain this trend.

---

23. INE (2016).

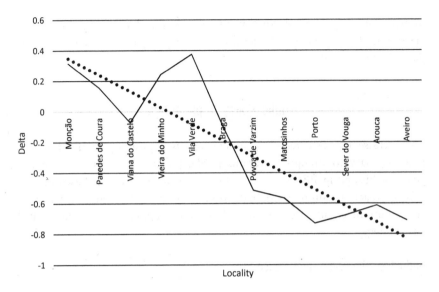

Figure 8.2. Variation of landfill deposits in 2002 and 2014.

Finally, Figure 8.3 shows the participation rates in CU projects and the increases in recycling of municipal waste. There appears to have been a positive relationship between the participation rates (i.e., with the installation

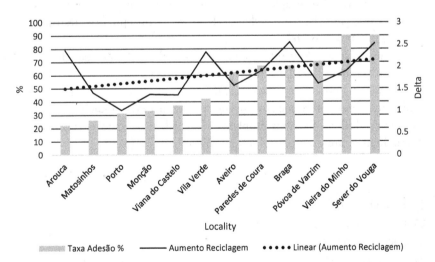

Figure 8.3. Participation rates in CU projects and urban waste recycling in 2002 and 2014.

of new containers for selective waste collection and recycling) in various cities and the percentage of recycled waste (e.g., paper, paperboard, and glass) in these localities.

Public Policy Implications

The increase in waste recycling in Portugal is a positive trend. However, it is necessary to strengthen various public policies in order to reach the goals established in PERSU 2020. Thus, a set of implications based on the 3Rs approach is summarized: reduction, recycling, and reuse; sustainable consumption; circular economy; and the implementation of a zero-waste city strategy.

Reduction, Recycling, and Reuse

Already in the last decade, there had been warning signs voiced for the need to achieve more sustainable urban planning based on reduction, recycling, and reuse strategies.[24] This perspective of environmental planning now appears applied not only to the environment but also, and above all, to urbanism in its various facets, whether in land use, transport, housing, or community and economic development initiatives. Other authors, have extended this triad to complementary strategies aimed at potentiating 6Rs or even 8Rs (e.g., recycle, reuse, reduce, reevaluate, reconceptualize, restructure, redistribute, and relocate).[25]

The reduction in land wasteful patterns through the requalification and reutilization of LULUs (i.e., local unwanted land uses) in NIMBY situations (i.e., not in my back yard),[26] the use of environmental impact studies to achieve more socially fair and consensual development patterns,[27] and the resolution of serious problems of spatial, social, and environmental discrimination are examples of sustainable urbanism goals.[28]

24. Fernandes (2007).

25. Cruz (2016).

26. Schively (2007).

27. Hostovsky (2006).

28. Mele (2011).

An example of recycling and reuse actions is the closure of the Fresh Kills landfill in New York, a symbol of the geography of waste, and its requalification as an urban park.[29] The 3Rs strategy can be complemented in extreme cases with carbon quota rationing policies to allow for a faster transition to the low-carbon economy.[30]

Sustainable Consumption

Living without consuming is difficult, since all living beings need energy and this energy is obtained through metabolic processes. However, it is possible to change consumption habits in order to reduce supplies and reuse materials capable of impacting our ecological footprint. Changes in behavior in order to achieve more sustainable consumption have been pointed out by several authors.[31] Environmental education and the use of the media to promote healthier environmental behaviors through "green minute" civic programs and service announcements seem to be relatively important.

There is a need for public policies that encourage sustainable consumption, thus enhancing the so-called green economy. The reduction of waste production also involves the purchase of rechargeable packaging, household packaging, products with less packaging, and products with returnable packaging. Shopping baskets with such characteristics reflect three times lower waste generations and guarantee savings in family incomes of around 15 percent.[32] The extreme role of markets in contemporary life has been questioned, which allows the articulation of a new perspective for the sharing economy in contexts of less harmful extractions and consumption of natural resources and greater environmental sustainability.[33] Finally, sustainable consumption may result from reconciling at least two different but complementary hierarchies: Abraham Maslow's hierarchy of needs (i.e., progressing from basic physiological needs to personal fulfillment needs at the top) and the hierarchy of waste reduction in the form of an inverted pyramid (i.e., prevention at the top and minimum generation at the base).

---

29. Gandy (1994) and Correia and Vauléon (2005).

30. Cohen (2014).

31. Jackson (2005) and Cruz (2016).

32. Ferreira (2002).

33. Sandel (2013).

Circular Economy

The circular economy arises in opposition to the unidirectional or linear mainstream economy, and its main objective is to reduce the consumption of raw materials, maintaining value chains and eliminating losses in the economic system.[34] Increasingly, waste should be seen as a raw material of significant value to be harvested and not disposed of in landfills. The circular economy also includes the integration of material streams and priority flows and increased use of ecodesign, natural and organic products, and the reuse of waste. The economic principles of this new economy make a distinction between growth and development (i.e., identified by certain authors as degrowth).[35] Moreover, this economy also needs fiscal measures to achieve the hierarchy of waste reduction in the form of an inverted pyramid, in order to change the paradigm of mostly depositing waste in landfills.

Zero-Waste City

The zero-waste city is an ambitious vision that needs to be operationalized and monitored, and once achieved, must be maintained. Five principles needed to achieve the goal of a zero-waste city have been identified: behavioral changes and sustainable consumption, increase of producer and consumer accountability, 100 percent waste recycling levels, legislation of the nonuse of landfills and incineration, and recover of 100 percent of waste resources.[36] The zero-waste city vision is already common practice in many cities. For example, San Francisco in the US has developed a no-waste-deposited-in-landfill strategy to be accomplished by 2020. Furthermore, San Francisco currently has waste management programs for the collection of organic waste for composting and future use as soil fertilizer.[37]

   Other successful waste management systems are selective door-to-door collection, mandatory selective collection with the PAYT system (i.e., "pay as you throw"), the use of fairer and more equitable criteria in the payment of garbage charges on the basis of generation and not through an indirect

34. European Commission (2014).

35. Cruz (2016).

36. Zaman and Lehmann (2011).

37. Friedman (2003).

calculation, as well as the utilization of land use planning regulations and municipal permits to achieve higher recycling levels.[38]

One of the few processes of separation and selective collection of waste in Portuguese public agencies has been analyzed and the conclusion was that more effective practices were needed. In addition to the example given previously of greater involvement of shopping center administrations in active waste management programs, it is also very important that independent traders, retail store owners and employees, consumers, as well as the political leaders and managers of public agencies orient themselves according to more responsible waste management behaviors in order to demonstrate the feasibility of these innovative programs.[39] The potential for achieving substantial environmental progress also exists in such areas as vehicle fleet management, reductions in energy consumption, and the establishment of local purchasing preference policies.

Conclusion

In Portugal, consumption has been used to leverage and boost the economy rather than to promote more environmentally correct behaviors. Commercial urbanism contributes to the revitalization of many urban centers, mainly through placemaking interventions in public spaces and commercial areas of cities, the modernization of some commercial establishments, and street entertainment programs. With a few exceptions,[40] CU results were apparently relatively positive. However, commercial urbanism projects in Portugal did not substantially address the management of solid municipal waste, that is, "the (undesired?) fruit of its own commercial activity," assuming that someone else would take it off the streets and beyond the public eye. It is important to recognize that this gap can bring harmful results in terms of unsustainable consumption patterns and less than desirable ecological habits, rituals, and behaviors.

This means that it is important to raise the awareness of not only consumers but also of retailers, chamber of commerce representatives, residents, local experts, and elected officials that a substantially large part of the

---

38. APA (2017).

39. Jackson (2005) and Ekström (2014).

40. Guimarães (2017).

waste resulting from consumption processes is still deposited in landfills, in opposition to both the European and national legislation currently in place. Placemarketing ecological campaigns alerting to the benefits of urban waste prevention, the advantages of the circular economy, fair trade acquisitions, and sustainable consumption patterns are proven to have a decisive impact on attaining lower levels of urban waste generation.

Rising patterns of consumption in developed countries have led to an increase in the ecological footprints and, quite often, have also constituted less than adequate examples for countries in the developing world. More efficient levels of energy consumption and the redesign of processes based on cleaner and greener materials can contribute to considerable reductions in the production of solid waste that is currently disposed of mostly in landfills. Decoupling the ecological footprint from the consumption of finite resources can also certainly contribute to cities with less pollution and better quality of life. Finally, this chapter has also identified the need to find concerted strategies to achieve more correct environmental behaviors, as well as broader notions of the citizen-consumer capable of changing current consumption habits and of creating more just, healthier, and equitable cities.[41]

---

41. Pires (1991) and Soromenho-Marques (2003).

Conclusion

Successful places in cities are difficult to find. Usually, they result from spontaneous appropriations by multiple publics. The essential characteristics of those places can be augmented by urban design techniques. Once deemed successful or promising, they may attract additional investment, which can also strengthen their endogenous essence. They might acquire renewed identities and be rebranded during requalification processes. However, questions remain regarding the appropriate levels of intervention and the extent of regulation and management, including design, maintenance, safety, funding, and promotion.

To recap, some of the most important findings of this book pertaining to the Iberian Peninsula include: the fact that many improvements to city centers have contributed to an increase in the leisure and night-time economy; many local governments are relying on their expertise, creative funding strategies, and established collaborations to maintain existing revitalization programs and eventually to start new ones; cities' scales, proactive collaboration climate, and political leadership are found to influence the dynamics, complexities, and opportunities for the continued success of commercial urbanism projects in medium-size cities; and walkability improvements to public spaces in downtown areas need to be coordinated with other appropriate legislative and management programs.

On the other hand, the findings pertaining to the Ibero-American world include: the observation that the downtowns of global cities in Latin America have undergone transformative experiences relatively similar to those of the global north, with a slight time lag and with a higher presence of the informal sector; the study of governance practices within contexts of urban revitalization in Latin American cities was important to understand that similar phenomena in distinct contexts have been dealt with slightly differently, even though it has produced relatively unique outcomes in terms of improved public spaces, a reinvigorated built environment, and more robust governance networks; the promotion of a culture of walking appears to be critical to the survival of livable cities; walk-only commercial precincts play an important role in ensuring urban vibrancy; and public interventions are needed to create quality urban spaces and to maintain adequate levels of urban vitality.

A very important finding of this book was that city centers undergo cycles of growth, decline, and revitalization, but not everyone benefits equally. The argument put forward is that the process of revitalizing urban areas ought to strive to eradicate homelessness. The lessons learned from examining homelessness in Phoenix include the following: cities ought not to hide homelessness; cities should invite and embrace new volunteers; cities must dedicate a percentage of their public funds to help fight homelessness and create affordable housing; cities can foster "social business enterprises"; cities must promote nonexclusionary urban design practices; cities should foster local and regional collaborations; and finally, cities also ought to develop a network of human services campuses.

The study of four innovative retail formats in the Phoenix metropolitan area elaborated on the similarities and differences between urban planning and commercial urbanism on both sides of the Atlantic Ocean. The fact that urbanization in the Phoenix metropolitan area is almost the mirror opposite of urban development in New York City, and that even in the greater Phoenix area there are growing tendencies to privilege walkability in contexts of commercial development, strengthens this book's case for more attention to walkability strategies in contexts of urban revitalization.

The recent walkability improvements to NYC's Times Square district made clear the research imperative that the existence of safe, attractive, and comfortable walking environments is of utmost importance to the vibrancy of downtowns and midtowns in global cities. The impacts of the redesign improvements from both management's and users' perspectives highlight four main findings: the world-class status of the Times Square area, the relevance of the urban acupuncture-like street improvements as part of a more comprehensive public spaces redesign program, real vibrancy gains for the district, and demonstrative potential for the creation of walkable areas elsewhere.

Even established tourism destinations, such as Figueira da Foz in central Portugal, are impacted by internal socioeconomic changes and leadership options as well as by exogenous forces and tendencies, events, and sectoral innovations. It was argued that over the last 50 years Figueira da Foz has had to reinvent its tourism branding and positioning multiple times through a myriad of city marketing and infrastructure development strategies to circumvent territorial and societal hurdles. The key finding is that tourism reinvention beyond consumption-oriented planning is necessary to withstand major socioeconomic and territorial transformations.

Finally, Chapter 8 demonstrates that the Portuguese commercial urbanism projects executed during the first decade of the 21st century created privileged arenas of consumption with negative consequences from a triple–bottom line sustainability perspective. Furthermore, those revitalization interventions also increased the pressures on other more peripheral and fragile, but equally important, urban areas of cities. The following strategies ought to be deployed in order to reduce the ecological concerns associated with higher levels of consumption: implement reduction, recycling, and reusing strategies at the local and regional levels; promote sustainable consumption practices; foster a more circular economy; and implement zero-waste city strategies.

The remainder of the conclusion synthesizes the main elements and procedures needed to operationalize the implementation of a city center revitalization strategy, ranging from setting up the city center management unit, accomplishing broad community representation, and creating an action plan to raising funds to implement the revitalization strategy and monitoring it accordingly. The international experiences analyzed in this book have shown that public-private partnerships are critical to the success of city center revitalization strategies. Some of the most important characteristics of partnerships include joint decision-making and the sharing of responsibilities among the different partners in order to benefit the entire community. More recently, the private sector through a myriad of organizations has been taking the lead in many revitalization partnerships and not only the public authorities as occurred in earlier decades.

The existence of a city center management office is crucial to the implementation of revitalization partnership and to the management of the city center. A city center manager helps the board of directors develop a strategy for the city center, including the implementation of an action plan and the program of activities and the creation and coordination of thematic working groups. The manager is also the coordinator of existing interests in the city center and the person responsible for raising more funds for the city center management office. The most successful revitalizations have included a clear, proactive, and consensual vision for the future of the city center, for instance, in the next 5 to 10 years. It is important that all partners contribute to the definition of this strategic vision and that all stakeholders are responsible for its implementation.

Before defining the intervention strategy, it is necessary to analyze the city center holistically in its different dimensions. For instance, the commercial position in the regional hierarchy, strengths (e.g., diversified offer), weaknesses (e.g., accessibility), opportunities (e.g., collaborative environment), and threats (e.g., peripheral retail areas). Many of these analyses may already be done in studies of the municipality or of the chamber of commerce; however, it is important that the partnership can produce a concise and clear strategy with the main diagnosis of the city center and an action plan.

The intervention strategies in the city center must contain an action plan that allows the management office to successfully achieve the previously defined vision and capture the opportunities identified in the market analysis. This action plan results directly from the diagnosis; it must identify all the activities that need to be done, their time frame, who is responsible for them, how much funding is allocated to each action, and where funds come from. This action plan must be revised and updated regularly, preferably every year.

With the exception of small cities, the city centers of medium and large cities can be quite large, which makes it difficult to resolve multiple problems through only one program. The most successful city center programs appear to be those that direct their limited resources to the target areas identified by the various partners. The concentration of resources in a certain geographical area makes it easier for the revitalization efforts to achieve a critical mass and to become more visible. Furthermore, it is also important to take incremental actions with realistic activities.

The existence of safe, attractive, and comfortable walking environments is critical to the vibrancy of downtowns and midtowns in global cities. This is a significant departure from the traditional transportation approach that catered mostly to the needs of drivers. This book has characterized the extent, significance, and public policy implications of walking improvements in the core commercial areas of a multitude of cities of various sizes in the Iberian Peninsula, Latin America, and North America. The city scales considered range from the small city of Guimarães with less than 50,000 inhabitants, Porto with 237 thousand, and Barcelona with 1.6 million to New York City, São Paulo, and Mexico City with approximately 10 million people each. Despite the differences in size and the local economic dynamics, a strong concern with creating, maintaining, and promoting safe, attractive, and comfortable walking environments in their central areas is a characteristic common to all of them.

The operationalization of the revitalization improvements includes city center partnerships with various emphases and with the collaboration of diverse stakeholders, depending on the city. A city center partnership must have a city marketing plan that allows the management office to communicate effectively with the targeted consumers. This plan must give a positive image of the city center and of its activities. Many of the cities analyzed in this book have regular activities in the newly created public spaces to portray the city center as an interesting and safe place to shop, reside, work, and recreate.

The Times Square case in Manhattan, New York, is paradigmatic of how walking improvements can augment a public space in order to create an exhilarating "theme park"–like setting in the core of Manhattan. In fact, the Times Square area is as much an example of American neoliberalism as it is a demonstration of liberty, and a human desire made so by physical improvements to the roadway system and by an immersive marketing apparatus displayed on the walls of adjacent buildings. Although this commercial precinct is now a victim of its own success, given its popularity and the number of people it attracts, its replication elsewhere is a cause for concern from a sustainable consumption perspective. Of course, the Times Square district in Manhattan is not alone among the global cities of the world, and places like Causeway Bay in Hong Kong and Shibuya in Tokyo are right *on par* in terms of diversity of retail offerings, settings, walkability levels, and patronage among residents and tourists alike.

Since there are many more small and medium-size cities in need of revitalization experiences than large downtowns and midtowns looking to exploit their successes, the following concluding remarks are mostly aimed at those particular cities. In order to create successful partnerships, it is also important that the leaders are from the local community and that they find resources within their own community. Sustainability, the assurance of triple–bottom line revitalization solutions, and incentives for less impactful consumption patterns ought to be integral goals of the city center revitalization strategy. Local leadership involves establishing and cultivating relationships with the most influential people in the community and between them and the merchants, not only the retailers located in the city center but especially those retailers with active roles in the city's chamber of commerce, which usually represents the entire business community within a certain region. It is important to communicate the results of partnership activities to the elected officials and to the people at large, so that they can keep their interest in the activities being implemented by the management office.

The management unit must have a mechanism that allows it to raise funds in adequate amounts to implement the action plan. The most successful partnerships seem to be those in which the public government subsidies are kept to a minimum. Normally, public funding is used to create the management office and to keep it functioning for a certain period of time, during which the office's staff is responsible for raising funds from other sources in order to achieve sustainable funding levels.

Voluntary contributions are also very important to the functioning of a revitalization partnership. These range from monetary contributions and various goods and services to time to participate in the affairs and deliberations of the thematic working groups. Public funds are usually given to revitalization partnerships with the condition that they have to be matched with local funds. In these cases, it is important that the city center management leadership can be very persuasive in showing potential contributors what they can gain from contributing to the partnership's endeavors. As demonstrated by the Phoenix case study, volunteering activities are also very important in helping to eradicate poverty and homelessness. No one ought to be excluded from a revitalization process.

The city center leadership must inspect the city center on a regular basis. In these inspections the manager should pay particular attention to cleanliness, safety, the attractiveness of the center, parking, and eventual conflicts between multiple constituents. The manager must also regularly monitor a set of statistic indicators that can provide the board of directors with an assessment of how the revitalization activities are evolving. These indicators include vacant properties, number of pedestrians, crime rates, and the number of new jobs created, among others.

The revitalization of the city center must be an economic development and political priority for the municipality. It is the municipality's responsibility to promote the identity and the diversity of the city center through its active participation in the partnership. To have competitive economic activities in the city center, municipalities have to review local ordinances and licensing processes in order to expedite investments in the precinct. These processes must be rapid, but without losing quality or rigor in the execution of interventions. These instruments are developed in order to coordinate commercial interventions. It is believed that the operationalization of such plans with traditional planning documents (e.g., master plans, ordinances, and regulations) and processes (e.g., licensing, permitting, and geographic information system analyses) can expedite the revitalization processes. It is a responsibility of the planning practitioners working for the municipality to include commercial activities in the city's municipal plans (e.g., strategic, master, urbanization, and site plans). It is important that retail activities are taken into consideration as any other businesses with profound implications in the organization of the territory.

The cleaning and maintenance of public spaces must have very high standards of quality and hygiene. These standards must apply to the mechanical and manual cleaning of streets and sidewalks, the emptying of litter and wastebaskets, and to the cleaning and removal of graffiti and other unwanted publicity. The maintenance of trees, flower pots, and bushes, as well as the maintenance of street furniture, signals, and lights is very critical to the appearance and safety of the city center.

The promotion of mixed-use developments and the control of suburbanization, while reducing the need to use individual automobiles in urban areas, must be critical objectives of municipal planning. The implementation of these objectives not only reinforces the livability of the city center but it also increases the quality of life for all city users.

The chambers of commerce have a critical role in the revitalization programs and in the creation of city center management offices, since their direct activity involves the promotion of commercial activity in the community. In many cities, the chamber of commerce temporarily houses the city center management office and allows the manager to utilize some of the resources (e.g., the facilities, equipment, and administrative support); this locational advantage may help the city center revitalization initiative. However, it is important to mention that the chamber of commerce usually has a territorial mandate broader than that of the city center precinct, which in theory can lead to long-term territorial conflicts over investment priorities.

The chamber of commerce can also have a critical role in making its members involved in the activities of the city center management office. This involves the organization of events, the coordination of promotions, festivals, and the production of marketing materials. The chamber of commerce can cooperate in the organization of events that aim to promote the activities in the center. The gathering of sponsorship, the naming of a coordinator, and the promotion of the event well ahead of time can make an important difference in terms of the target audience.

The chamber of commerce must also be ready to promote best practices of commercial management to its members. It can also organize and promote professional training sessions capable of increasing the competitiveness of small businesses. In cooperation with the city center management office and the municipality, the chamber of commerce can develop and promote alternative ways of doing business. It can, for instance, promote businesses over the Internet such as e-commerce. It can also identify niche markets of traditional local products and sell them in cooperation with the tourism services of the municipality.

The realization of a market study is critical to know who the customers are, which other customers can be attracted, what kind of products customers want, what their preferences are, and finally, how to incentivize loyalty among customers. In order to compete, the city center retail must be able to create and be known for certain types of products. This calls forth the notion of a niche market. The retail located in the city center cannot sell the exact same merchandise as the stores in peripheral shopping malls. They can instead target certain themes and privilege certain age groups, for instance. The goal is to coexist with the shopping malls located elsewhere and not to compete directly with them. So, fundamentally the difference should not be in price but in the type of product. Even though now there are many new ways to buy the same product, city center retail can prosper by providing a friendly and quality service to its customers. For instance, this might involve personalized services and an after-sale assistance program.

The mission to create a livable center capable of attracting and retaining customers is not a responsibility of the municipality alone. It is up to the individual merchants to keep their establishments attractive, as well as to participate in the resolution of the problems of the city center. Their support of the city center management office ought to go beyond monetary contributions, to also include goods and services, time, equipment, and even installations to aid the city center revitalization intervention.

City center retailers, as well as all other stakeholders involved in urban revitalization and pedestrianization programs, ought to be aware of the need for more sustainable consumption practices, which do not necessarily entail higher growth levels but instead aim at improving quality of life in cities. City center management offices are expected to play a crucial role in the implementation of policy actions aimed at encouraging higher levels of reduction, recycling, and reuse of finite natural resources; fostering sustainable consumption patterns; simultaneously strengthening the establishment of more circular economy developments; and ultimately, helping to attain a zero-waste city strategy. Finally, emphasis should be placed on conciliating marketplace success with the imperatives of a more sustainable and less impactful community development in cities.

References

Ahrentzen, S. (2001). Choice in housing. *Harvard Design Review*, 8, 1–6.

Alcoforado, L., Cordeiro, A., and Ferreira, A. (2013). Tourism as a strategic vector in municipal educational project promoters of sustainable development: Reflections about the case of Figueira da Foz (pp. 357–368). In F. Cravidão and N. Santos (Eds.), *Turismo e cultura: Destinos e competitividade*. Coimbra: Coimbra University Press.

Alfonzo, M. (2005). To walk or not to walk? The hierarchy of walking needs. *Environment and Behavior*, 37, 808–836.

Allett, T. (2012). More than a makeover. *Airports International*, October, 34–36.

Alves, D., Barreira, A., Guimarães, M., and Panagopoulos, T. (2016). Historical trajectories of currently shrinking Portuguese cities: A typology of urban shrinkage. *Cities*, 52, 20–29. doi.org/10.1016/j.cities.2015.11.008

Angotti, T. (2008). *New York for sale: Community planning confronts global real estate*. Cambridge: MIT Press.

APA. (2003). *Policy guide on homelessness*. Online policy guide. Retrieved from http://planning.org/policyguides/homelessness.htm (accessed July 29, 2007).

APA. (2017). *Planning for sustainable material and waste management*. PAS Report 587. Chicago: Planners Press.

Appleyard, D. (1981). *Livable streets*. Berkeley: University of California Press.

Arefi, M. (2014). *Deconstructing placemaking: Needs, opportunities, and assets*. New York: Routledge.

Arizona Town Hall. (2009). *From here to there: Transportation opportunities for Arizona*. Tucson: Arizona Town Hall.

Arranz-López, A., Soria-Lara, J., López-Escolano, C., and Campos, Á. (2017). Retail mobility environments: A methodological framework for integrating retail activity and non-motorized accessibility in Zaragoza, Spain. *Journal of Transport Geography*, 58, 92–103.

Ashworth, G., Kavaratzis, M., and Warnaby, G. (2015). The need to rethink place branding (pp. 1–11). In M. Kavaratzis, G. Warnaby, and G. Ashworth (Eds.), *Rethinking place branding: Comprehensive brand development for cities and regions*. Heidelberg: Springer.

Ashworth, G. J., and Voogd, H. (1994). Marketing of tourism places: What are we doing? *Journal of International Consumer Marketing*, 6(3–4), 5–19. doi. org/10.1300/J046v06n03_02

Asociación Vallisoletana de Comercio. (2011). *Estructura de estabelecimientos comerciales del centro urbano de Valladolid*. Valladolid: Agrupación Vallisoletana de Comercio.

ASU. (2004). Downtown Phoenix campus. Online report. Retrieved from: http://www.asu.edu/cdp/dtn.html (accessed December 20, 2006).

ATCM. (1998). *A guide to good practice*. London: ATCM.

AZDES. (2006). *Current status of homelessness in Arizona: 15th annual report*. Phoenix: Arizona Department of Economic Security.

AZDH. (2006). *Arizona's housing market, a glance*. Phoenix: Arizona Department of Housing.

Bagli, C. (2010). After 30 years, Times Square rebirth is complete. *New York Times*, December 3.

Bagli, C. (2015). Times Square's crushing success raises questions about its future. *New York Times*, January 26.

Balsas, C. (1999). *Urbanismo comercial em Portugal, e a revitalização do centro das cidades*. Lisbon: GEPE/Ministério da Economia.

Balsas, C. (2000). *O urbanismo comercial e as parcerias público-privado para a cestão do centro das cidades, ensinamentos da experiência estrangeira*. Lisbon: Observatório do Comércio, Ministério da Economia.

Balsas, C. (2001). Building dreams of mass-consumption across the Atlantic, a comparative study of two mega malls. *Passages: Journal of Transnational and Transcultural Studies*, 3(2), 137–162.

Balsas, C. (2002). *Urbanismo comercial e parcerias público-privado: Ensinamentos da experiência estrangeira*. Lisbon: GEPE.

Balsas, C. (2003). Urbanismo comercial: Mitos e boas práticas na revitalização de centros urbanos. *Sociedade e Território: Revista de Estudos Urbanos e Regionais*, 36, 116–130.

Balsas, C. (2004a). City center revitalization in the context of the 2001 European capital of culture in Porto. *Local Economy*, 19(4), 396–410.

Balsas, C. (2004b). Measuring the livability of an urban center: An exploratory study of key performance indicators. *Planning Practice and Research*, 19(1), 101–110.

Balsas, C. (2006). The 2005 Phoenix capitol mall studios as examples of community embeddedness. *Open House International*, 31(3), 67–76.

Balsas, C. (2007). City centre revitalization in Portugal: A study of Lisbon and Porto. *Journal of Urban Design*, 12(2), 231–259.

Balsas, C. (2012). Sustainable development in Portugal: An analysis of Lisbon and Porto (pp. 633–651). In I. Vojnovic (Ed.), *Building sustainable communities: A Global urban perspective*. East Lansing: Michigan State University Press.

Balsas, C. (2014). Walking and urban vibrancy: An international review of commercial pedestrian precincts. *Cidades*, 11(18), 230–260.

Balsas, C. (2017a). The right to walk in cities: A comparative review of Macau, Lisbon and Las Vegas. *International Journal of Law in the Built Environment,* 9(2), 123–142.

Balsas, C. (2017b). Where the rubber meets the road: Walking, riding, and driving or walking, walking, walking for our health. *Journal of Transport and Health,* 5, 182–188.

Balsas, C. (2018). Country marketing and planning implications of the European soccer championship EURO 2004. *Journal of Urban Technology,* 25(3), 29–46.

Bandeira, M., and Vilaça, A. (2013). Braga: A centralidade de um mercado bimilenar (pp. 151–170). In J. Fernandes and M. Sposito (Eds.), *A nova vida do velho centro nas cidades Portuguesas e Brasileiras.* Porto: CEGOT.

Banerjee, T. (2001). The future of public space: Beyond invested streets and reinvented places. *Journal of the American Planning Association,* 67(1), 9–24.

Banister, D. (2005). *Unsustainable transport.* New York: Routledge.

Barber, B. (2007). *Consumed: How markets corrupt children, infantilize adults, and swallow citizens Whole.* New York: Norton.

Barber, B. (2013). *If mayors ruled the world.* London: Yale University Press.

Barreira, A. P., Cesário, M., and de Noronha, M. T. (2017). Pull attributes of the Algarve: The tourists' view. *Tourism Planning and Development,* 14(1), 87–109.

Barreta, J. (2011). Mercados municipales en Portugal. *Distribución y Consumo,* 11/12, 1–17.

Barreta, J. (2012). *Comércio de próximidade e regeneração urbana.* Lisbon: CIP.

Barrett, L., Price-Spratlen, T., and Kanan, J. (2003). Determinants of homelessness in metropolitan areas. *Journal of Urban Affairs,* 25(3), 335–355.

Baudrillard, J. (1998). *The consumer society: Myths and structures.* London: Sage.

Beatley, T. (2000). *Green urbanism: Learning from European cities.* Washington, DC: Island Press.

Beatley, T. (2004). *Native to nowhere.* Washington, DC: Island Press.

Beauregard, R. (2003a). City of superlatives. *City and Community,* 2(3), 183–199.

Beauregard, R. (2003b). *Voices of decline: The postwar fate of US cities.* 2nd edition. New York: Routledge.

Bell, D., and Jayne, M. (2009). Small cities? Towards a research agenda. *International Journal of Urban and Regional Research,* 33(3), 683–699.

Bennett, R., and Koudelova, R. (2001). Image selection and the marketing of downtown areas in London and New York. *The International Journal of Public Sector Management,* 14(3), 205–220.

Berry, J. (2007). Sky Harbor study to look at diversity of vendors. *Arizona Republic,* September 25.

Birch, E. (2006). Hopeful signs: US urban revitalization in the 21st century. Paper presented at the Land Policies for Urban Development Conference. Lincoln Institute of Land Policy. Cambridge, September.

Blomley, N. (2007). Civil rights meet civil engineering: Urban public space and traffic logic. *Canadian Journal of Law and Society,* 22(2), 55–72.

Bolin, B., Declet-Barretto, J., Hegmon, M., Meirotto, L., and York, A. (2013). Double exposure in the Sunbelt: The sociospatial distribution of vulnerability in Phoenix, Arizona (pp. 159–178). In C. Boone and M. Fragkias (Eds.), *Urbanization and sustainability: Linking urban ecology, environmental justice and global environmental change.* Heidelberg: Springer. doi:10.1007/978-94-007-5666-3

Borgers, A., and Timmermans, H. (2005). Modelling pedestrian behavior in downtown shopping areas. *Proceedings of CUPUM 05.* London: Centre for Advanced Spatial Analysis, University College London.

Boston, T., and Ross, C. (2001). *The inner city, urban poverty and economic development in the next century.* New Brunswick: Transaction.

Bowers, F. (2007). Sun-scorched Phoenix takes more heart for its homeless. *Christian Science,* July 9.

Boyer, C. (2003). X marks the spot: Times Square dead or alive? (pp. 430–436) In G. Bridge and S. Watson (Eds.), *A companion to the city.* Oxford: Blackwell.

Bradley, T., and Hall, T. (2006). The festival phenomenon: Festivals, events and the promotion of small urban areas (pp. 77–90). In D. Bell and M. Jayne (Eds.), *Small cities: Urban life beyond the metropolis.* London, UK: Routledge.

Bright, E. (2000). *Reviving America's forgotten neighborhoods: An investigation of inner city revitalization efforts.* New York: Garland.

Brinegar, S. (2000). Response to homelessness in Tempe, Arizona: Public opinion and government policy. *Urban Geography,* 21(6), 497–514.

Brinegar, S. (2003). The social construction of homeless shelters in the Phoenix area. *Urban Geography,* 24(1): 61–74.

Brown, K. (2001). *Getting it right: A good practice guide to successful town centre management initiatives.* London: ATCM.

Bunnell, G. (2002). *Making places special.* Chicago: Planners Press.

Burayidi, M. (Ed.) (2001). *Downtowns: Revitalizing the centers of small urban communities.* New York: Routledge.

Burwell, S. (2007). The downtown Phoenix public market. *Java Magazine,* May 12–13.

Cabrita, J. (1991). Prioridades e métodos para a reabilitação em áreas urbanas. In *Colóquio viver (n)a cidade.* Lisbon: LNEC/ISCTE.

Cachinho, H. (2006). Consumator: Da condição do individuo na cidade pós-moderna. *Finisterra,* 41(81), 33–56. doi.org/10.18055/Finis1461

Cachinho, H., and Salgueiro, T. (2016). Os sistemas comerciais urbanos em tempos de turbulência: Vulnerabilidades e níveis de resiliência. *Finisterra,* 101, 89–109.

Calavita, N., and Ferrer, A. (2000). Behind Barcelona's success story. *Journal of Urban History,* 26(6), 793–807.

Caldwell, N., and Freire, J. R. (2004). The differences between branding a country, a region and a city: Applying the Brand Box model. *Journal of Brand Management,* 12(1), 50–61. doi:10.1057/palgrave.bm.2540201

Câmara Municipal da Figueira da Foz (CMFF). (2014a). *Figueira 2030, território sustentável do Atlântico: Plano estratégico de desenvolvimento da Figueira da Foz.* Figueira da Foz: CMFF.

Câmara Municipal da Figueira da Foz (CMFF). (2014b). *Relatório de avaliação da execução do PDM da Figueira da Foz.* Figueira da Foz: CMFF.

Câmara Municipal da Figueira da Foz (CMFF). (2016). *Figueira invista.* Figueira da Foz: CMFF.

Campbell, R. (2005). Universities are the new city planners. *Boston Globe,* March 20.

Capel, H. (2009). Las pequeñas ciudades en la urbanización generalizada y ante la crisis global. *Investigaciones Geográficas,* 70, 7–32.

Carley, M., Chapman, M., Hastings, A., Kirk, K., and Young, R. (2000). *Urban regeneration through partnership.* Bristol: The Policy Press.

Carmona, M. (2001). Sustainable urban design: A possible agenda (pp. 165–192). In A. Layard, S. Davoudi, and S. Batty (Eds.), *Planning for a sustainable future.* London: Spon Press.

Carmona, M. (2014). The place-shaping continuum: A theory of urban design process. *Journal of Urban Design,* 19(1), 2–36.

Carmona, M., Magalhães, C., and Hammond, L. (Eds.) (2008). *Public space: The management dimension.* New York: Routledge.

Carreras, C. (2003). *Atlas comercial de Barcelona.* Barcelona: Ajuntament de Barcelona.

Carrizo, I., and Gardon, P. (2003). Regulacion comercial basada en cuotas de mercado. *Boletin Económico de ICE,* 2787, 23–34.

Cars, G., Healey, P., and Magalhães, C. (2002). *Urban governance, institutional capacity and social milieux.* Aldershot: Ashgate.

Cascão, R. (1985). Demografia e sociedade: A Figueira da Foz na primeira metade do século XIX. *Revista de História Económica e Social,* 15, 83–122.

Castello, L. (2007). *A percepção do lugar: Repensando o conceito de lugar em arquitetura-urbanismo.* Porto Alegre, Brazil: PROPAR-UFRGS.

Castello, L. (2010). *Rethinking the meaning of place, conceiving place in architecture-urbanism.* London: Ashgate.

Castells, M., Conill, J., Cardenas, A., and Servon, L. (2012). Beyond the crisis: The emergence of alternative economic practices (pp. 210–248). In M. Castells, J. Caraça, and G. Cardoso (Eds.), *Aftermath: The cultures of the economic crisis.* Oxford: Oxford University Press.

Castillo-Manzano, J., and Lopez-Valpuesta, L. (2009). Urban retail fabric and the metro: A complex relationship. Lessons from middle-size Spanish cities. *Cities,* 26, 141–147.

Castillo-Manzano, J., Lopez-Valpuesta, L., and Asencio-Flores, J. (2014). Extending pedestrianization processes outside the old city centre: Conflict and benefits in the case of the city of Seville. *Habitat International,* 44, 194–201.

Cavaco, C. (2005). O turismo e as novas dinâmicas territoriais (pp. 367–428). In C. Medeiros (Ed.), *Geografia de Portugal: Actividades económicas e espaço geográfico.* Lisbon: Circulo dos Leitores.

Cavaco, C. (2010). *Dinamização económica dos centros históricos.* Lisbon: CECOA. April 21, Correspondence exchanged with the author.

Chesluk, B. (2008). *Money jungle imagining the New Times Square*. New Brunswick: Rutgers University Press.

Chung, C., Inaba, J., Koolhaas, R., Leong, S., and Cha, T. (2002). *Harvard Design School guide to shopping*. New York: Taschen.

Clark, C. (1994). *101 Ideas on economic development*. Omaha: Peoples Natural Gas.

Coca-Stefaniak, A., and Bagaeen, S. (2013). Strategic management for sustainable high street recovery. *Town and Country Planning*, 82(12), 532–537.

Coca-Stefaniak, A., Parker, C., Quin, S., Rinaldi, R., and Byrom, J. (2009). Town centre management models: A European perspective. *Cities*, 26, 74–80.

Cochran, S. (1999). *Inventing Nanjing Road: Commercial culture in Shanghai, 1900–1945*. Ithaca: Cornell East Asia Series.

Cohen, M. (2014). Supplementing the conventional 3R waste hierarch: Considering the role of carbon rationing (pp. 215–224). In K. Ekström (Ed.), *Waste management and sustainable consumption: Reflections on consumer waste*. New York: Routledge.

College of Design. (2005). *Arizona capitol mall district revitalization plan*. Retrieved from http://www.design.asu.edu/azcapitalmall/ (accessed July 29, 2007).

Collin, R. (1992). Homelessness in the United States: 1980–1990. *Journal of Planning Literature*, 7(1), 22–37.

Collins, T., and Grineski, S. (2007). Unequal impacts of downtown redevelopment: The case of stadium building in Phoenix, AZ. *Journal of Poverty*, 11(1), 23–54.

Collins, W. (2005). *The emerging metropolis: Phoenix, 1944–1973*. Phoenix: Arizona State Parks Board.

Community Food Connections (CFC) (2014). Community Food Connections 2014 annual report. Retrieved from http://phxpublicmarket.com/openair/wp-content/uploads/2013/10/2014-CFC-Annual-Report-web-version.pdf (accessed January 6, 2016).

Connolly, P. (1999). Mexico City: Our common future? *Environment and Urbanization*, 11(1), 53–78.

Cordeiro, A., and Barros, C. (2011). Uma cidade sustentável, um território coeso: O exemplo da Figueira da Foz (pp. 1336–1345). In *Actas do 17º Congresso da Associação Portuguesa para o Desenvolvimento Regional (APDR) and 5º Congresso de Gestão e Conservação da Natureza*.

Correia, D., and Y. Vauléon. (2005). A geografia do desperdício. *Arquitectura e Vida*, 57, 74–77.

Costa, C. (2001a). *Avaliação do II quadro comunitário de apoio componente do turismo: Síntese e recomendações*. Aveiro: Universidade de Aveiro.

Costa, C. (2001b). An emerging tourism planning paradigm? A comparative analysis between town and tourism planning. *International Journal of Tourism Research*, 3(6), 425–441. doi:10.1002/jtr.277

Crawford, J. (2000). *Carfree cities*. Utrecht: International Books.

Crawford, M. (2002). Suburban life and public space (pp. 21–30). In D. Smiley (Ed.), *Sprawl and public space: Redressing the mall.* Washington, DC: National Endowment for the Arts.

Crossa, V. (2009). Resisting the entrepreneurial city: Street vendors' struggle in Mexico City's historic centre. *International Journal of Urban and Regional Research,* 33(1), 43–63.

Crow, M. (2002). *A new America university: Setting the new gold standard—white paper.* Arizona State University, Tempe.

Cruz, I. (2016). Consumo sustentável e ambiente: O papel do Estado e das políticas públicas na inculcação de disposições ambientalistas. *Sociologia: Revista da Faculdade de Letras da Universidade do Porto,* 32, 33–60.

Culhane, D., and Metraux, S. (2008). Rearranging the deck chairs or relocating the lifeboats? *Journal of the American Planning Association,* 74(1), 111–121.

Cunha, L., and Cravidão, F. (1997).Tourism and environmental degradation on the west coast of Portugal (pp. 113–116). In J. Machado and J. Ahern (Eds.), *Environmental challenges in an expanding urban world and the role of emerging information technologies.* Lisbon: CNIG.

Dalsgaard, A. (2012). *The human scale brings cities to life.* Documentary. New York: Kimstim.

Davis, D. (1994). *Urban leviathan: Mexico City in the twentieth century.* Philadelphia: Temple University Press.

Davis, P. (1999). *Ecomuseum: A sense of place.* London: Leicester University Press.

Davoudi, S. (2009). Governing waste: Introduction to the special issue. *Journal of Environmental Planning and Management,* 52(2), 131–136.

De Certeau, M. (1984). *The practice of everyday life.* Berkeley: University of California Press.

Dear, M., and Flusty, S. (1998). Postmodern urbanism. *Annals of the Association of American Geographers,* 88(1), 50–72.

Delgado, C. (2016). Formerly with the Parque Expo Polis Vila Nova de Gaia, Lisbon, June 3.

DeLisle, J. (2005). The evolution of shopping centre research: A 12-year retrospective. *Journal of Shopping Center Research,* 12(2), 1–83.

Design Trust for Public Space. (2003). *Times Square: The next 100 years, problems and possibilities.* Timessquarenyc.org. (accessed February 27, 2015).

DeVerteuil, G. (2006). The local state and homeless shelters: Beyond revanchism? *Cities,* 23(2), 109–120.

DGAE. (2010) *Dinamização económica dos centros históricos: O balanço de uma década 1997/2007.* CECOA, April 21. Retrieved from http://gis.cm-agueda.pt/pru/docs/ seminario_tema tico1/tema2_ clotildecavaco_dgae.pdf (accessed August 22, 2017).

DoE. (1997). *Town centre partnerships.* London: The Stationary Office.

Domingues, A. (2006). *Cidade e democracia: 30 anos de transformação urbana em Portugal.* Lisbon: Argumentum.

Dubasik, S. (2006). KJZZ radio series on homelessness in Phoenix: Part 1. Recording archived at KJZZ.com.

Eeckhout, B. (2001). The "Disneyfication" of Times Square: Back to the future? (pp. 379–428). In K. Gotham (Ed.), *Critical perspectives on urban redevelopment,* vol. 6. New York: JAI.

Ehrenfeucht, R., and Loukaitou-Sideris, A. (2010). Planning urban sidewalks: Infrastructure, daily life and destinations. *Journal of Urban Design,* 15(4), 459–471.

Ehrenhalt, A. (2012). *The great inversion and the future of the American city.* New York: Random House.

Eisenschitzs, A. (2010). Neo-liberalism and the future of place marketing. *Place Branding and Public Diplomacy,* 6(2), 79–86.

Ekström, K. (Ed.) (2014), *Waste management and sustainable consumption: Reflections on consumer waste.* New York: Routledge.

El-Geneidy, A., Kastelberger, L. and Abdelhamid, H. (2011). Montréal's Roots: Exploring the growth of Montréal's indoor city. *Journal of Transport and Land Use,* 4(2), 33–46.

Ellin, N. (1997). *Architecture of fear.* New York: Princeton Architectural Press.

Ellin, N. (2006). Desert metropolis. (pp. 18–25) In E. Booth-Clibborn (Ed.), *Phoenix: 21st century city.* Hong Kong: Booth-Clibborn Editions.

Ellin, N. (2006). *Integral urbanism.* New York: Routledge.

European Commission. (2014). *Towards a circular economy: A zero waste programme for Europe.* Brussels, 2.7.2014—COM(2014) 398 final. Retrieved from http://ec.europa.eu/environment/ circular-economy/pdf/circular-economy-communication.pdf (accessed August 18, 2017).

Eusébio, M. (2006). *Avaliação do impacte económico do turismo a nível regional: O caso da região centro de Portugal.* Unpublished doctoral dissertation. Aveiro: Universidade de Aveiro. http://hdl.handle.net/10773/1839.

Evans, G. (2001). *Cultural planning, an urban renaissance?* New York: Routledge.

Ewing, R., and Handy, S. (2009). Measuring the unmeasurable: Urban design qualities related to walkability. *Journal of Urban Design,* 14(1), 65–84.

Fadigas, L. (2015). *Urbanismo e território: As políticas públicas.* Lisbon: Edições Sílabo.

Fainstein, S. (1999). Can we make the cities we want? (pp. 249–271) In R. Beauregard and S. Body-Gendrot (Eds.), *The urban moment.* Thousand Oaks: Sage.

Fainstein, S. (2000). New directions in planning theory. *Urban Affairs Review,* 35(4), 451–478.

Fainstein, S. (2006). *Planning and the just city.* Paper presented at the Conference on Searching for the Just City, GSAPP, Columbia University, April 29.

Fainstein, S., and Stokes, R. (1998) Spaces for play: The impacts of entertainment development on New York City. *Economic Development Quarterly,* 12(2), 150–165.

Farrell, M. (2005). Spain and Portugal in the European Union: Assessing the impact of regional integration. *Journal of Southern Europe and the Balkans,* 7(3), 409–415.

Featherstone, M. (2007). *Consumer culture and postmodernism.* 2nd edition. Los Angeles: Sage.

Fernandes, J. (1989). Circulação, peões e baixa, o caso do Porto. *Revista da Faculdade de Letras Geografia,* 5, 33–43.

Fernandes, J. (1995). Urbanismo comercial: A experiência Portuguesa. *Revista da Faculdade de Letras,* 10(11), 105–125.

Fernandes, J. (2007). Urbanismo sustentável: Redução, reciclagem e reutilização da cidade. *Revista da Faculdade de Letras: Geografia. Universidade do Porto* 2(1), 163–178.

Fernandes, J. (2012). Os projetos de urbanismo comercial e a revitalização do centro da cidade. *Revista Memória em Rede,* 4(6), 71–84.

Fernandes, J., and Chamusca, P. (2014). Urban policies, planning and retail resilience. *Cities,* 36, 170–177.

Fernandes, J., and Martins, L. (1988). A área central dos aglomerados urbanos do noroeste de Portugal. *Revista da Faculdade de Letras: Geografia,* 4, 33–52.

Fernandes, J., Cachinho, H., and Ribeiro, C. (2000). *Comércio tradicional em contexto urbano, dinâmicas de modernização e políticas públicas.* Lisbon: Observatório do Comércio, Ministério da Economia.

Fernández, Ó. (2007). Towards the sustainability of historical centres: A case-study of Léon, Spain. *European Urban and Regional Studies,* 14(2), 181–187.

Ferrão, J., Henriques, E., and Neves, A. (1994). Repensar as cidades de média dimensão. *Análise Social,* 129: 1123–1147.

Ferrão, P., Lorena, A., and Ribeiro, A. (2016). Industrial ecology and Portugal's national waste plans (pp. 275–289). In R. Clift and A. Druckman (Eds.), *Taking stock of industrial ecology.* Heidelberg: Cham Springer Open International.

Ferreira, A. (2013). Turismo, cultura e regeneração urbana, o renascimento das pequenas e médias cidades. *Revista Turismo e Desenvolvimento,* 20, 31–39.

Ferreira, F. (2002). Resíduos Urbanos: Os novos desafios (pp. 252–261). In E. Brito (Ed.), *Gestão urbana: Passado, presente e future.* Lisbon: Parque Expo'98.

Ferreira, P. (2010). *A rua direita, em Viseu: Importância histórica, património e memória desta artéria.* Unpublished Thesis. Lisbon: Universidade Aberta.

Fidélis, T., and Pires, S. (2009). Surrender or resistance to the implementation of Local Agenda 21 in Portugal: The challenges of local governance for sustainable development. *Journal of Environmental Planning and Management,* 52(4), 497–518.

Fiedler, R., Schuurman, N. and Hyndman, J. (2006). Hidden homelessness: An indicator-based approach for examining the geographies of recent immigrants at-risk of homelessness in Greater Vancouver. *Cities,* 23(3), 205–216.

Figueiredo, E. (2008). Imagine there's no rural: The transformation of rural spaces into places of nature conservation in Portugal. *European Urban and Regional Studies*, 15(2), 159–171. doi.org/10.1177/0969776407081939

Filion, P., Hoernig, H., Bunting, T., and Sands, G. (2004). The Successful Few: Healthy downtowns of small metropolitan regions. *Journal of the American Planning Association*, 70(3), 328–343.

Florida, R. (2005a). *Cities and the creative class.* New York: Routledge.

Florida, R. (2005b). The world is spiky. *The Atlantic Monthly*, 296(3), 48–51.

Ford, L. (2003). *America's new downtowns: Revitalization or reinvention?* Baltimore: Johns Hopkins University Press.

Forsyth, A. (2015). What is a walkable place? The walkability debate in urban design. *Urban Design International*, 20(4), 274–292.

Fortuna, C. (2016). Património com futuro . . . Ou sobre a resiliência das cidades. *Revista Património*, 4, 6–13.

Fraser, J. (2004). Beyond gentrification: Mobilizing communities and claiming space. *Urban Geography*, 25(5), 437–457.

Frechoso-Remiro, J., and Villarejo-Galende, H. (2011). Town centre management at a crossroad in central Spain. *Journal of Town and City Management*, 2(2), 117–131.

Frieden, B., and Sagalyn, L. (1989). *Downtown, Inc.: How America rebuilds cities.* Cambridge: MIT Press.

Friedman, A. (2003). Recycling redux. *Planning*, November, 5–9.

Friedman, T. (2005). The World is flat. New York: Farrar, Straus and Giroux.

Friedmann, J. (2000). The good city: In defense of utopian thinking. *International Journal of Urban and Regional Research*, 24(2), 460–472.

Frúgoli, H., Jr. (2000). *Centralidade em São Paulo, trajetórias, conflictos e negociações na metrópole.* São Paulo: Editora da Universidade de São Paulo.

Fuller, D. (1994). Shopping centers and the environment: Recycling strategies for the 1990s. *Journal of Shopping Center Research*, 1(1), 7–37.

Fulton, W., Weaver, S., and Waits, M. (2004). *Playing the inside game: The challenge of urban revitalization in Arizona.* Tempe: Morrison Institute for Public Policy.

Gaiger, L. (2004). A economia solidária no Brasil e o sentido das novas formas de produção não capitalistas. *Revista Venezolana de Economía Social*, 8, 9–37.

Gammage, G. (2003). *Phoenix in perspective: Reflections on developing the desert.* 2nd edition. Tempe: Herberger Center for Design Excellence and Arizona State University.

Gammage, G., and Fink, J. (2004). The Phoenix experiment. Paper delivered at the conference *On the Edge: Metropolitan Growth and Western Environments.* Stanford University, April 15–16.

Gandy, M. (1994). *Recycling and the politics of urban waste.* London: Earthscan.

García, C. (2015). Peatonalización de la Calle Madero del centro histórico de la Ciudad de México: Análisis del cambio en el ámbito comercial. In *Seminario*

Internacional de Investigación en Urbanismo: VII Seminario Internacional de Investigación en Urbanismo, Barcelona–Montevideo, June 2015. Barcelona, DUOT. Retrieved from http://hdl.handle.net/2117/81110 (accessed August 31, 2016).

Garcia, J. (2015). Formerly with the Secretaria de Transporte y Vivienda, Gobierno del Distrito Federal, Mexico City, October 24.

Garcia, M., Rodríguez, R. and Moreno, R. (2005). Urban regeneration policy from the integrated urban development model in the European Union. *Local Government Studies*. doi:10.1080/03003930.2015.1110520

Garreau, J. (1992). *Edge City: Life on the new frontier*. New York: First Anchor Books.

Garza, G. (1999). Global economy, metropolitan dynamics and urban policies in Mexico. *Cities*, 16(3), 149–170.

Gaspar, J. (1987). Do pelourinho ao centro comercial. *Póvos e Culturas*, 2, 243–259.

Gehl, J. (2010). *Cities for people*. Washington, DC: Island Press.

Getz, D., and Page, S. (2016). Progress and prospects for event tourism research. *Tourism Management*, 52, 593–631. doi.org/10.1016/j.tourman.2015.03.007

Gibbs, R. (2012). *Principles of urban retail, planning and development*. Hoboken: John Wiley and Sons.

Gibson, T. (2004). *Securing the spectacular city: The politics of revitalization and homelessness in downtown Seattle*. Lanham: Lexington.

Gober, P. (2006). *Metropolitan Phoenix, place making and community building in the desert*. Philadelphia: University of Pennsylvania Press.

Gomes, P., and Veiga, A. (2002). *Figueira da Foz: Memória, conhecimento, e inovação*. Paços de Ferreira: Néstia Editores.

Gonzalez, S., and Waley, P. (2012). Traditional retail markets: The new gentrification frontier? *Antipode*, 45(4), 965–983.

Gospodini, A. (2004). Urban morphology and place identity in European cities. *Journal of Urban Design*, 9(2), 225–248.

Goss, J. (1993). The "Magic of the Mall": An analysis of form, function, and meaning in the contemporary retail-built environment. *Annals of the Association of American Geographers*, 83(1), 18–47.

Gotham, K. (Ed.) (2001). *Critical perspectives on urban redevelopment*. New York: JAI/Elsevier.

Graham, A. (2009). How important are commercial revenues to today's airports? *Journal of Air Transport Management*, 15, 106–111.

Gratz, R., and Mintz, N. (1998). *Cities back from the edge: New life for downtown*. New York: John Wiley and Sons.

Greed, C. (2003). *Inclusive urban design*. Oxford: Architectural Press.

Greenberg, M. (2003). The limits of branding: The World Trade Center, fiscal crisis and the marketing of recovery. *International Journal of Urban and Regional Research*, 27(2), 386–416.

Greenberg, M., and Fox, K. (2013.) *Crisis cities: Disaster and redevelopment in New York and New Orleans*. New York: Routledge.

Gross, J. S. (2013). Business improvement districts in New York: the private sector in public service or the public sector privatized? *Urban Research & Practice*, 6(3), 346–364.

Groth, P. (1994). *Living downtown: The history of residential hotels in the United States*. Berkeley: University of California Press.

Guathakurta, S., and Stimson, R. (2007). What is driving the growth of new "sun-belt" metropolises. *International Planning Studies*, 12(2), 129–152.

Guimarães, P. (2009). *O comércio no centro da cidade de Braga Face aos impactos provenientes da implantação de dois novos centros comerciais*. Unpublished thesis. Braga: University of Minho.

Guimarães, P. (2017). An evaluation of urban regeneration: The effectiveness of a retail-led project in Lisbon. *Urban Research and Practice*, 10(3), 350–366.

Gunder, M. (2006). Sustainability, planning's saving grace or road to perdition? *Journal of Planning Education and Research*, 26, 208–221.

Guy, C. (2007). *Planning for retail development*. London: Routledge.

Hack, G. (2011). Urban flux (pp. 446–462). In T. Banerjee and A. Loukaitou-Sideris (Eds.), *Companion to urban design*. New York: Routledge.

Hack, G., and Sagalyn, L. (2011). Value creation through urban design (pp. 258–281). In S. Tiesdell and D. Adams (Eds.), *Urban design in the real estate development process*. Oxford: Wiley-Blackwell.

Hackworth, J. (1999). Local planning and economic restructuring: A synthetic interpretation of urban redevelopment. *Journal of Planning Education and Research*, 18, 293–306.

Hackworth, J. (2007). *Neoliberal city: Governance, ideology, and development in American urbanism*. Ithaca: Cornell University Press.

Halebsky, S. (2004). Superstores and the politics of retail development. *City and Community*, 3(2), 115–134.

Hall, C. (1997). Geography, marketing and the selling of places. *Journal of Travel and Tourism Marketing*, 6(3–4), 61–84.

Hall, C. (2009). *El turismo como ciencia social de la movilidad*. Madrid: Síntesis.

Hall, C. M. (2013). Vanishing peripheries: Does tourism consume places? *Tourism Recreation Research*, 38(1), 71–92. doi.org/10.1080/02508281.2013.11081730

Hall, C. M., and Lew, A. (2009). *Understanding and managing tourism impacts: An integrated approach*. New York: Routledge.

Hall, C. M., and Sharples, L. (2003). The consumption of experiences or the experience of consumption? An introduction to the tourism of taste (pp.1–24). In C. M. Hall, L. Sharples, R. Mitchell, N. Macionis, and B. Cambourne (Eds.), *Food tourism around the world: Development, management and markets*. Oxford: Butterworth-Heinemann.

Hall, P. (2014). *Good cities, better lives: How Europe discovered the lost art of urbanism*. London: Routledge.

Hall, T., and Hubbard, P. (1998). *The entrepreneurial city, geographies of politics, regime and representation*. New York: John Wiley and Sons.

Hardin, G. (1968). The tragedy of the commons. *Science*, 162(3859): 1243–1248.

Harter, L. M., Berquist, C., Scott Titsworth, B., Novak, D., and Brokaw, T. (2005). The structuring of invisibility among the hidden homeless: The politics of space, stigma, and identity construction. *Journal of Applied Communication Research*, 33(4), 305–327.

Harvey, D. (1992). Social justice, postmodernism and the city. *International Journal of Urban and Regional Research*, 16(4), 588–601.

Harvey, D. (2010). *The enigma of capital and the crisis this time*. Paper prepared for the American Sociological Association Meeting in Atlanta, August 16.

Hass-Klau, C. (2015). *The pedestrian and the city*. New York: Routledge.

Heim, C. (2001). Leapfrogging, urban sprawl and growth management: Phoenix 1950–2000. *American Journal of Economics and Sociology*, 60(1), 246–283.

Herzog, L. (2006). *Return to the centre: Culture, public space, and city building in a global era*. Austin: University of Texas Press.

Hoch, C., and Slayton, R. (1989). *New homeless and old: Community and the skid row hotel*. Philadelphia: Temple University Press.

Hoffman, A. (2003). *House by house, block by block: The rebirth of America's urban neighborhoods*. New York: Oxford University Press.

Holleran, M. (2006). Director of CASS. Personal interview by the author. June 26.

Homeless campus is testament to community's sense of humanity. (2003). *Arizona Republic*, April 13.

Hopkins, E., and Nackerud, L. (1999). An analysis of Atlanta's ordinance prohibiting urban camping: Passage and early implementation. *Journal of Social Distress and the Homeless*, 8(4), 1999.

Hostovsky, C. (2006). The paradox of the rational comprehensive model of planning: Tales from waste management planning in Ontario, Canada. *Journal of Planning Education and Research*, 25(4), 382–395.

Hou, J. (2011). Citizen design participation and beyond (pp. 329–340). In T. Banerjee and A. Loukaitou-Sideris (Eds.), *Companion to urban design*. New York: Routledge.

HRA. (2007). *Valuing Times Square: The economic impact of Times Square*. Timessquarenyc.org (accessed February 27, 2015).

HUD. (2005). *The strategies for preventing homelessness*. Washington, DC: US Department of Housing and Urban Development.

HUD. (2007). *The annual homeless assessment report to Congress*. Washington, DC: US Department of Housing and Urban Development.

Hume, C. (2005). You are not welcome: Urban planners are subtly making the downtown core a less hospitable place. *Toronto Star*, February 5.

ICCH. (2004). *Ending homelessness in Arizona: Phase 1, improving services*. Phoenix: Arizona.

ICCH. (2005). *Plan to end homelessness: Plan for housing*. Phoenix: Arizona.

IDA. (2000). *Addressing homelessness: Successful downtown partnerships*. Washington, DC: International Downtown Association.

Inam, A. (2005). *Planning for the unplanned: Recovering from crises in megacities.* New York: Routledge.

INE. (2016). *Estatísticas dos resíduos (2016 edition).* Lisbon: INE.

Inskeep, E. (1988). Tourism planning: An emerging specialization. *Journal of the American Planning Association,* 54(3), 360–372.

Jabareen, Y. (2013). Planning for countering climate change: Lessons from the recent plan of New York City—PlaNYC 2030. *International Planning Students,* 18(2), 221–242.

Jackson, E. (2001). Physical regeneration: Learning from the American experience (pp. 53–56). In C. Balsas (Ed.), *Urbanismo comercial em Portugal, e a necessidade de uma nova gestão urbana.* Lisbon: URBE and CMPV.

Jackson, T. (2005). Motivating sustainable consumption. *Sustainable Development Research Network—SDRN.* Retrieved from http://sustainablelifestyles.ac.uk/sites/default/files/ motivating_sc_final.pdf (accessed August 22, 2017).

Jacobs, A. (1993). *Great streets.* Cambridge: MIT Press.

James, K., Thompson-Fawcett, M., and Hansen, C. J. (2016). Transformations in identity, governance and planning: The case of the small city. *Urban Studies,* 53(6), 1162–1177. doi.org/10.1177/0042098015571060

Janoschka, M., Sequera, J. and Salinas, L. (2014). Gentrification in Spain and Latin America: A critical dialogue. *International Journal of Urban and Regional Research,* 38(4), 1234–1265.

Jayne, M. (2006). *Cities and consumption.* New York: Routledge.

Jencks, C. (1994). *The homeless.* Cambridge: Harvard University Press.

Johnson, A. (2008). Wary developers use caution. *Arizona Republic,* February 24, D1 and D2.

Judd, D., and Fainstein, S. (1999). *The tourist city.* New Haven: Yale University Press.

Karrholm, M. (2008). The territorialisation of a pedestrian precinct in Malmo: Materialities in the commercialization of public spaces. *Urban Studies,* 45(9), 1903–1924.

Kasarda, J. (2008). Shopping in the Airport City and Aeropolis. *Research Review,* 15(2), 50–56.

Kasarda, J., and Lindsay, G. (2011). *Aerotropolis: The way we'll live next.* New York: Farrar, Straus and Giroux.

Kavaratzis, M., Warnaby, G., and Ashworth, G. (2015). *Rethinking place branding: Comprehensive brand development for cities and regions.* Heidelberg: Springer.

Kearney, B. (2006). Copper Square and downtown Phoenix: The next great American downtown. Presentation made to the ULI Arizona District Council. August 30.

Keating, W. (1986). Linking downtown development to broader community goals. *Journal of the American Planning Association,* 52(2), 133–141.

Kelling, G., and Coles, C. (1996). *Fixing broken windows: Restoring order and reducing crime in our communities.* New York: Martin Kessler Books.

Kennedy, M. (1979). Generalizing from single case studies. *Evaluation Quarterly,* 3(4), 661–678.

Kirby, A. (2005). The changing character of metropolitan Phoenix: Notes on sprawl. Paper given at the seminar *The Changing City and Suburbs of Phoenix: Downtown Regeneration and Sprawl.* February 23.

Kortekaas, K. H. (2004). Sustainable tourism initiatives in European saltscapes (pp. 199–207). In F. Pineda, C. A. Brebbia, and M. Mugica (Eds.), *Sustainable tourism: First International Conference on Sustainable Tourism.* Southampton: WIT Press.

Kostopoulou, S. (2013). On the revitalized waterfront: Creative milieu for creative tourism. *Sustainability,* 5, 4578–4593. doi:10.3390/su5114578

Kotkin, J. (2005). *Phoenix rising: A city of aspirations.* Phoenix: Goldwater Policy Report No. 204. April 27.

Kotler, P., Haiderr, D., and Rein, I. (1993). *Marketing places: Attracting investment, industry, and tourism to cities, states, and nations.* New York: The Free Press.

Kowinski, W. (1985). *The malling of America: An inside look at the great consumer paradise.* New York: W. Morrow.

Krumholz, N. (1999). Equitable approaches to local economic development. *Policy Studies Journal,* 27(1), 83–95.

Kunzmann, K. (2011). Spaces of consumption (pp. 391–404). In T. Banerjee and A. Loukaitou-Sideris (Eds.), *Companion to urban design.* New York: Routledge.

Kyle, K. (2005). *Contextualizing homelessness, critical theory, homelessness, and federal policy addressing the homeless.* New York: Routledge.

Ladner, M. (2006). *How to win the war on poverty: An analysis of state poverty trends.* Goldwater Institute Policy Report No. 215.

Landry, C. (2000). *The creative city.* London: Earthscan.

Larsen, L., Poortinga, E., and Hurdle, D. (2004). Sleeping rough: Differences between shelter users and non-users in Phoenix. *Environment and Behavior,* 36(4), 578–591.

Law, R. (2001). "Not in my city": Local governments and homelessness policies in the Los Angeles metropolitan region. *Environment and Planning C,* 19, 791–815.

Lee, B., and Price-Spratlen, T. (2004). The geography of homelessness in American communities: Concentration or dispersion? *City and Community,* 3(1), 3–27.

Leinberger, C. (2008). *The option of urbanism: Investing in a new American dream.* Washington, DC: Island Press.

Leite, C. (2009). Reshaping the metropolitan territory: Contemporary urban interventions in São Paulo (pp. 246–265). In V. del Rio and W. Siembieda (Eds.), *Contemporary Urbanism in Brazil: Beyond Brasilia.* Gainesville: University of Florida Press.

Leme, M., and Ventura, D. (2000). *O calçadão em questão: 20 anos de experiência do calçadão paulistano.* São Paulo: Belas Artes.

Leontidou, L. (1990). *The Mediterranean city in transition: Social change and urban development.* Cambridge: Cambridge University Press.

Lewis, J., and Williams, A. (1998). Portugal: Market segmentation and economic development (pp. 125–149). In A. Williams and G. Shaw (Eds.), *Tourism and economic development: European experiences.* Chichester: John Wiley and Sons.

Lima, M., and Cardenete, M. (2008). The impact of European structural funds in the south of Spain. *European Planning Studies,* 16(10), 1445–1457.

Lincoln Institute of Land Policy. (2003). *Phoenix: The urban desert, a documentary film.* Boston: Lincoln Institute of Land Policy.

Litman, T. (2011). *Economic value of walkability.* Victoria: Victoria Transport Policy Institute.

Lloyd, R., and Clark, T. (2001). The city as an entertainment machine (pp. 357–377). In K. Gotham (Ed.), *Critical perspectives on urban redevelopment,* vol. 6. New York: JAI.

Lo, R. (2009). Walkability: What is it? *Journal of Urbanism,* 2(2), 145–166.

Logan, J., and Molotch, H. (1987). *Urban fortunes: The political economy of place.* Berkeley: University of California Press.

Logemann, J. (2009). Where to shop? The geography of consumption in the twentieth-century Atlantic world. *Bulletin of the GHI,* 45, 55–68.

Loukaitou-Sideris, A. (2002). Regeneration of urban commercial strips: Ethnicity and space in three Los Angeles neighborhoods. *Journal of Architectural and Planning Research,* 19(4), 334–350.

Loukaitou-Sideris, A., and Banerjee, T. (1998). *Urban design downtown: Poetics and politics of form.* Berkeley: University of California Press.

Loukaitou-Sideris, A., and Ehrenfeucht, R. (2009). *Sidewalks: Conflict and negotiation over public space.* Cambridge: MIT Press.

Lovasi, G., Schwartz-Soicher, O., Neckerman, K., Konty, K., Kerker, B., Quinn, J., and Rundle, A. (2013). Aesthetic amenities and safety hazards associated with walking and bicycling for transportation in New York City. *Annals of Behavioral Medicine,* 45(1 Suppl.), S76–S85.

Low, S., and Smith, N. (Eds.) (2006). *The politics of public space.* New York: Routledge.

LSE. (2011). *Urban age cities compared. Retrieved from* http://lsecities.net/media/objects/articles/urban-age-cities-compared/en-gb/ (accessed April 6, 2015).

Luckingham, B. (1989). *Phoenix: The history of a southwestern metropolis.* Tucson: The University of Arizona Press.

Luna-Garcia, A. (2003). Cities of Spain: Localities on the edge of an identity breakdown. *Cities,* 20(6), 377–379.

Lydon, M., and Garcia, A. (2015). *Tactical urbanism.* Washington, DC: Island Press.

Madureira, C., Martins, M., and Rodrigues, M. (2010). Processos de separação e recolha selectiva de resíduos nos organismos públicos: O caso português. *Finisterra,* 45(89), 141–156.

MAG. (2003). *Ending homelessness is everyone's responsibility: Regional plan to end homelessness*. Phoenix: Maricopa Association of Governments.

Magahern, J. (2004). Big time mallin': Living, loving and loathing in the mini-cities of the valley's malls. *Phoenix New Times*, December 9–15, 20–21, 25–26, 30, 34.

Makagon, D. (2004). *Where the ball drops days and nights in Times Square*. Minneapolis: University of Minnesota Press.

Mallard, A. (2016). Exploring urban controversies on retail diversity (pp. 85–103). In A. Blok and I. Farias (Eds.), *Urban cosmopolitics: Agencements, assemblies, atmospheres*. New York: Routledge.

Mappin, G., and Allmendinger, P. (2000). Retail development (pp. 191–214). In P. Allmendinger and J. Raemaekers (Eds.), *Introduction to planning practice*. Chichester: John Wiley and Sons.

Marcuse, P. (1998). Sustainability is not enough. *Environment and Urbanization*, 10(2), 103–112.

Marcuse, P. (2007). *Visions of a just city in critical planning*. Distinguished planning lecture, School of Planning at Arizona State University, February 22.

Marcuse, P. (2014). The paradoxes of public space. *Journal of Architecture and Urbanism*, 38(1), 102–106.

Marques, N., and Santos, N. (2013). O centro litoral de Portugal como destino de turismo de negócios: Análise à oferta de alojamento e de espaços para reuniões (pp. 75–110). In F. Cravidão and N. Santos (Eds.), *Turismo e cultura: Destinos e competitividade*. Coimbra: Coimbra University Press.

Marques, T. (1999). Gestor de projecto ou gabinete de gestão. *Comércio e concorrência*. October 11–18.

Martins, P. (2015). Sea bathing and seaside tourism in Portugal in the nineteenth and twentieth centuries: An overview. *Journal of Tourism History*, 7(3), 246–267. doi.org/10.1080/1755182X.2015.1114685

Matos, F. (2012). Movimentos sociais pela sustentabilidade das cidades. *Finisterra*, 94, 81–102.

Mayer, H., and Knox, P. (2006). Slow cities: Sustainable places in a fast world. *Journal of Urban Affairs*, 28: 321–334.

Mayer, H., and Knox, P. (2010). Small-town sustainability: Prospects in the second modernity. *European Planning Studies*, 18(10), 1545–1565. doi.org/10.1080 /09654313.2010.504336

McIntosh, J. (Ed.) (1997). *Renaissance of the capitol mall district*. Tempe: ASU Herberger Center for Design Excellence.

McQuiad, R. (1999). The role of partnerships in urban economic regeneration. *International Journal of Public-Private Partnerships*, 2(1), 3–28.

Mega, V. (2016). *Conscious coastal cities*. New York: Springer.

Mehta, V. (2008). Walkable streets: Pedestrian behavior, perceptions and attitudes. *Journal of Urbanism*, 1(3), 217–245.

Mehta, V. (2013). *The street: A quintessential social public space.* New York: Routledge.

Mele, C. (2011). Casinos, prisons, incinerators, and other fragments of neoliberal urban development. *Social Science History,* 35(3), 423–452.

Meunier, J. (2012). Making desert cities sustainable (pp. 107–124). In K. Pijawka and M. Gromulat (Eds.). *Understanding Sustainable cities: Concepts, cases, and solutions.* Dubuque: Kendall Hunt.

Miles, S. (2012). The neoliberal city and the pro-active complicity of the citizen consumer. *Journal of Consumer Culture,* 12(2), 216–230.

Millard, B. (2014). Challenging motorism in New York City. *Contexts,* 13(1), 32–37.

Miller, K. (2007). *Designs on the public: The private lives of New York's public spaces.* Minneapolis: University of Minnesota Press.

Mitchell, D. (2003). *The right to the city: Social justice and the fight for public space.* New York: The Guilford Press.

Mitchell, J. (2001). Business improvement districts and the 'new' revitalization of downtown. *Economic Development Quarterly,* 15(2), 115–123.

MJ. (2008). *Personal interview with a Sky Harbor volunteer.* March 1.

Monahan, T. (2006). Electronic fortification in Phoenix: Surveillance technologies and social regulation in residential communities. *Urban Affairs Review,* 42(2), 169–192.

Monheim, R. (1992). Town and transportation planning and development of retail trade in metropolitan areas of West Germany. *Landscape and Urban Planning,* 22(2), 121–136.

Montgomery, J. (1998). Making a city: Urbanity, vitality and urban design. *Journal of Urban Design,* 3(1), 93–116.

Mullin, J. (2001). Planning for retail activities in small downtowns, towards a pragmatic approach (pp. 15–19). In C. Balsas (Ed.), *Urbanismo comercial em Portugal, e a necessidade de uma nova gestão urbana.* Lisbon: URBE and CMPV.

NCH and NLCHP. (2006). *A dream denied: The criminalization of homelessness in the US.* Los Angeles: The National Law Center on Homelessness and Poverty.

Nelson, K. (2005). Homeless get their own court—will clear charge as incentive to rehabilitate. *Arizona Republic,* November 12.

Nemeth, J. (2009). Defining a public: The management of privately owned public space. *Urban Studies,* 46(1), 2463–2490.

Neuman, M., and Gavinha, J. (2005). The planning dialectic of continuity and change: The evolution of metropolitan planning in Madrid. *European Planning Studies,* 13(7), 987–1012.

Nevárez, J. (2009). *Spectacular mega-public space art and the social in Times Square* (pp. 163–176). In S. McQuire, M. Martin, and S. Niederer (Eds.), *Urban screens reader.* Amsterdam: Institute of Network Cultures.

New Solutions Group. (2013). *Place-making in legacy cities: Opportunities and good practices.* Washington, DC: Center for Community Progress.

Newman, P., and Kenworthy, J. (1999). *Sustainability and cities: Overcoming automobile dependence.* Washington, DC: Island Press.

Newtown, C. (2006). Capitol a "disaster" area—growing lament about mall. *Arizona Republic,* February 14.

NYC. (2013). *Mayor Bloomberg cuts ribbon on first phase of permanent Times Square reconstruction.* NYC Press release. December 23. Retrieved from www1.nyc.gov (accessed March 9, 2015).

NYCDOT. (2008). *Sustainable streets strategic plan for the New York City Department of Transportation 2008 and beyond.* New York: NYCDOT.

NYCDOT. (2010). *Green light for Midtown evaluation report.* Timessquarenyc.org. (accessed February 27, 2015).

NYCDOT and Gehl Architects. (2012). *World class streets: Remaking New York City's public realm.* New York: NYCDOT and Gehl Architects.

Oakley, D. (2002). Housing homeless: Local mobilization of federal resources to fight NIMBYism. *Journal of Urban Affairs,* 24(1), 97–116.

ÓhUallacháin, B., and Leslie, T. (2013). Spatial pattern and order in Sunbelt retailing: Shopping in Phoenix in the twenty-first century. *Professional Geographer,* 65(3), 396–420.

Oliveira, E. (2015). Place branding in strategic spatial planning. *Journal of Place Management and Development,* 8(1): 23–50. doi.org/10.1108/JPMD-12-2014-0031

Page, S., and Hardyman, R. (1996). Place marketing and town centre management: A new tool for urban revitalization. *Cities,* 13(3), 153–164.

Palma, D. (2000). Ten myths about downtown revitalization (pp. 374–371). In R. Kemp (Ed.), *Main Street renewal: A handbook for citizens and public officials.* Jefferson: McFarland and Company.

Parker, C., Nikos, N., Quin, S., and Grime, I. (2014). High street research agenda: Identifying high street research priorities. *Journal of Place Management and Development,* 7(2), 176–184.

Paumier, C. (2004). *Creating a vibrant city centre, urban design and regeneration principles.* Washington, DC: Urban Land Institute.

Peck, L. (2004). Do anti-poverty serving non-profit organizations locate where people need them? Evidence from a spatial analysis of Phoenix. Paper presented at the *Public Policy Analysis and Management Conference.* Atlanta.

Pérez, J. (2007). Urban planning system in contemporary Spain. *European Planning Studies,* 15(1), 29–50.

Pèrez-Eguiluz, V. (2014). El patrimonio urbano y la planificación. Interpretación de los conjuntos históricos de Castilla y Léon y sus instrumentos urbanísticos. *Ciudades,* 17, 212–242.

Perry, D., and Wiewel, W. (2005). *The university as urban developer: Case studies and analysis.* Armonk: M. E. Sharpe.

Peterson, M., and McDonogh, G. (Eds.) (2011). *Global downtowns*. Philadelphia: University of Pennsylvania Press.

Pile, S. (2005). *Real cities: Modernity, space and the phantasmagorias of city life*. London: Sage.

Pine, J., and Gilmore, J. (1999). *The experience economy: Work is theatre and every business a stage*. Boston: Harvard Business School Press.

Pires, A. (1991). O consumo da cidade ou o planeamento e o desafio da cidadania (pp. 117–130). In *Futuro para uma Europa dos Cidadãos*. Lisbon: CIVITAS and Federação Internacional para os Direitos Humanos.

Pires, A., Martinho, G., and Chang, G. (2011). Solid waste management in European countries: A review of systems analysis techniques. *Journal of Environmental Management, 92*(4), 1033–1050.

Pitt, M. (2005). Trends in shopping centre waste management. *Facilities, 23*(11/12), 522–533.

Pojani, D. (2008). Santa Monica's third street promenade: The failure and resurgence of a downtown pedestrian mall. *Urban Design International, 13*(3), 141–155.

Portas, N., Domingues, A., and Cabral, J. (2002). *Políticas urbanas, tendências, estratégias e oportunidades*. Lisbon: Fundação Calouste Gulbenkian.

Porter, M. (1995). The competitive advantage of the inner city. *Harvard Business Review,* May–June, 55–71.

Porter, M. (1997). New strategies for inner-city economic development. *Economic Development Quarterly, 11*(1), 11–27.

Portney, K. (2003). *Taking sustainable cities seriously: Economic development, the environment, and quality of life in American cities*. Cambridge: MIT Press.

Project for Public Spaces (PPS). (1996). *Public markets and community revitalization*. Washington, DC: The Urban Land Institute.

Prytherch, D. (2007). Urban geography with scale: Rethinking scale via Wal-Mart's "Geography of Big Things." *Urban Geography, 28*(5), 456–482.

Pursue a centennial dream. (2005). *Arizona Republic*, December 8.

QCAII. (2001/2007). Anexo 1: Projetos apresentados no âmbito do urbanismo comercial (pp. 161–163). In J. Barreta, *Comércio, cidade e projectos de urbanismo comercial*. Setúbal: Diversas Áreas.

Rahaman, K., Lourenço, J., and Viegas, J. (2012). Perceptions of pedestrians and shopkeepers in European medium-sized cities: Study of Guimarães, Portugal. *Journal of Urban Planning and Development, 138*(1), 26–34.

Ramos, M. (2010). Trampling over paradoxical trends and visions of European walkability. In PQN Report: The future of walking. Retrieved from http://www.walkeurope.org/ (accessed May 9, 2012).

Ravenscroft, N. (2000). The vitality and viability of town centres. *Urban Studies, 37*(13), 2533–2549.

Redón, S. (2015). Formerly with the Observatorio del Comercio Urbano, Barcelona, October 20.

Richardson, G., and Pancrazio, A. (2007). Multiple projects key to downtown's revival. *Arizona Republic*, April 8.

Richardson, G., and Stearns, J. (2005). Downtown Rocks: Area is abuzz with lofty plans. *Arizona Republic*, May 15.

Rifkin, J. (2004). *The European dream: How Europe's vision of the future is quietly eclipsing the American dream*. New York: Jeremy P. Tarcher/Penguin.

Rigby, D. (2011). The future of shopping. *Harvard Business Review*, December, 65–76.

Roberts, P., and Sykes, H. (2000). *Urban regeneration: A handbook*. Sage: London.

Roberts, S. (2009). *A kind of genius: Herb Sturz and society's toughest problems*. New York: Public Affairs.

Robertson, K. (1994). *Pedestrian malls and skywalks*. Avebury: Aldershot.

Robertson, K. (1995). Downtown redevelopment strategies in the United States. *Journal of the American Planning Association*, 61, 429–437.

Robertson, K. (1997). Downtown retail revitalization: A review of American development strategies. *Planning Perspectives*, 12, 383–401.

Robertson, K. (1999). Can small-city downtowns remain viable? A national study of development issues and strategies. *Journal of the American Planning Association*, 65(3), 270–283.

Rodin, J. (2005). The 21st century urban university. *Journal of the American Planning Association*, 71(3), 237–249.

Rodrigues, L. (2016). *Manual de crimes urbanísticos: Exemplos práticos para compreender os negócios insustentáveis da especulação imobiliária*. 2nd edition. Lisbon: Guerra e Paz.

Roger Evans Associates. (2007). *Delivering quality places: Urban design compendium 2*. London: English Partnerships and Housing Corporation.

Roland Berger and Partner. (1993). *Assistência na definição da estratégia de desenvolvimento turístico da Figueira da Foz*. Unpublished final presentation to the steering committee. Figueira da Foz, December 20.

Romero, C. (2004). A mall for the future. *Arizona Republic*, September 17.

Roost, F. (1998). Recreating the city as entertainment center: The media industry's role in transforming Postdamer Platz and Times Square. *Journal of Urban Technology*, 5(3), 1–21.

Rosan, C. (2012). Can PlaNYC make New York City "greener and greater" for everyone? Sustainability planning and the promise of environmental justice. *Local Environment*, 17, 959–976.

Ross, A. (2011). *Bird on fire: Lessons from the world's least sustainable city*. Oxford: Oxford University Press.

Ross, C., and Leigh, N. (2000). Planning, urban revitalization, and the inner city: An exploration of structural racism. *Journal of Planning Literature*, 14(1), 367–380.

Rotenberg, R. (2011). Toward a genealogy of downtowns (pp. 29–47). In M. Peterson and G. McDonogh (Eds.), *Global downtowns*. Philadelphia: University of Pennsylvania Press,

Rowe, P. (2011). *Emergent architectural territories in East Asian cities.* Basel: Birkhauser.

Rowley, J., and Slack, F. (1999). The retail experience in airport departure lounges: Reaching for timelessness and placelessness. *International Marketing Review,* 16(4/5), 363–375.

Roy, A. (2012). Urban informality: The production of space and practice of planning (pp. 669–690). In R. Weber and R. Crane (Eds.), *The Oxford handbook of urban planning.* Oxford: Oxford University Press.

RUDI and Academy of Urbanism. (2009). *PLACEmaking: Celebrating quality and innovation in urban life.* London: Resource for Urban Design Information.

Russo, R. (2012). Left turns and pedestrian safety. *TRB annual meeting.* Washington, January 23.

Ruth, M., and Franklin, R. (2014). Livability for all? Conceptual limits and practical implications. *Applied Geography,* 49, 18–23.

Sadik-Khan, J., and Solomonow, S. (2016). *Streetfight: Handbook for an urban revolution.* New York: Viking.

Sagalyn, L. (2001). *Times Square roulette: Remaking the city icon.* Cambridge: MIT Press.

Salgueiro, T. (1996). *Do comércio à distribuição.* Celta: Oeiras.

Salgueiro, T. (1999). A cidade e o comércio nos finais do século (pp. 22–27). In *Comércio, cidade e qualidade de vida.* DGCC and DGOTDU.

Salgueiro, T., and Cachinho, H. (2007). *As relações cidade—comércio: Dinâmicas de evolução e modelos interpretativos.* Apontamentos de Geografia: Série Investigação No. 20.

Salvati, L. (2014). In-between Europe and the Mediterranean: Urban culture and the economic structure of the post-war "southern city." *Current Politics and Economics of Europe,* 25(1), 39–63.

Sandel, M. (2012). *What money can't buy: The moral limits of markets.* New York: Farrar, Straus and Giroux.

Sandercock, L. (2004). Towards a planning imagination for the 21st century. *Journal of the American Planning Association,* 70(2), 237–249.

Santos, M. (2013). *Profetas do consumo: Amanhã é o primeiro dia do nosso sonho de consumo.* Lisbon: Âncora.

Sanz, J. (2007). Dificultades del urbanismo comercial: El plan general de equipamiento comercial de Castilla y León. *Ciudades,* 10, 109–144.

Sassen, S. (2001). *The global city, New York, London and Tokyo.* 2nd edition. Princeton: Princeton University Press.

Sassen, S. (2014). *Expulsions brutality and complexity in the global economy.* Cambridge: The Belknap Press of Harvard University Press.

Scarpaci, J. (2004). *Plazas and barrios: Heritage tourism and globalization in the Latin American centro histórico.* Tucson: University of Arizona Press.

Schaller, B. (2010). New York City's congestion pricing experience and implications for road pricing acceptance in the United States. *Transport Policy,* 17, 266–273.

Scharoun, L. (2012). *America at the mall: The cultural role of a retail utopia.* Jefferson: McFarland & Company.

Schively, C. (2007). Understanding the NIMBY and LULU phenomena: Reassessing our knowledge base and informing future research. *Journal of Planning Literature,* 21(3), 255–266.

Schmandt, M. (1995). Postmodern Phoenix. *Geographical Review,* 85(3), 349–363.

Schmidt, L. (2016). *Portugal: Ambientes de Mudança.* Lisbon: Círculo de Leitores.

Schmookler, A. (1993). *The illusion of choice: How the market economy shapes our destiny.* Albany: State University of New York Press.

Schwartz, S. (2015). *Street smart.* New York: Public Affairs.

Seidman, K. (2004). *Revitalizing commerce for American cities: A practitioner's guide to urban Main Street programs.* Washington, DC: Fannie Mae Foundation.

Seixas, P. (2014). Theming and exception in Europe's west coast: The transnational quaternary production of space (pp. 83–108). In P. Santos and P. Seixas (Eds.), *Metropolization, globalization and Beyond: Europe's west coast.* Berkeley: Berkeley Public Policy Press.

Sepe, M. (2013). *Planning and place in the city: Mapping place identity.* New York: Routledge.

Sertich, R. (1980). *Comparative analysis of regional shopping centers in the Phoenix, Arizona planning area.* Unpublished master's thesis. Tempe, Arizona State University.

Servon, L., and Pink, S. (2015). Cittaslow: Going glocal in Spain. *Journal of Urban Affairs,* 37(3), 327–340.

Sheridan, M. (2015). Special section retail. *Urban Land,* November–December, 107–114.

Shortell, T. (2016). Walking as urban practice and research method (pp. 1–22). In E. Brown and T. Shortell (Eds.), *Walking in cities: Quotidian mobility as urban theory, method, and practice.* Philadelphia: Temple University Press.

Shulman, A. (2009). *Miami modern metropolis.* Miami: Bass Museum of Art.

Silva, E. (2004). The DNA of our regions: Artificial intelligence in regional planning. *Futures,* 36(10), 1077–1094.

Sinnett, D., Williams, K., Chatterjee, K., and Cavill, N. (2011). *Making the case for investment in the walking environment: A review of the evidence.* London: Living Streets.

Slater, T. (2006). The downside of upscale: The battle over the skid row. *Los Angeles Times,* July 30.

Smiley, D. (Ed.) (2002). *Sprawl and public space: Redressing the mall.* Washington, DC: National Endowment for the Arts.

Smith, K. (2006). The homeless situation in Los Angeles and the BID response (pp. 403–410.) In D. Feehan and M. Feit (Eds.), *Making business districts work.* New York: Haworth Press.

Smith, R. (1955). Colonial towns of Spanish and Portuguese America. *Journal of the Society of Architectural Historians,* 14(4), 3–12.

Sohn, D., Moudon, A., and Lee, J. (2012). The economic value of walkable neighborhoods. *Urban Design International,* 17(2), 115–128.

Solnit, R. (2000). *Wanderlust: A history of walking.* New York: Viking.

Soni, N., and Soni, N. (2016). Benefits of pedestrianization and warrants to pedestrianize an area. *Land Use Policy,* 57, 139–150.

Soromenho-Marques, V. (2003). Economia, política e desenvolvimento sustentável: Os desafios da crise global e social do ambiente. *Educação, Sociedade e Culturas,* 21, 9–22.

Southworth, M. (2005). Designing the walkable city. *Journal of Urban Planning and Development,* 131(4), 246–257.

Speck, J. (2012). *Walkable city: How downtown can save America, one step at a time.* New York: North Point Press.

Spencer, J. (2005). How to think about place and people approaches to poverty. *Journal of Planning Education and Research,* 24(3), 292–303.

Stearns, J. (2004). Public market set to open in Phoenix. *Arizona Republic,* September 30.

Stitt, B. (1996). The lies of downtown. *Small Town,* 27(1), 18–25.

Stone, C. (1989). *Regime politics: Governing Atlanta, 1946–1988.* Lawrence: University Press of Kansas.

Stone, J. (2007). Fate of Phoenix, feeding Phoenix's (hopeful) economic boom. *944TM Magazine,* May, 128.

Sunnucks, M. (2004). Sky Harbor Terminal 4 to expand retail offerings. *Business Journal of Phoenix.* March 7.

Takahashi, L. (1996). A decade of understanding homelessness in the USA: From characterization to representation. *Progress in Human Geography,* 29, 291–310.

Takahashi, L., and Dear, M. (1997). The changing dynamics of community opposition to human services facilities. *Journal of the American Planning Association,* 63(1), 79–93.

Takahashi, L., and Gaber, S. (1998). Controversial facility sitting in the urban environment. *Environment and Behavior,* 30(2), 184–215.

Talen, E. (2002). Pedestrian access as a measure of urban quality. *Planning, Practice and Research,* 17(3), 257–278.

Talen, E. (2011) Sprawl retrofit: Sustainable urban form in unsustainable places. *Environment and Planning B: Planning and Design,* 38, 952–978.

Tallon, A. (2013). *Urban regeneration in the UK.* 3rd edition. London: Routledge.

Teixeira, J., and Pereira, M. (1999). Les projects speciaux d'urbanisme commercial: Un partenariat pour la qualification du commerce et du centre-ville (pp. 193–214). In T. Salgueiro (Ed.), *The globalization of consumption and retail places.* Lisbon: GECIC.

Tejedor, A., Jerez, F., and Sánchez, M. (2009). *Proceso de peatonalización y nueva sociabilidad: Los casos de Sevilla y Malaga.* Sevilla: Centro de Estudios Andaluces.

Teles, P. (2014). *A cidade das (i) mobilidades manual técnico de acessibilidade e mobilidade para todos*. Lisbon: Vida Económica.

Thompson, R. (2006). Pastor at the Grace Lutheran Church. Personal interview by the author. June 26.

Times Square Alliance. (2012). *Twenty years twenty principles*. Timessquarenyc.org (accessed February 27, 2015).

Torrens P. (2012). Moving agent pedestrians through space and time. *Annals of the Association of American Geographers*, 102(1), 35–66.

Townsend, A. (2004). Digitally mediated urban space: New lessons for design. *Praxis*, 6, 100–105.

Traub, J. (2004). *The devil's playground: A century of pleasure and profit in Times Square*. New York: Random House.

Turismo de Portugal. (2017). *Estratégia turismo 2017*. Lisbon: Turismo de Portugal.

ULI. (2001). *Light-rail transit in Phoenix, Arizona: Economic development along the planned light-rail line*. Online short report. Retrieved from http://www.valleymetro.org/ METRO_light_rail/ (accessed December 20, 2006).

Universidade Internacional da Figueira da Foz (UIFF) and Associação Comercial da Figueira da Foz (ACIFF). (2002). *O comércio tradicional na Figueira da Foz*. Unpublished report. Câmara Municipal da Figueira da Foz.

Untermann, R. (1984). *Accommodating the pedestrian: Adapting towns and neighborhoods for walking and bicycling*. New York: Van Nostrand Reinhold.

Urry, J. (1995). *Consuming places*. New York: Routledge.

Urry, J. (2011). *The tourist gaze 3.0*. Los Angeles: Sage.

Valencia, E. (2002). *Principles of solidary economics*. Retrieved from http://www.jesuit.ie/ijnd/SolidarityEconomics.pdf (accessed March 2, 2008).

Valente, S. (2015). A (in)comunicação entre políticas públicas do "lixo" e os cidadãos (pp. 95–102). In J. Ferrão and A. Horta (Eds.), *Ambiente, território e sociedade, novas agendas de investigação*. Lisbon: Imprensa de Ciências Sociais.

Van Leeuwen, E., and Nijkamp, P. (2009). Operational advances in tourism research. *Revista Portuguesa de Estudos Regionais*, 22, 5–20.

Vargas, H. (2000). O comércio varejista e políticas urbanas. *Sinopses*, 34, 20–30.

Vargas, H., and Castilho, A. (2006). *Intervenções em centros urbanos, objectivos, estratégias e resultados*. Barueri: Editora Manole.

Vargas, H., and Castilho, A. (Eds.) (2015). *Intervenções em centros urbanos, objectivos, estratégias e resultados*. 3rd edition. Barueri: Manole.

Vasconcellos, E. (2005). Urban change, mobility and transport in São Paulo: Three decades, three cities. *Transport Policy*, 12(2), 91–104.

Vaz, E., Nainggolan, D., Nijkamp, P., and Painho, M. (2011). Crossroads of tourism: A complex spatial systems analysis of tourism and urban sprawl in the Algarve. *International Journal of Sustainable Development*, 14(3–4), 225–241. doi:10.1504/IJSD.2011.041963

Viana, L., and Fonseca, F. (2011). Impactos sociais e econômicos da atuação do Banco Interamericano de Desenvolvimento nas políticas públicas. *Cadernos do Desenvolvimento, 6*, 199–213.

Viola, R., Hostetter, S., Riscica, V., Kay, A., and Peck, H. (2015). *Manhattan pedestrian safety action plan.* New York: New York City Department of Transportation.

Viteritti, J. (2010). Is New York forsaking the poor? *Urban Affairs Review, 45*(5), 693–704.

Vogel, R., Savitch, H., Xu, J., Yeh, A., Wu, W., Sancton, A., Kantor, P., and Newman, P. (2010). Governing global city regions in China and the West. *Progress in Planning, 73*, 1–75.

Wachs, M. (2013). Turning cities inside out: Transportation and the resurgence of downtowns in North America. *Transportation, 40*, 1159–1172.

Waits, M., and Henton, D. (2001). *The downtowns of the future: Opportunities for regional stewards.* Mountain View: Alliance for Regional Stewardship.

Walker, D. (2013). Resisting the neoliberalization of space in Mexico City (pp. 170–194). In T. Samara, S. He, and G. Chen (Eds.), *Locating right to the city in the global South.* New York: Routledge.

Walker, R., and Seasons, M. (2002). Planning supported housing: A new orientation in housing for people with serious mental illness. *Journal of Planning Education and Research, 21*(3), 313–319.

Wall, A. (2005). *Victor Gruen: From urban shop to new city.* Barcelona: Actar.

Wall, J. (2006). Program Director. Personal interview by the author. November 10.

Weinstein, B., and Clower, T. (2004). *Homelessness as an impediment to urban revitalization: The case of Dallas, Texas.* Working paper, Center for Economic Development and Research. University of North Texas.

Weis, W. (2013). Hypocrisy at the lectern. *Journal of Management for Global Sustainability, 1*, 29–45.

Whitehead, T., Simmonds, D., and Preston, J. (2006). The effects of urban quality improvements. *Journal of Environmental Management, 80*, 1–12.

Whyte, W. (1988). *City: Rediscovering the centre.* New York: Doubleday.

Williams, A., and Shaw, G. (1998). Tourism policies in a changing economic environment (pp. 375–391). In A. Williams and G. Shaw (Eds.), *Tourism and economic development: European experiences.* Chichester, UK: John Wiley and Sons.

Wilson, W. (1987). *The truly disadvantaged: The inner city, the underclass, and public policy.* Chicago: University of Chicago Press.

Winterberg, S., and Bender, S. (2002). Back to basics: Creating revitalization projects that work. *Paper presented at the Annual Conference of the American Planning Association.* Chicago, April 13–17.

World Tourism Organization (UNWTO). (2016). *Tourism highlights: 2016 edition.* Madrid: World Tourism Organization.

Wright, J., Rubin, B., and Devine, J. (1998). *Beside the golden door: Policy, politics, and the homeless.* New York: Aldine de Gruyter.

Wu, J., Jenerette, G., Buyantuyev, A., and Redman, C. (2011). Quantifying spatiotemporal patterns of urbanization: The case of the two fastest growing metropolitan regions in the United States. *Ecological Complexity,* 8(1), 1–8.

Wu, T., Xie, P. F., and Tsai, M. (2015). Perceptions of attractiveness for salt heritage tourism: A tourist perspective. *Tourism Management,* 51, 201–209. doi. org/10.1016/j.tourman.2015.05.026

Yan, R., and Eckman, M. (2009). Are lifestyle centres unique? Consumers' perceptions across locations. *International Journal of Retail and Distribution Management,* 37(1), 24–42.

Yiu, C. (2011). The impact of a pedestrianisation scheme on retail rent: An empirical test in Hong Kong. *Journal of Place Management and Development,* 4(3), 231–242.

Zacharias, J. (2001). Pedestrian behavior and perception in urban walking environments. *Journal of Planning Literature,* 16(1), 3–18.

Zagatto, A. (2012). *Aliança pelo Centro Histórico de São Paulo,* June 8.

Zaman, A., and Lehmann, S. (2011). Challenges and opportunities in transforming a city into a "zero waste city." *Challenges,* 2, 73–93.

Zavattaro, S. (2013). *Cities for sale: Municipalities as public relations and marketing firms.* Albany: State University of New York Press.

Zhang, H., and Lei, S. (2012). A structural model of residents' intention to participate in ecotourism: The case of a wetland community. *Tourism Management,* 33(4), 916–925.

Zukin, S. (1995). *The cultures of cities.* Oxford: Blackwell.

Zukin, S. (2003). Whose culture, whose city? (pp. 136–146). In R. LeGates and F. Stout (Eds.), *The city Reader.* 2nd edition. New York: Routledge.

Index